Poultry

by
THE EDITORS OF TIME-LIFE BOOKS

Cover: A roast turkey, among the most festive of poultry dishes, is carved easily with a two-pronged fork and a sharp, flexible blade (see Chapter 3). For the most satisfactory results, the turkey should be allowed to rest for about 10 minutes at room temperature before the first cut is made.

EUROPEAN EDITOR: George Constable
Assistant European Editor: Kit van Tulleken
Design Consultant: Louis Klein
Chief Designer: Graham Davis
Director of Photography: Pamela Marke
Chief of Research: Vanessa Kramer

THE GOOD COOK
Series Editor: Windsor Chorlton

EDITORIAL STAFF FOR POULTRY
Deputy Editor: Deborah Thompson
Picture Editor: Anne Angus
Anthology Editor: Liz Clasen
Designer: Douglas Whitworth
Staff Writers: Norman Kolpas, Alan Lothian,
Anthony Masters
Researchers: Ursula Beary, Sally Crawford,
Suad McCoy, Karin Pearce
Sub-Editors: Gillian Boucher, Nicoletta Flessati
Permissions Researcher: Mary-Claire Hailey
Design Assistant: Martin Gregory

EDITORIAL PRODUCTION FOR THE SERIES
Production Editor: Ellen Brush
Art Department: Julia West
Editorial Department: Kathy Eason, Joanne
Holland, Rosemarie Hudson, Molly Sutherland
Picture Department: Eleanor Lines

TIME
LIFE
BOOKS

THE GOOD COOK
THE TIME-LIFE ENCYCLOPAEDIA OF GARDENING
HUMAN BEHAVIOUR
THE GREAT CITIES
THE ART OF SEWING
THE OLD WEST
THE WORLD'S WILD PLACES
THE EMERGENCE OF MAN
LIFE LIBRARY OF PHOTOGRAPHY
FOODS OF THE WORLD
TIME-LIFE LIBRARY OF ART
GREAT AGES OF MAN
LIFE SCIENCE LIBRARY
LIFE NATURE LIBRARY
YOUNG READERS LIBRARY

THE CHIEF CONSULTANT:
Richard Olney, an American, has lived and worked since 1951 in France, where he is a highly regarded authority on food and wine. A regular contributor to the influential journals *Cuisine et Vins de France* and *La Revue du Vin de France,* he has also written numerous articles for other gastronomic magazines in France and the United States, and is the author of *The French Menu Cookbook* and the award-winning *Simple French Food.* He has directed cooking courses in France and the United States and is a member of several distinguished gastronomic societies, including *La Confrérie des Chevaliers du Tastevin, La Commanderie du Bontemps de Médoc et des Graves* and *Les Amitiés Gastronomiques Internationales.*

THE PHOTOGRAPHER:
Alan Duns was born in 1943 in the north of England and studied at the Ealing School of Photography. He has undertaken many advertising assignments, but specializes in food photography. His work has appeared in major British publications.

THE INTERNATIONAL CONSULTANTS:
Great Britain: *Jane Grigson* was born in Gloucester and brought up in the north of England. She is a graduate of Cambridge University. Her first book on food, *Charcuterie and French Pork Cookery,* was published in 1967; since then, she has published a number of cookery books, including *Good Things, English Food* and *The Mushroom Feast.* She became cookery correspondent for the colour magazine of the London *Observer* in 1968. **France:** *Michel Lemonnier* was born in Normandy. He began contributing to the magazine *Cuisine et Vins de France* in 1960, and also writes for several other important French food and wine periodicals. The co-founder and vice-president of the society *Les Amitiés Gastronomiques Internationales,* he is a frequent lecturer on wine and vineyards, and a member of most of the vinicultural confraternities in France. He lives in the south of France, near Avignon. **Germany:** *Jochen Kuchenbecker* trained as a chef, but worked for 10 years as a food photographer in many European countries before opening his own restaurant in Hamburg. *Anne Brakemeier,* who also lives in Hamburg, has published articles on food and cooking in many German periodicals. She is the co-author of three cookery books. **The Netherlands:** *Hugh Jans,* a resident of Amsterdam, has been translating cookery books and articles for more than 25 years. He has also published two books of his own, *Bistro Koken* and *Koken in Casserole,* and his recipes appear in many Dutch magazines. **The United States:** *Carol Cutler,* a resident of Washington, DC, is the author of *Haute Cuisine for Your Heart's Delight* and the award-winning *The Six-Minute Soufflé and Other Culinary Delights.* A contributing editor of both *International Food and Wine* and *Working Woman* Magazines, she frequently lectures about food and gives demonstrations of cooking techniques. *Shirley Sarvis,* a freelance food writer and consultant in San Francisco, is the author and co-author of a dozen cookery books. Her interest in national cuisines has led her to travel extensively and she was a consultant on the Time-Life Books' *Foods of the World* series. *José Wilson* moved to the United States from England in 1951. The food editor of *House and Garden* Magazine for 15 years, she has written many books on food and interior decoration, including *American Cooking: the Eastern Heartland* in Time-Life Books' *Foods of the World* series and, with Arthur Leaman, *The Complete Food Catalog.*

Valuable help was given in the preparation of this volume by the following members of Time-Life Books: *Michele le Baube, Maria Vincenza Aloisi, Josephine du Brusle* (Paris); *Jeanne Buys* (Amsterdam); *Hans-Heinrich Wellman* (Hamburg); *Bona Schmid* (Milan); *Elisabeth Kraemer* (Bonn).

CONTENTS

Making Fare of Fowl

"Poultry," wrote the 19th-century French gastronome Jean Anthelme Brillat-Savarin, "is for the cook what canvas is to the painter. It is served to us boiled, roasted, fried, hot or cold, whole or in pieces, with or without sauce, boned, skinned, stuffed, and always with equal success."

This volume explores all these possibilities. The first half of the book presents the techniques involved in preparing poultry as the main course of a meal. It aims at nothing less than teaching all the skills necessary to make a first-class poultry cook.

Some techniques, such as cutting up a bird into serving portions (*pages 16-19*) or trussing it whole (*page 40*), are so basic you will resort to them regularly. Others, such as boning a bird without breaking the skin (*page 20*), are more unusual; you will probably save them for special occasions.

To complement the techniques, the second half of this volume offers a unique anthology of published recipes—for chicken, turkey, duck, goose, guinea-fowl and pigeon squab—drawn from around the world and across the centuries. Used together, the two sections will not only give you access to a complete repertoire of poultry dishes, they will also inspire you with the confidence to experiment with ingredients and devise your own recipes.

Selecting a bird

An important consideration in choosing a recipe should be the age of the bird. As a rule, young birds are tender and subtly flavoured; they are ideal for roasting, grilling or sautéing—cooking methods that work rapidly, sealing in flavour and preserving succulence. The breast meat of the lean birds—chicken, turkey and guinea-fowl—is particularly delicate, and cooks in a shorter time than the darker meat of the legs.

As a bird matures, it becomes increasingly tough—especially its active leg muscles. However, the flesh develops a depth of flavour that is rarely found in young birds. In addition, it acquires a gelatinous quality that enables it to tolerate the long cooking required to tenderize the muscle fibres. If an old bird is gently braised or poached with vegetables and seasonings, it will retain its flavour; and the liquid in which it is cooked will itself become suffused with enough of the bird's essence to stand on its own as a soup, stock or sauce.

The age of freshly killed poultry can be gauged without difficulty. The beak and the tip of the breastbone are flexible to the touch in young birds, rigid in old ones. However, when you buy pre-packaged birds, whether fresh or frozen, you will have to rely on labels and what you can see through the wrappings. The skin of a young bird should look smooth, with no visible hairs.

The colour of the skin differs from breed to breed and varies according to diet; it is not a reliable guide to age or quality.

In the past, young poultry was sold on a seasonal basis. Roasting chickens, for example, were widely available only in the spring and commanded as high a price, weight for weight, as prime beef. They were usually male birds; the hens were too valuable as breeders to be sacrificed for the table until they stubbornly refused to lay any more eggs. Since the introduction of scientific, intensive breeding techniques, however, young birds of both sexes have become available all year round at prices comparable to that of the most inexpensive minced beef. They are guaranteed to be plump and tender; but since they are fed on standard diets and are allowed very little exercise, they require a more imaginative—if judicious—use of marinades, sauces and stuffings than their farmyard cousins.

The universal chicken

It would be a pardonable exaggeration to say that the chicken was created especially for the table. Descended from the red jungle fowl of south-east Asia, and domesticated as early as 2500 BC in the Indus Valley, the chicken has by now become an established part of almost every cuisine. Its ease of rearing and its value as an egg-layer may have contributed to its popularity, but the chicken owes its culinary reputation to the sheer variety of dishes for which it is suited.

In every country where chicken is reared for the table, cooks use local produce to prepare characteristic dishes. The Italians, for example, sauté chicken with tomatoes, mushrooms and wine to make *cacciatora*; the Japanese grill chicken pieces that have been marinated in a mixture of ginger, soy sauce and rice wine to produce *toriniku no tatsuta-age*. Chicken *tandoori*, a roast or grilled dish seasoned with yogurt and hot spices, is a speciality of cooks in India; Circassian chicken, which incorporates pounded nuts, is characteristic of Middle Eastern cuisine.

Chickens are marketed under different names according to their age, and range from the six-week-old poussin to the more-than-one-year-old boiling fowl or rooster. In between, there is the so-called spring chicken—traditionally a young cockerel, but nowadays a two-to-four-month-old bird of either sex—and the roasting chicken, which is in its prime at four to six months.

Any chicken younger than six months is best grilled, sautéed or roasted. Grilling is an ideal way to coax flavour from a poussin or a spring chicken. If such a bird is first marinated in a piquant blend of oil and herbs, then grilled under fierce heat—or, better still, over a glowing bed of charcoal or fragrant wood embers—its flavour is heightened while the flesh remains moist and tender.

A roast chicken, cooked until the skin is crisp and golden and served with a gravy made from the juices left in the roasting pan, represents the best in home cooking. There is a comforting familiarity in the ritual of its preparation—the trussing, basting and, finally, the carving at table. Today, most roasts are prepared in ovens. But in medieval Europe, a bird was impaled on a spit and roasted in front of an open fire—a method that continued to be used up to the end of the 19th century and still has its enthusiastic adherents. As the bird cooked, it was basted with the juices that dripped into a pan beneath it. To prevent the bird from cooking unevenly, it was rotated on the spit—either by a servant, by a wound-up spring device or, in some households, by a dog hitched to a treadwheel connected to the spit. Great value was attached to the technique of carving such a bird at table, and every nobleman's house had its professional carver, called a trencher, after the wooden board on which the meat was cut up and served. (The word "trencherman", meaning a hearty eater, is a legacy of the period.)

Whether cooked on a spit or in an oven, a farmyard bird, with flesh firm and flavoursome from exercise and a natural diet of grain and insects, may require no more elaboration than a sprinkling of salt and pepper inside and a generous pat of butter outside. But a mass-produced chicken that is to be roasted benefits from a stuffing that will heighten the flavour of its meat as it cooks. The stuffing chosen may range from the forthright to the intricate, from a simple breadcrumb mixture to a robust blend of minced veal and chopped vegetables or an exotic marriage of nuts, fruit and spices.

Cut up into pieces, a roasting bird is also a suitable candidate for sautéing in butter or oil, or for deep frying in sizzling hot fat.

As for the superannuated egg-layer, called a boiling fowl or stewing hen, it may be poached in water or stock. Or it may be presented in the guise of a roasting chicken: when braised for an hour or so with a little water in a lidded casserole, then baked in the oven, a boiling fowl will emerge golden-brown and as tender as a bird half its age. The same treatment can be bestowed on an old rooster, but the one-year-old bird, called a cockerel, is best reserved for a braise, such as the French *coq au vin* (*pages 54-57*).

Then, there is that martyr to the cause of cooking, the capon— a castrated male chicken. Caponizing originated in ancient Greece, but only became widespread in classical Rome after a law was passed forbidding the consumption of fattened hens, which were considered to be a delicacy. With a simple surgical operation, Roman poultry breeders not only circumvented the ban, but produced a bird that grew to twice the size of an untreated chicken while retaining all the succulence of a young bird.

Although relatively expensive, capons are still prized, especially as roasting birds. Unlike that of ordinary chickens, their flesh is marbled throughout with fat which melts during cooking, nourishing the flesh and preserving its tenderness.

The turkey

When the Spanish *conquistadores* invaded Mexico in the 16th century, they discovered a large, gobbling curiosity of a bird, prized by the Aztecs who had domesticated it centuries earlier.

Goose
4.5 to 8 kg (10 to 18 lb)

Turkey
4 to 14 kg (9 to 30 lb)

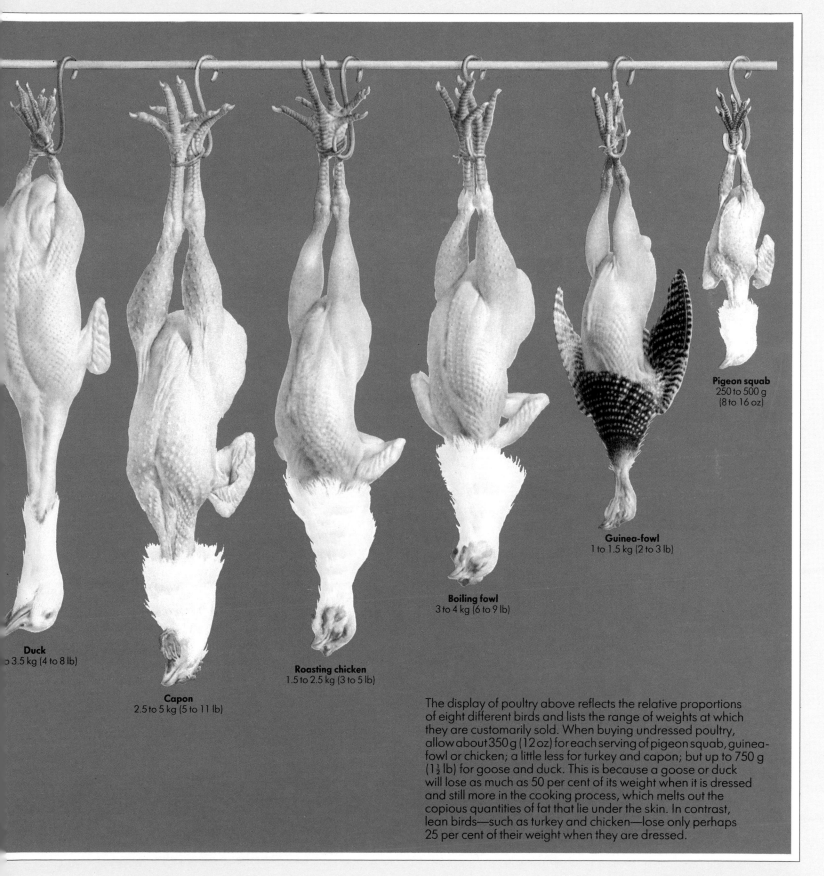

Duck
to 3.5 kg (4 to 8 lb)

Capon
2.5 to 5 kg (5 to 11 lb)

Roasting chicken
1.5 to 2.5 kg (3 to 5 lb)

Boiling fowl
3 to 4 kg (6 to 9 lb)

Guinea-fowl
1 to 1.5 kg (2 to 3 lb)

Pigeon squab
250 to 500 g
(8 to 16 oz)

The display of poultry above reflects the relative proportions of eight different birds and lists the range of weights at which they are customarily sold. When buying undressed poultry, allow about 350 g (12 oz) for each serving of pigeon squab, guinea-fowl or chicken; a little less for turkey and capon; but up to 750 g (1½ lb) for goose and duck. This is because a goose or duck will lose as much as 50 per cent of its weight when it is dressed and still more in the cooking process, which melts out the copious quantities of fat that lie under the skin. In contrast, lean birds—such as turkey and chicken—lose only perhaps 25 per cent of their weight when they are dressed.

Discovering for themselves that the bird was good to eat, the Spaniards introduced it to Europe, where it soon became immensely popular—"one of the finest gifts given to the Old World by the New," according to Brillat-Savarin. With apparent disregard for geography, the English dubbed the newcomer the turkey—probably after the merchants who traded between Turkey and England, and who are reputed to have discovered the bird when they called at Cadiz on their return voyages.

Although turkey is nowadays available in pieces, the size of the whole bird makes it most suitable for family gatherings. In England, a plump roast turkey, bulging with chestnut, sausage meat or sage and onion stuffing and accompanied by redcurrant jelly and bread sauce, marks the high point of the Christmas dinner. In America it is a roast turkey with cranberry sauce that crowns the Thanksgiving table. But turkey need not always be treated in the traditional way and served with all the familiar accompaniments. The great French chef Auguste Escoffier describes a dinner menu featuring a simple roast turkey that epitomizes French provincial cooking: after a day's hunting, he sat down to a meal "composed of a cream of pumpkin soup with little croûtons fried in butter, a young turkey roasted on the spit and accompanied by a large country sausage and a salad of potatoes, dandelions and beetroots, and followed by a big bowl of pears cooked in red wine and served with whipped cream".

Duck and goose

Of the several breeds of duck raised for the table, the most esteemed are the Nantais and Rouennais ducks of France, the Aylesbury duck of England and the Long Island duck of the United States. The Long Island ducks trace their lineage to nine white ducks brought in 1873 by a clipper ship captain from China, where ducks have been domesticated for at least 2,000 years. The Chinese, in fact, have a special reverence for the duck, which in times past they regarded as a symbol of fidelity. They are masters at making the most of the rich, succulent flesh that is the duck's greatest virtue while minimizing its major disadvantage—a body that, in the case of most breeds, contains a relatively large proportion of bone and fat, and which has inspired the saying: "A duck is too much for one, but not enough for two." One way in which Chinese cooks—as well as knowledgeable European ones—extend the duck is to remove the skeleton and fill the boned bird with a savoury stuffing (*demonstration, page 62*). Thus supplemented, the duck will serve six generously.

Strictly speaking, the term "duck" applies to birds that are more than two months old; younger specimens are called ducklings and have a fine flavour that is tasted to good advantage if the bird is plain-roasted, without stuffing or elaborate garnishes. Once a duck has reached its optimum size—at about three months—it will have a rich flavour that can be appreciated to the full in roast or braised dishes garnished or sauced with tart fruit—cherries, apples or oranges. The English cooking authority Elizabeth David suggests that a duck is one of the most difficult birds to roast properly, since the legs remain underdone when the breast is cooked to perfection: with a hint of pink left in the meat. A traditional solution to this particular culinary problem is to serve the breast alone for one course and then grill the legs for another 10 to 15 minutes and serve them—accompanied by a simple salad—as another course.

Before the introduction of the turkey to Europe, goose was the bird for festive occasions: "Christmas is coming; the goose is getting fat," runs an old English rhyme—evoking Dickensian scenes of feast and plenty. In Germany—where geese were domesticated as early as 1500 BC—and in Scandinavia as well as Central Europe, roast goose is still traditional Christmas fare. Typically, the stuffings chosen to accompany goose are based on fruits and vegetables—apples and prunes, potatoes and cabbage—that both provide a contrast to the rich flesh and make a substantial contribution to the dish.

Most geese are sent to the market at an age of eight or nine months; once they have passed their prime, they become too tough for roasting. With Gallic initiative, the French rejuvenate such a bird by braising it with vegetables, pork rinds and calf's feet for many hours in a tightly sealed pot (*demonstration, page 60*), until the meat is so tender that, in the words of an expert French chef, "it can be cut with a spoon". The French, in fact, make particularly enterprising use of the goose. Not only is the large liver, or *foie gras*, prized as a delicacy in itself, the intestines and giblets are incorporated in sausages (wrapped in the skin of the bird's neck) and the copious internal fat is used for cooking and for preserving salted goose flesh (*demonstration, page 84*). For domestic consumption, goose fat is to south-western France what butter is to Normandy or olive oil to Provence.

Guinea-fowl and pigeon

The guinea-fowl is as delicious to eat as its voice—a harsh, metallic cry—is unpleasant to hear. The Greeks are credited with bringing the bird from its native Africa before the fifth century BC. In size, it is equivalent to a spring chicken; in flavour, it combines the delicate taste of chicken with a faint suggestion of game that may be heightened in Britain and Europe by hanging the birds, unbled, in a cool place for one or two days after they are slaughtered and before they are cooked.

Hanging tenderizes the meat, but the domesticated guinea-fowl, like its wild relatives, remains a little on the dry side. To prevent the breast meat from drying out, a guinea-fowl requires regular basting during roasting and it may benefit from a protective layer of bacon rashers placed on its breast or a generous portion of seasoned butter spread under the breast skin before cooking (*demonstration, page 39*). Alternatively, it can be flattened and stuffed beneath the skin with a mixture of vegetables and any fresh white cheese (*demonstration, pages 47-49*). Basted from within by the liquid from the vegetables and cheese, the bird stays moist; while the flavours of the stuffing lend a delicious nuance to the breast meat.

The several breeds of domesticated pigeon are not to be confused with their wild relatives, which have dark meat and a gamey flavour. The domestic bird's meat is pale and has a mellow flavour. As in medieval times, when manorial dovecotes provided a welcome supply of fresh meat in early spring, the young birds—called squabs—are killed when they are about four weeks old and barely fledged. Once pigeons have been on the wing for a while, their muscles toughen. So that the pigeons may have the best possible flavour, they are never bled. The young birds are usually sautéed, roasted or split and grilled; the older ones can be braised or pot-roasted or incorporated into a pie.

Tips on frozen poultry

All kinds of poultry make better eating if freshly killed. And frozen poultry is undeniably inferior. Yet a freezer can be a great asset if it is used to store farm-reared birds. Even when deep-frozen, a farmyard chicken will have more flavour than its pampered cousin. If a bird is fresh when it is put into the freezer it will keep for up to six months; the giblets, which have a shorter storage life, should be packed separately and used within three months. Since many recipes do not call for a whole bird, a freezer is also invaluable for storing the unused portions; for ease of thawing when you are ready to use the meat, wrap each piece individually before placing it in the freezer.

When buying frozen poultry, avoid packages that are limp or contain pinkish ice—signs that the bird was accidentally defrosted and then refrozen. When cooking poultry, always be sure the bird has first been thoroughly defrosted; if it is only partly thawed, it will not cook through evenly. To preserve its flavour, thaw the wrapped bird in the refrigerator—a process that may take two or three days for a heavy turkey. Allow at least four hours for each kilogram (two hours for each pound).

When you buy any bird, make sure it is sold complete with its giblets: the neck and the edible parts of the entrails—the liver, the heart and the gizzard. Occasionally, the giblets are removed and sold to food processors before the bird is marketed. If that is the case, complain; giblets are nutritious and full of flavour. Use them chopped in a stuffing or to add flavour to a sauce.

Preparing poultry for cooking

Before cooking a bird, check to see that it has been properly prepared. Plucked birds often retain a few small feathers, especially around the vent and wings; these feathers can be easily removed by hand. If the flesh has any visible hairs, carefully pass the bird over a low flame and brush the singed hairs away. Both the neck and breast cavity should be clean. Sometimes, however, the kidneys are left in place and, occasionally, shreds of lung tissue remain attached on each side of the backbone. You can remove them, if you wish, although it is not strictly necessary as they will not affect the flavour of the cooked bird.

Sometimes, too, you will purchase a duck or goose that still has its oil glands—two small nodules on the upper side of the tail that help keep the bird's plumage waterproof. Contrary to widespread belief, the oil glands of most birds are innocuous and are removed only for aesthetic reasons; however, those of Muscovy duck—and all wild duck—will impart a musky taste to the flesh if they are not removed before cooking. You can cut out the glands easily with the tip of a sharp knife.

Cook any fresh bird within two days; poultry cannot be refrigerated longer without deteriorating in quality.

Serving wine with poultry

Like most food, poultry dishes are enhanced by wine, which stimulates the digestion and heightens the flavours of food it accompanies. There is a popular fallacy that white wines are the logical choice for most poultry dishes. In fact, wines suitable for serving with any kind of poultry may be either white or red, and can run the gamut from light-bodied and simple to full-bodied and complex, from rough and rustic to restrained and elegant, from direct and fruity to intricately bouqueted. However, each type of bird has a natural affinity with certain types of wines.

The full flavour of goose and duck is usually complemented by a correspondingly full-bodied red wine, such as a mature claret or Burgundy, although a well-aged Sauternes can marry surprisingly well with goose. Guinea-fowl, which retains the subtle gamey flavour of its wild relatives, is best appreciated with a relatively young claret, a red Burgundy or a dryish white wine, such as a Graves. When simply roasted or casseroled, chicken and turkey are equally at home with any wine of quality—whether it be a brittle six-month-old white, a young Zinfandel from California, a venerable claret, a perfumed Gewürztraminer from Alsace or a fruity Sauternes.

If you are serving a poultry dish as the main course of a menu, your choice of wine may be affected by the wines that you plan to serve with the preceding and following courses. As a rough guide, it is logical to work from white wines to red, young to old, light-bodied to full-bodied. Another consideration will be the other ingredients used in the preparation of the poultry dish. If a bird's natural flavour has been elaborated upon by a marinade or sauce, the accompanying wine should be selected accordingly. Marinades may detract from a mature red wine, but a dry white has enough natural acidity to counter their sharpness. Sauces thickened with egg yolk, as used in chicken fricassée (*page 58*), meld best with a fine white wine. The depth and vigour of a red wine sauce deserve to be matched by a red wine for drinking—perhaps a wine that is less robust, but more intricately flavoured than the wine used in the cooking.

Like the methods of cooking poultry described in this book, these suggestions are not meant to be cast-iron rules; they represent merely a framework of principles that has been formed by experience and tempered by common sense. Taste, however, is an individual thing; and once the basic principles of cooking poultry are understood, the cook is free to use imagination and improvisation—in preparing a chicken for the table or in choosing a wine to accompany it.

In the words of Louis Diat, a distinguished French chef and author: "The end result of learning the basic cookery methods . . . is that you develop versatility and flexibility obtainable in no other way. You come to understand recipes far more quickly and easily—the very reading of them can be a pleasure—and you become, also, less dependent on them. And this kind of assurance is, I believe, a test of a good cook."

Vegetable Garnishes that Marry Poultry Flavours

Sometimes, garnishes are mere embellishments, designed—like a sprinkling of parsley—to make foods look more appealing. Even vegetable garnishes are usually cooked separately and arranged on a platter around a roast or other meat dish. In poultry cooking, however, you can give new purpose to garnish vegetables such as the ones shown here. By adding them to the bird while it is cooking, you invite the flavours of the vegetables to mingle with those of the bird; the garnish thus becomes an integral part of the finished dish

while still contributing colour and contrast to the serving platter.

Braising (*pages 52-63*) and poaching (*pages 64-69*) rely for sturdy support on the group of vegetables known as aromatics: carrots, turnips and onions, for example, whose robust flavours are drawn out during long cooking to flavour the bird and its sauce. Sautéing, however, offers the cook the most opportunities to use garnishes imaginatively (*pages 22-29*). In sautés, the vegetables—once prepared—are generally added only a few

minutes before the end of the cooking time. In this way delicately textured and flavoured types, such as new peas, cucumbers or mushrooms, keep their shape, colour and essences.

For any method of cooking, most fresh vegetables have to be cleaned, peeled, shelled or trimmed. A few, including the six shown immediately below, require some special preparation.

Many garnishes used in sautés also require brief pre-cooking. Trimmed fennel is usually sliced and parboiled, as are

Stringing mange-tout peas. Break off the stem end of each pod and pull away the fibrous strings from each edge *(above)*.

Cleaning leeks. Insert a knife tip into the white part, and slice through the trimmed green leaves. Rotate the leek a quarter-turn and repeat *(above)*. Rinse or soak in water.

Seeding tomatoes. Put each tomato in boiling water for 30 seconds, skin it, halve it horizontally, then remove the seeds and the acidic juice.

Trimmed artichoke

Leek

Fennel

Skinned tomatoes

Peas

Mushrooms

Peeled turnip

Broad beans

Mange-tout peas

such root vegetables as turnips, carrots and potatoes. Mange-tout should be parboiled for a minute and added to the sauté at the last moment. But tender celery, green spring onions, young broad beans and peas may be scattered raw on the sauté for the last few minutes of cooking.

To prepare artichokes, pull back the tough outer leaves until they break away, snap off the stem, slice off the upper tough part of the remaining leaves and, spiral-fashion, peel the outer part of the green base. If the artichoke is young and tender, remove the fibrous choke; if it is old, parboil it before removing the choke. Halve or quarter the artichoke and stew the segments in butter for 10 minutes; or until they are tender but still firm. Then add them to the sauté and cook them for a few minutes more.

Mushrooms need only be tossed quickly in butter over a high heat, then incorporated into the sauté just before serving. Okra, too, should be cooked briefly in butter before being added to the sauté. First prepare them by cutting off the thick stem ends; do not pierce the hollow pod. Peppers should be grilled, skinned and seeded (*below*). Leeks and small onions can be stewed in butter until tender. Cucumbers can be parboiled in salted water and stewed in butter. Aubergines are usually peeled and cubed and added raw or part-cooked in olive oil.

Any one of the vegetables shown here will complement or invigorate your sauté. Putting together your own combinations will also give you the satisfaction of inventing distinctive new dishes.

Removing carrot cores. Winter carrots often have a tough, woody core. Halve each carrot lengthwise, loosen the centre with a knife, and prize out the core *(above)*.

Peeling peppers. Bake a pepper briefly under a hot grill, rotating it frequently; its skin will peel off easily. Halve the pepper and remove seeds, core and ribs.

Removing cucumber seeds. Halve each cucumber lengthwise and scoop out the seeds with a ball-cutter or spoon.

Courgettes

Carrots

Pepper

Trimmed celery

Onions

Seeded cucumber

Aubergine

Okra

Spring onions

Peeled potatoes

Soy sauce

Wine vinegar with tarragon

Lemon

Olive oil

Red-wine vinegar

Orange rind

Tarragon

Chives

Chervil

Rosemary

Thyme

Parsley

Herbs, Spices and Liquids for Marinades

A delicious and subtle way to give a new edge to the taste of poultry is to steep it in a marinade before cooking. A classic marinade combines herbs, spices and other flavourings with oil and usually an acidic liquid such as lemon juice, wine or vinegar. The raw meat absorbs the flavours, while the acid breaks down the fibres to make the flesh more tender. The acid also lends a welcome piquancy of its own to bland, commercially raised chickens.

A marinade takes two basic forms. A blend of fruity olive oil, herbs and spices rubbed into the skin of a bird before cooking constitutes a simple "dry" marinade—so called because it incorporates no water-based fluid, or, at most, a few drops of lemon juice. To allow the flavours to penetrate, marinate the bird for a few hours at room temperature, or overnight in the refrigerator; and then use the leftover marinade to baste the bird at intervals during the cooking process.

The more copious "wet" marinades, in which poultry is partly or wholly immersed, include a quantity of acidic liquid that helps the herbs and spices to permeate the flesh with their essences as it softens the fibres. Turn the poultry from time to time so that each side absorbs the marinade, and wipe it dry before frying or grilling so it will brown properly.

For flavourings, you can select from the whole range of herbs (*above*) and spices (*below*), as well as such assertive vegetables as onions. Experiment with different liquids, too: try a little sherry, for instance; or follow oriental practice and use pungent soy sauce.

Juniper

Nutmeg

Cinnamon

Mixed dried herbs

Mace

Cardamom

Coriander

White wine

Onion

Sherry

Garlic

Red wine

Ginger

Bay

Basil

Marjoram

Winter savory

Lovage

Rosemary and a "dry" marinade perfume a flattened bird.

Cayenne pepper and onions sharpen a wine-based marinade.

White pepper

Paprika

Cayenne pepper

Black pepper

Cumin

Saffron threads

Cloves

Allspice

13

Nature's Herbal Fragrances in Your Kitchen

Herbs are the soul of good cooking. Most poultry dishes would be poorer without them, and chicken is especially enlivened by imaginative use of these natural flavouring agents. Of the hundreds of different herbs grown, the 16 illustrated here are among those that marry best with poultry. Each has its own character—sweet or pungent, subtle or strong. Each may be used alone, the quantity varied by the type of bird, its size and the degree of herb flavour desired. Herbs can also be used in combinations chosen carefully to prevent powerful ones from overwhelming the more delicate.

The surest way to get to know herbs is to try them out in your own cooking. As a beginning, explore the classic combination of the bouquet garni (*box, opposite*) for braising and poaching, and experiment with *fines herbes*—a mixture of finely chopped fresh parsley, chives, tarragon and chervil—when making sauces. Although you can generally substitute one teaspoon of dried herb for one tablespoon of fresh, use fresh ones for the truest flavours wherever possible. Most herbs are easily grown in a garden or window-box. Herbs will stay fresh for days if you put them in a damp towel or a polythene bag and refrigerate them.

Chervil. One of the most delicate and subtle relations of parsley, chervil is best added at the end of cooking. In combinations its hint of anise flavour helps accentuate the taste of other herbs.

Tarragon. A pungent herb with a subtle anise flavour, tarragon is often used alone, but is one of the elements of *fines herbes*. It is especially good with chicken—fresh tarragon sprigs tucked into the body cavity will give a delicious lift to a simple roast.

Parsley. A basic in bouquets garnis, parsley combines well with most other herbs. Flat-leaf parsley (*far left*) has a more pronounced and finer flavour than the curly-leafed variety (*left*) and it withstands long cooking.

Bay. Aromatic bay leaves can be used fresh or dried. An indispensable part of the classic bouquet garni, they can also be skewered on brochettes (*page 50*) or tucked between the wings and body of a roasting bird.

Chives. Chives are the most delicately flavoured member of the onion family. The slender, bright green leaves should be used fresh, cut into tiny pieces, and added to a hot dish or sauce at the last moment: cooking destroys the flavour.

Sweet Marjoram. Pungent yet mild, stems of marjoram add a pleasant bitterness to a bouquet garni. The crushed leaves (fresh or dried) may be used to perfume a sauce; or the flower buds can be finely chopped to season a bread or herb butter stuffing.

Hyssop. Popular in medieval cookery, hyssop has a resinous perfume that is offset by a refreshing edge of bitterness. The leaves lend sprightliness to a poultry marinade or may be incorporated in a bouquet garni.

Savory. Grilled poultry benefits particularly from the peppery and piquant winter savory (*above*) as well as its milder relative, summer savory. Both can be used in a bouquet garni, *fines herbes* or a dried herb mixture.

Lovage. A giant herb, similar in appearance and flavour to celery, lovage has dark green leaves that can be chopped and added in small amounts to stuffings for duck, goose and turkey, or included in a bouquet garni.

Thyme. This herb is sweet but powerful; it should be used with restraint for grills, but can be employed more generously in braises. Common thyme (*below*), either fresh or dried, is an essential ingredient of a bouquet garni. Lemon thyme enlivens sautés and simple sauces.

Rosemary. Intense and spicy, rosemary can easily be overpowering: a single fresh sprig placed in the body cavity of a roasting chicken will flavour the whole bird. On an outdoor grill, a few bits of rosemary burned on the coals will add fragrance to poultry (*page 51*).

Fennel. The feathery leaves of common, or wild, fennel give a mild liquorice flavour to a stuffing. The dried stalks of the plant can be used to scent a pot-roasted chicken. Take care only to combine fennel with complementary herbs, such as tarragon.

Basil. The spicy flavour of basil is best on its own in tomato mixtures and sauces for chicken and duck. Tear the leaves by hand if they are too large to use whole, and, since they discolour rapidly when cut or torn, do this at the last possible moment.

Sage. A traditional seasoning for poultry stuffing, sage has an aggressive flavour that not everyone finds pleasant. Try putting a small branch of it into the cavity of a roasting chicken. Avoid dried sage, which can taste musty.

Oregano. Unlike most herbs, oregano is more potent dried than fresh. It marries well with tomato sauces and is useful in marinades. The flowers are the most valuable part of the plant, but the stems and leaves are pleasantly perfumed. Crumbled and sprinkled on a charcoal grill, they add savour to poultry.

Sorrel. The sharp, clean acidity of fresh young sorrel leaves in a sauce complements the delicacy of poached chicken (*page 69*). You can also chop up the leaves to enliven a stuffing.

A Neat Bundle of Seasonings

A bouquet garni is simply a bunch of mixed herbs that flavours stocks, soups and braises while they cook, and is discarded at the end of the process. In its commercial form—a spoonful of dried herbs in a little muslin bag—a bouquet garni is usually stale and expensive. The real thing is cheap, easy to make, and packed with flavour. The heart of a classic bouquet garni is the triple alliance of fresh or dried bay leaf, fresh parsley (including the flavourful stalks and root) and fresh or dried thyme. The herbs are wrapped in a celery stalk or leek green—or both, as here. There are no unbreakable rules about the composition of a bouquet garni. The three classic components are nearly always present, but other herbs—and even dried orange or lemon peel—can be used.

1 Assembling the bouquet. Wash a suitably sized celery stick and place in it your chosen flavourings: shown here are fresh flat-leaf parsley, dried thyme, fresh bay, celery tops and leek green. Fold the celery stick and leek green around the herbs.

2 Tying with string. Holding the bouquet together, wind enough kitchen string tightly around to make a secure bundle. Leave a loop of string hanging free so that you can remove the herb bundle easily when cooking is completed.

A Waste-Free Way of Jointing

Poultry pieces purchased from a shop or supermarket are sometimes of poor quality and, weight for weight, are more expensive than a whole bird. By learning how to cut up poultry at home, you can save money and also provide neater looking, more appetizing portions. And there is a bonus, too, in the giblets.

The process is simpler than it appears and, approached with confidence, can be accomplished in a few minutes. All you need are a chopping board and a heavy cook's knife with a sharp edge and pointed blade. But the key to cutting up poultry into tidy pieces lies in your own hands. Learn to locate the joints by feel so that, when you bear down on the knife, you avoid the bones and cut through the less resistant tendons and cartilage.

On these pages, a chicken is used to demonstrate the technique, but since all birds have the same basic anatomy, you can adapt the steps to cut up duck, turkey, guinea-fowl and other poultry.

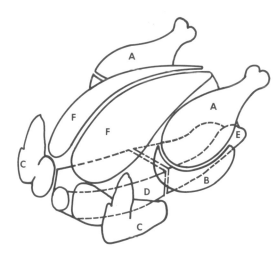

The lettered diagram above summarizes the simplest way to divide up a whole chicken. The most convenient place to begin is at the legs, which yield drumsticks (A) and thigh pieces (B). After the wings (C) are removed, the ribcage is cut through (Step 4) to separate the back and breast. The back is divided into two pieces (D and E) by cutting across the spine. The final step is cutting the breast into two portions (F) by splitting it lengthwise.

1 Removing the legs. Place the chicken, breast side up, on a board. Pull one leg gently away from the body and cut through the skin between the body and the thigh. Now bend the whole leg firmly outwards until the ball of the thigh bone pops from its socket. Cut down between ball and socket, and the leg will come cleanly away. Repeat this procedure with the other leg.

2 Dividing the legs. Place each whole chicken leg in turn on the board, skin side down, and cut firmly down through the joint to separate drumsticks from thighs. If the bird is a very small one, this step may be omitted.

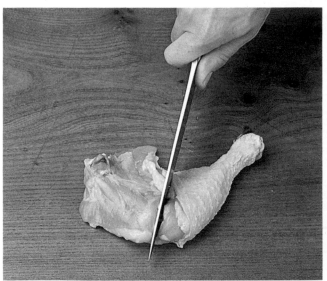

3 Removing the wings. Press one wing against the body of the bird; both parts of the shoulder joint will now be visible beneath the skin. Make an incision between the ball and socket of the joint, then pull the wing outwards and cut down through the skin at the base of the wing. Remove the other wing by the same method.

Splitting the carcass. Place the knife blade inside the cavity of the bird and pierce one side between the shoulder joint and the ribcage. Cutting towards yourself, parallel to the backbone, carefully slit the ribcage. Repeat the same steps on the bird's other side.

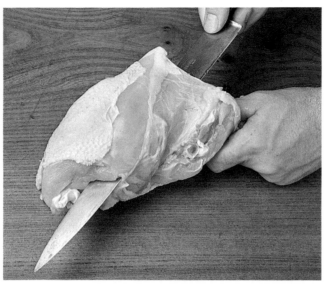

**Separating the breast.** Pull the breast away from the back to expose the shoulder bones. Cut down between these bones to detach the breast section (*right*). Next, divide the back into two pieces by cutting widthwise across the spine at the point where the ribcage ends.

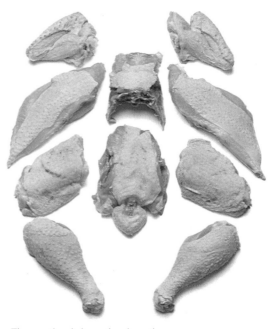

**Halving the breast.** Place the breast skin side up on the chopping board. Using a strong, steady pressure on the knife, cut down through the breastbone on one or the other side of its keel. Larger birds, such as turkey or goose, can be cut again widthwise to yield between four and six breast portions.□

The method described on these pages yields 10 pieces. No part of the carcass is wasted, but the sizes of the pieces differ widely. An alternative procedure that provides fewer but more equal portions is explained on the following pages.

Equal Portions and How to Obtain Them

Although the jointing method shown on the previous pages is quick and economical, professional chefs cut up poultry by a variation of the method shown here when they want to produce larger and more attractive pieces—all with roughly the same amount of meat on them.

In this method, demonstrated here on a chicken, the wing tips are removed for neatness and then the wings themselves are cut off the carcass with some of the tender breast and a piece of the back attached to them. The legs are not divided into thighs and drumsticks; instead, they are each detached in one piece, together with an "oyster"—the succulent button of dark meat on the bird's back that usually disappears into the stock-pot with the carcass. The rest of the back is reserved for stock or soup, along with the wing tips and any oddments trimmed off in the process of tidying up for cooking.

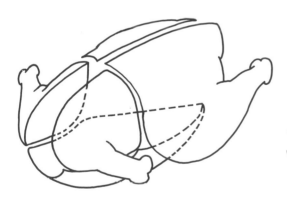

The diagram above, with the chicken back uppermost, indicates the lines along which the bird is divided. Note that as much flesh as possible from the back is included in the leg and wing cuts. And most of the meat from the rest of the carcass is included in the breast cut so that the bones left behind have very little flesh on them. The bones may be used for stock.

1 **Cutting along the spine.** Lay the chicken on its breast and feel for the ends of the shoulder-blades with your fingers. Make a shallow cut across the back below the shoulder-blades, and a perpendicular cut along the spine from the centre of the first cut (*right*). Do not slice through the bone. These cuts outline the area that contains the morsels known as oysters.

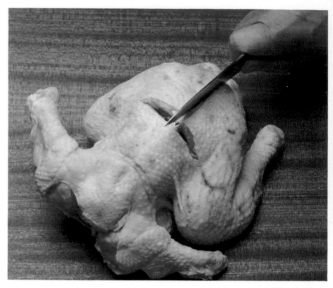

2 **Freeing the oysters.** Each oyster nestles snugly in a small hollow alongside the backbone. Use the point of the knife to free it from the bone (*right*), leaving the oyster attached to the skin.

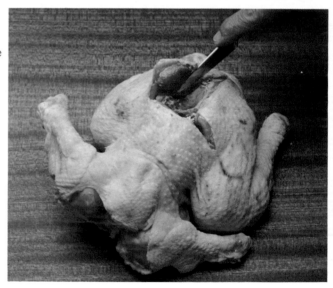

3 **Removing the legs.** Turn the chicken breast uppermost. Cut through the skin where one thigh joins the body. Bend the leg outwards to pop the bone from its ball-and-socket joint. Cut down between the ball and socket (*right*) and remove the leg, bringing the oyster with it. Take care to keep the oyster clear of the knife blade as you cut. Repeat with the other leg. Trim off the bony knobs from the drumstick ends and, to prevent the legs from distorting as they cook, nick the strong tendons between the drumsticks and the thighs.

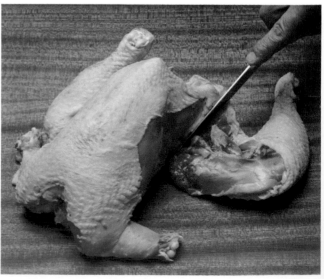

Freeing the shoulders. Turn the chicken over, breast side down. Insert the knife between the backbone and one shoulder-blade, and cut down firmly through the back into the cavity, leaving the wing attached to the breast. Repeat this step on the other side of the backbone.

Splitting the carcass. Place the knife inside the cavity of the bird and pierce one side between a shoulder joint and the ribcage (*right*). Next, cut carefully towards yourself, slitting right the way through the ribcage parallel to the backbone. Repeat the same steps on the other side of the bird. Since the shoulders have already been cut free (*Step 4*), the back may now be pulled away.

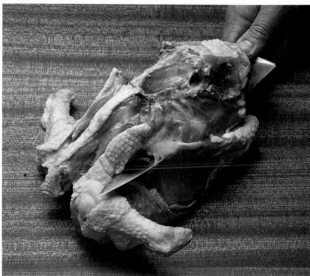

Removing the wings. Turn the whole breast, with wings attached, skin side up. Sever the wing portions by cutting firmly through the skin and flesh from the point at which the collar-bone meets the breastbone. Make the cuts diagonally so that some of the breast meat is included in each wing portion.□

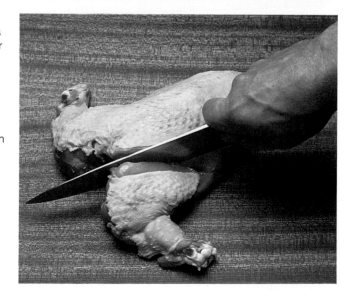

Cut up by the method described on these pages, an average-sized chicken will yield five pieces. The breast of a larger chicken or a goose or turkey can further be divided into two or even more pieces. All the pieces are of similar proportions, and will provide servings of equal size.

An Ingenious Method for Boning Whole Birds

If it is prepared with a savoury stuffing, boned poultry is an impressive demonstration of the cook's art—and an economy, too. With its bones removed, a stuffed bird can be served in slices (*page 62*)—a simple method of carving that wastes no meat. The extracted bones can furnish rich stock to be used in cooking the bird. Best of all, the method will provide six portions from a duck, instead of the usual two or three.

The apparently intricate boning technique can easily be mastered by any cook who has learned to cut up a chicken (*previous pages*); it is identical for all types of poultry. All you need are a small, very sharp knife and patience. The first try may take up to an hour; the second time it will go more quickly.

The boning process, demonstrated here on a duck, keeps the skin intact, with no slits except the openings where the butcher cleaned the bird. First, the structure comprising the wishbone, collar-bones and shoulder-blades is removed. The flesh can then be carefully peeled back from the carcass. At this stage the boned bird resembles a limp meaty sack (*above*). The main wing and leg bones are left in place, so that the bird—after it has been stuffed, trussed and cooked—will have a natural, untouched appearance. Carving then reveals the surprise within.

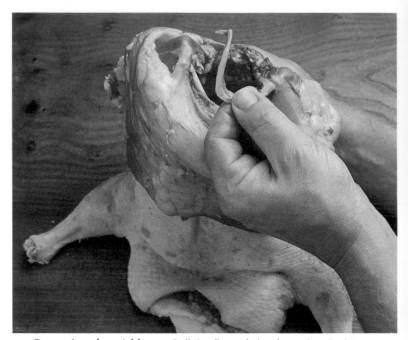

1 **Removing the wishbone.** Pull the flap of skin from the duck's neck down around the shoulders, turning it inside out until you can locate the wishbone with your fingers. Slit just deep enough into the surrounding flesh to expose the wishbone fully. Snap the wishbone from its attachment at the shoulder joints, where it meets the collar-bones, shoulder-blades and wing bones.

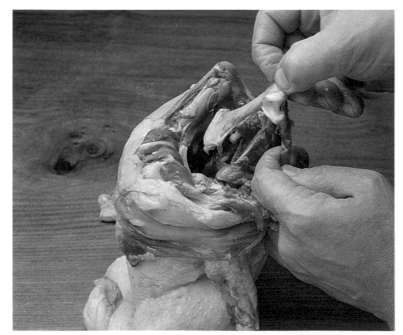

4 **Removing the collar-bones and shoulder-blades.** Each collar-bone is now attached only to a shoulder-blade—a thin strut whose other end is embedded in the flesh. Remove both bones together by pulling steadily on the connecting joint. To help free the shoulder-blade from the flesh without tearing the muscles, draw it out between a firmly pinched finger and thumb (*above*). If the bone breaks, cut out any remaining pieces with the knife.

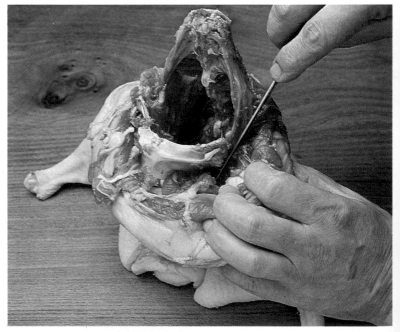

5 **Exposing the skeleton.** Pull back the flesh around the shoulders to reveal the top of the skeletal structure comprising ribcage, breastbone and backbone. Working towards the legs, scrape the flesh from the skeleton, using fingers and knife (*above*). To avoid damaging the skin, always cut towards the carcass. Where the backbone is attached by the cartilaginous tips of the vertebrae, slice through these tips, but leave them in the flesh.

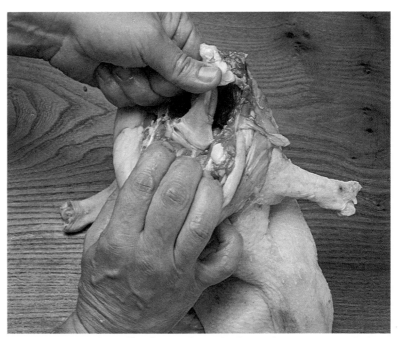

2 **Freeing the wings.** Pull back one wing, as shown above, until you have exposed the tough bands of sinew that hold the wing bone to the collar-bone and the shoulder-blade. Cut through these sinews to separate the wing, but do not pull out the wing bone. Repeat the procedure with the other wing.

3 **Snapping the collar-bones from the breastbone.** One end of each collar-bone is attached to the corresponding shoulder-blade; the other end is joined to the breastbone by a weak and easily broken seam of cartilage. First, clear the surrounding flesh from the collar-bones with your fingers, scraping with the knife where necessary; then, snap them free from the breastbone.

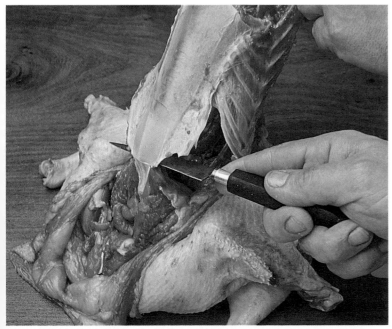

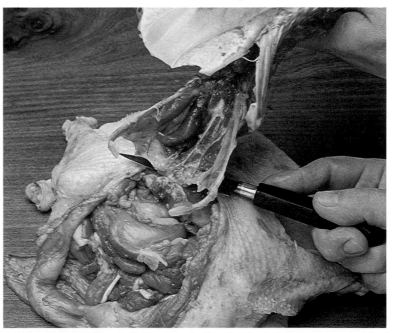

6 **Separating the breastbone.** When the knife reaches the legs, pop the bones from the ball-and-socket joints where they join the spine and cut through the connecting cartilage. Leave the leg bones in place. Continue peeling back the flesh until you reach the end of the breastbone: a thin strip of cartilage connects it to the body. Cut through this strip (*above*) to free the breastbone.

7 **Removing the skeleton.** The flesh will now be almost completely peeled away from the skeleton. Lift up the skeleton and cut through the backbone at the tail (*above*), leaving behind the last three or four vertebrae—the tail's bone structure. If the lower ribs, which are not firmly attached to the rest of the skeleton, remain in the flesh, cut them out. The boned duck is now ready to be filled with a stuffing (*page 38*), trussed and cooked.□

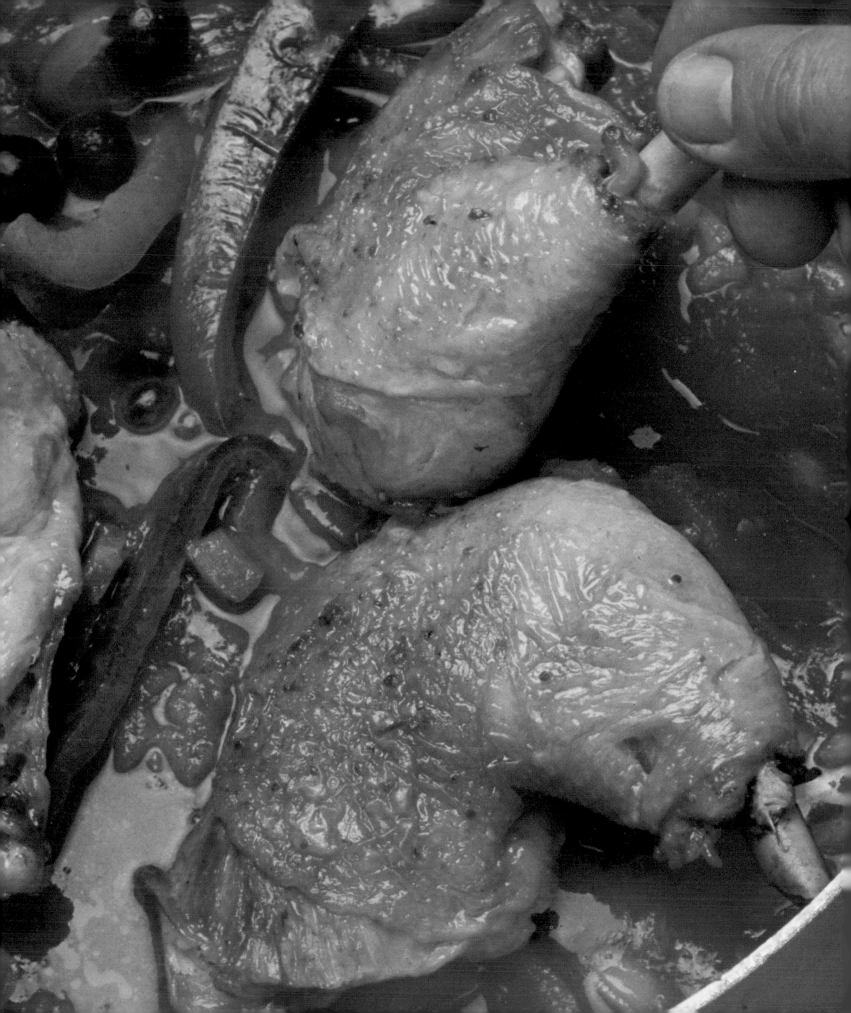

1
Pan Frying
Sealing in the Succulence

In the final assembly of an eye-catching sauté with a Provençal flavour, tender pan-fried chicken pieces are combined with a red wine sauce and a garnish of green peppers, seeded tomatoes, black olives, onion slices and garlic.

To be savoured at its best, young poultry should be cooked by a method that preserves its natural succulence and tenderness. Pan frying, a method particularly appropriate for chicken pieces, is one of the easiest ways of ensuring this. The pan—coated inside with just enough oil or fat to keep the chicken from adhering to it—transmits heat directly to the meat, searing its surfaces and sealing in its juices. All you need is a pan of highly conductive metal: copper, an excellent conductor, is a natural choice, but good results can be achieved with a heavy iron or aluminium pan.

This simple way to cook poultry is called sautéing—from the French *sauter*, "to jump". Strictly speaking, the term is applied to the technique of tossing small chunks of meat or vegetables in a pan set over a high heat; making the pieces "jump" promotes even cooking and prevents sticking. But in the more usual application of the method, the pieces are turned, rather than tossed, to keep them from burning on the outside before being cooked within. Usually the poultry pieces are first browned over a high heat and then, with the heat reduced, cooked until done. The time varies, depending on whether dark or white meat is involved.

A second method of pan frying calls for dipping the poultry pieces in seasoned flour at the outset. The oil or fat does not come directly into contact with the meat, but transforms the flour into a crisp, golden crust that locks in the poultry juices. Unlike sautéing, where a minimum of oil or fat is used, this method calls for up to 1 cm ($\frac{1}{2}$ inch) of oil or fat—a deep enough layer to immerse the food half-way and seal the crust quickly, first on one side, then on the other.

Both methods of pan frying are the foundation of a limitless number of finished poultry dishes. Sautéing, in particular, is so easy to master that it invites improvisation with different sauces and garnishes. It is a universal cooking method; in Chinese cookery, for example, morsels of food are sautéed by being rapidly stirred as they fry in a large, curved pan, or *wok*.

In addition, sautéing is an important preliminary step in the preparation of braises and casseroles. Its vital role in these different cooking methods makes it one of the most important of all culinary techniques.

A Cooking Method that Produces its own Sauce

In the three-stage sautéing process illustrated here, the poultry pieces are first browned in an open pan to seal the meat and prevent flavoursome juices from escaping. Then the pan is covered and they are cooked through gently. Finally, when the pieces are done, they are removed, and the juices and the caramelized residue remaining in the pan are put to use as the base of a sauce.

Ideally, the pan for sautéing should be just wide enough to hold the chicken pieces side by side. If they overlap, the moisture they exude will not evaporate readily and the pieces will start to stew instead of browning. On the other hand, too much space between the pieces will allow the oil or fat to overheat and burn.

Butter enriches the taste of poultry, and many sauté recipes call for it to be used to brown the pieces. Olive oil and poultry fat also produce good results.

During the gentle-cooking stage, a vegetable garnish may be added to the poultry to enhance the flavour of the finished dish. The vegetables should always be introduced after the poultry has browned, so that their moisture does not interfere with the sealing process.

The range of garnishes is boundless (see box on this page and the detailed instructions for preparing garnishes on page 10). The vegetables can be raw or may be partly cooked before they are added to the pan. In the illustrated cooking sequence here, the chicken pieces are garnished with parboiled chunks of cucumber. In Prosper Montagné's chicken sauté Archduke(*recipe, page 91*), the cucumber is cooked in butter separately and then added as a final garnish.

When the meat and garnish are done, the excess fats are poured off and a liquid is used to dissolve the brown bits of caramelized juices adhering to the bottom of the pan. This process is called deglazing and it is the first step in making the sauce. In this demonstration, white wine is used to deglaze the pan, but any liquid—such as stock or water—will do.

1 **Sealing in the flavour.** In a sauté pan, heat enough oil or fat to coat the bottom. Dry the chicken pieces—any moisture clinging to them will interfere with the sealing process—and arrange them in the pan. Fry the pieces, turning them with tongs until they are evenly browned. This will take 15 to 20 minutes.

2 **The gentle-cooking phase.** Reduce the heat and cover the pan. The breasts will be done in about 8 to 10 minutes. You could test for doneness by pricking with a skewer; if the juices that run out are untinted by blood, the breasts are done. Remove them to a warm dish, replace the lid, and cook the other pieces for about 10 minutes more.

Elaborating a Sauté with Vegetables and Herbs

A Mediterranean sauté

A sauté with mushrooms and leeks

By adding various garnishes to sautéed poultry pieces and finishing the sauce in different ways, a surprising number of original dishes can be created. A small bundle of fresh herbs, for example, contributes an aromatic presence that eliminates the need for any additional garnish; simply add the herbs at the start of the gentle-cooking phase and remove them when cooking is completed. You can prepare a sauce in the same pan by bringing wine to a boil and simmering it to half its original volume.

For a dish in the tradition of Provençal cookery, garnish the poultry with tomatoes, green peppers, black olives, garlic and parsley (*above, left*). Or create a medley of contrasting flavours by garnishing the chicken with rapidly sautéed mushrooms and sliced leeks stewed in butter (*above, right*). Finish the sauce with white wine and butter, as here, or with cream and chicken stock thickened with flour (*recipe, page 91*).

3 **Adding the garnish.** After the breasts have been removed, add a vegetable garnish if you want one. The exact moment depends on the ingredients chosen and the time they take to cook (*recipes, pages 88-92*). Here, chunks of cucumber that were first parboiled in salted water and drained, then stewed in a little butter, constitute the garnish.

4 **Pouring off excess fat.** The juices exuded by the chicken are a delicious complement to the flesh, but the frying fat is unpalatable. Put the remaining chicken pieces and the garnish in the warm dish containing the breasts. Pour off and discard the fat, but stop before the darker meat juices in the pan run out.

5 **Deglazing.** Add a generous dash of liquid—in this case, white wine—to the pan..Over high heat, stir and scrape with a wooden spoon until the coagulated meat juices sticking to the pan have been loosened and dissolved in the liquid. Boil the enriched liquid briskly for a few minutes to reduce and concentrate it.

6 **Finishing the sauce.** Sauces for sautéed poultry dishes are usually completed by adding an element that enhances the flavour and consistency. Here, double cream is added to the pan liquid and stirred constantly over a high heat until the sauce thickens to a consistency that will smoothly coat the poultry pieces.

7 **Assembling the finished sauté.** Reduce the heat to low, then return the chicken pieces and the garnish to the sauce in the sauté pan. Replace the lid and warm the assembled dish through for a few minutes before serving it. □

Fried Chicken in a Crisp Coating

Fried chicken is one of the world's great basic dishes. In the United States it ranks as a national institution—albeit one subject to infinite variations from region to region and cook to cook.

Some people insist that the chicken be fried in the fat from smoked bacon; others swear by lard, still others by peanut oil. In the United States especially, inventive cooks test their ingenuity by devising original and sometimes exotic coating mixtures. Although the dish demonstrated here uses ordinary white flour (*recipes, pages 96-97*), some cooks supplement or replace it with buckwheat, rye or wholemeal flours; others add ground-up nuts and cereals flavoured with different combinations of herbs and spices.

In some parts of the world, chicken is marinated before being coated for frying, as in the Greek recipe on page 95—a process that both flavours the flesh and guarantees its tenderness.

The cooking, too, can be subject to variations: although chicken is normally pan fried until done, an alternative is to give the pieces an initial browning in the frying pan, and finish by baking them in a moderate oven.

However the coating is prepared, there are two keys to accomplishing a perfect finished dish. Do not wipe the chicken pieces dry first, as you would for sautés; a slight moistness helps the coating to adhere. Flour the pieces an hour or so before frying them; this allows time for the coating to stick firmly, making it less likely that bits will become detached during cooking and burn.

Unlike the more elaborate sautés, with their garnishes and sauces, simple fried chicken tastes as good cold as it does hot. If prepared a day in advance, it makes excellent picnic fare that can conveniently be eaten with your fingers.

Coating the chicken. An hour or so before frying, season the chicken pieces on all sides with salt and pepper. Spread flour—or any suitable coating mixture—on a dinner plate and roll each chicken piece in the flour until it is evenly covered. Place the pieces on a wire rack so that any loose flour will drop off them.

Flouring in a Bag

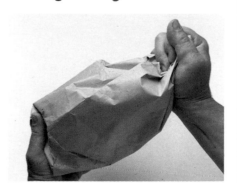

A neat trick for coating chicken pieces is to put the seasoned coating mixture in a sturdy paper or plastic bag, then add the poultry a piece or two at a time and shake the bag vigorously, holding it tightly closed. When the chicken is removed, it will be completely covered. Any flour left in the bag can be used for a gravy (see box on the right).

An Easy-to-Make Pan Gravy

While cooks may argue about the relative merits of different coatings for pan-fried chicken, most would agree that milk gravy is a worthy accompaniment to the dish. The gravy is made by first browning a sprinkling of flour in a few tablespoons of the fat in the pan, and then deglazing the savoury scrapings in the pan with milk. The resulting smooth sauce provides a suitable contrast to the crisply fried chicken.

You can improve on this basic sauce by substituting other liquids, such as cream, for the milk, as in the recipe on page 97. You can add fried chopped giblets or a sprinkling of herbs. Try replacing some of the milk with chicken stock for a richer flavour. Whatever gravy you make, you can serve it either poured over the platter of chicken or on the side in a gravy boat.

2 **Frying the chicken.** In a heavy skillet or frying pan, heat a shallow layer of oil or fat. Place the chicken pieces in the fat: if you use tongs, you avoid spattering your hands with hot fat but risk damaging the flour coating (wooden tongs reduce the risk). Do not overcrowd the pan, which would make the pieces difficult to turn and cause uneven cooking. As the surface being fried begins to take on colour, gently turn the pieces over.

3 **Cooking until done.** Keep turning the pieces occasionally to ensure that they cook evenly. After about 30 minutes, the tender breasts will be cooked through; remove them to a serving platter and put in a warm oven. After another 15 minutes or so, remove the remaining chicken, add the pieces to those that have been kept warm in the oven, and serve from the platter.☐

1 **Making a roux.** After frying the chicken, pour from the pan all but a couple of tablespoons of fat. Return the pan to a low heat and sprinkle flour into the fat. With a wooden spoon, briskly stir the fat and flour together until the mixture begins to bubble. This mixture—which is the thickening agent of many sauces—is called a *roux*.

2 **Adding the liquid.** Slowly pour milk, single cream or any other suitable liquid into the pan and stir and scrape rapidly to blend together the fat, flour and pan juices. Add salt and pepper to taste.

3 **Removing the taste of flour.** Gravies and sauces thickened with flour have a pasty flavour if they are not cooked long enough. Simmering gently for 15 minutes (longer for some sauces) will remove the floury taste and reduce the gravy to a consistency that will coat the chicken. Stir the gravy occasionally to prevent it from caking on the bottom of the pan.

Boned Chicken Suprêmes for Elegant Sautés

Chicken breasts that have been skinned, boned and halved are known in culinary parlance as *suprêmes*. Rapidly sautéed and coated with a vinegar-and-butter sauce (*opposite page*), or with a delicate wine-and-almond sauce, as in the recipe on page 93, *suprêmes* are perfect for a luncheon or light supper. Each *suprême* makes an elegant single serving.

To prepare the chicken, start with a whole skinned breast prepared by the method shown on page 16. The bones and cartilage all have well-defined forms: using your fingers and a small, sharp knife, it is short work to remove them.

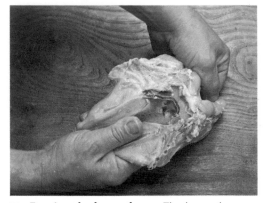

1 Freeing the breastbone. The breastbone is attached to the collar-bone. Place the breast skin side down and slit along the membrane covering the breastbone. Grasp the collar-bone and twist back the breastbone to snap them apart.

2 Removing the breastbone. Snap the breastbone from the piece of white cartilage attached to the narrow end of the breast. Gently prize the breastbone out of the breast. The ribs (*foreground*) may come away with it, as here.

3 Removing the ribs. Any ribs left attached to the breast can be pulled away with your fingers: if they resist, cut them away with the knife. Trim the tips of the ribs from the sides of the breast (*above*).

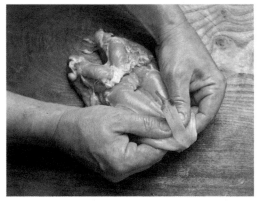

4 Removing the cartilage. Push your thumbs underneath the thin, flat piece of cartilage attached to the narrow end of the breast and pry the cartilage free.

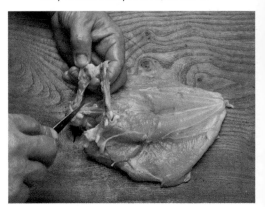

5 Removing the collar-bone. With the knife tip, cut through the thin layer of flesh that covers the collar-bone, carefully following the contours of the bone. When the bone is attached only at its two ends, pull it loose or cut it free.

6 Removing the wishbone. Feel the shape of the wishbone beneath the flesh, and carefully cut away the surrounding flesh with the knife tip. When it is uncovered, firmly grasp its prongs and pull it out.

7 Trimming the breast. Halve the breast along the cleft that held the breastbone. Trim off any fat or nervous tissue to shape each piece into a neat fillet.

8 Cooking the suprêmes. Heat one or two tablespoons of oil or fat in a small sauté pan. Place the breast pieces in the pan and, over a moderate heat, cook first one side and then the other until they are firm and springy to the touch.□

A Piquant Vinegar-and-Butter Sauce

A good sauce highlights the qualities of the food it accompanies without disguising its taste. The delicate texture and taste of sautéed, boned chicken breasts is enhanced by a sauce that is light in flavour and texture, with just a hint of sharpness to lend vigour to the dish. The sauce prepared here, which pairs well with plain sautéed chicken pieces (*recipe, page 93*), is flavoured with red-wine vinegar and chopped shallots.

The vinegar is reduced to concentrate its flavour and give it more body. To finish, pieces of butter are stirred into the sauce to bind it and give a velvety texture. When the butter is melted in the hot—not boiling—vinegar it goes into suspension: the sauce will separate if it is further heated. As soon as the butter and vinegar have blended together, pour the sauce over the chicken and serve.

1 **Deglazing with vinegar.** In the pan used to fry the chicken, sauté finely chopped shallots over a low heat. Cook, stirring, until they are lightly coloured but not brown. After pouring off any excess fat, add the vinegar and deglaze.

2 **Transferring to a saucepan.** Pour the vinegar and shallots into a small saucepan. The smaller diameter of the pan will make it easier to control the rate at which the liquid reduces.

3 **Reducing the liquid.** Boil the vinegar over brisk heat until it has reduced to the consistency of a light syrup. While it is reducing, test the consistency frequently with a wire whisk (*above*).

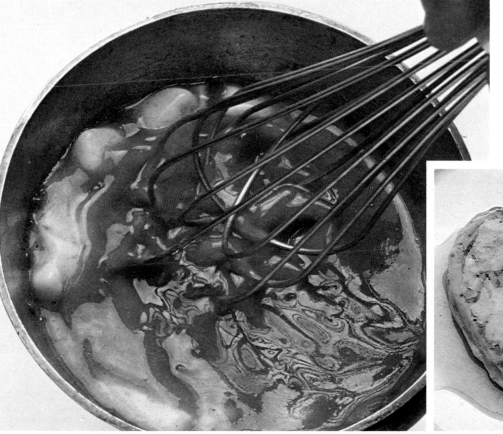

4 **Enriching with butter.** Cut the butter into small chunks that will melt quickly. Take the vinegar off the heat and add the butter all at once to the saucepan. Whisk (*left*) until the butter has blended into the vinegar. Add salt and pepper to taste, then pour the sauce directly from the pan on to the chicken breasts (*below*).

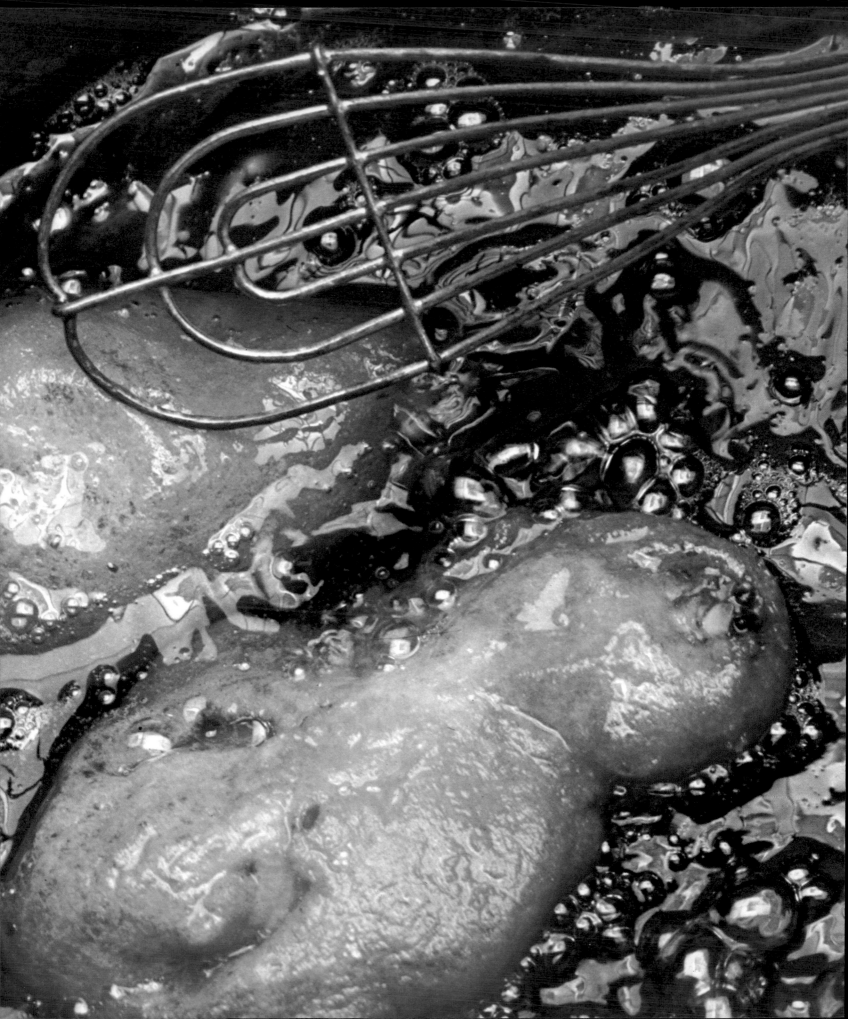

2
Deep Frying
A Sizzling Way to Ensure Crispness

Deep-fried chicken pieces turning golden in sizzling oil are ready for turning with a wire scoop or "spider". Such a scoop will not damage the batter coating and, when it is used to lift out the chicken, permits excess oil to drain off quickly.

In his book *The Physiology of Taste*, the 19th-century French gastronome Jean Anthelme Brillat-Savarin expounded an accurate, if somewhat eccentric, theory of deep frying. "The whole merit of deep frying," he wrote, "comes from the surprise"—a term he used to describe the instantaneous sealing of a piece of food when it is immersed in hot oil or fat. "By means of this surprise," Brillat-Savarin explained, "a sort of shell is formed around the food, which prevents the fat from penetrating and seals in the food's juices."

Brillat-Savarin noted that the success of deep frying depends on the high temperature to which the cooking medium of oil or fat is heated. "The boiling liquid," he stressed, "must be hot enough to make its action rapid and immediate; but it cannot arrive at this point unless it has been exposed for a considerable time to a high and lively fire." In precise terms, "hot enough" means that the oil or fat must reach a temperature between 180°C and 195°C (350°F and 385°F). Among the best oils and fats for deep frying are vegetable oils, lard and rendered suet—none of which burn at these temperatures. Butter is not suitable for deep frying.

A simple way to gauge the temperature of the oil or fat is to drop into it a small piece of bread; if the bread turns golden-brown in about a minute, the oil or fat has reached at least 180°C (350°F). When you deep fry poultry pieces coated with batter, you can use a spoonful of the batter to test the temperature (*overleaf*). Many cooks prefer to take the temperature of the oil or fat more accurately with deep-frying thermometers; others do away with testing by using thermostatically controlled deep-frying pans.

The initial heating of the fat is only the first step. When you put in poultry pieces, the temperature of the fat will fall, and the heat under the pan must be raised to compensate. Thereafter you must regulate the heat so that the food cooks evenly and without excessive browning. Chicken pieces with the bones in will cook through in 15 to 20 minutes, depending on size. Bearing these figures in mind, lower the heat if the food is browning too quickly; raise the heat if the food is not colouring fast enough. Larger pieces, such as turkey legs, will burn on the outside before being cooked within and are therefore not suitable for deep frying. Duck and goose are too fatty to be cooked by this method.

Marinated Chicken with a Batter Coating

The variety of poultry dishes that may be created by deep frying depends mostly on pre-cooking preparations. Chicken can be cut into pieces (*pages 16-19*) and cooked with the bones left in. Turkey as well as chicken can be chopped into chunks or carved into boneless, skinless morsels. The raw meat can be seasoned imaginatively with spices or a marinade before deep frying. The most tempting variations, though, are those achieved by coating marinated pieces in a batter, such as the one shown here, that cooks to a light, golden crispness.

When deep frying, you should observe a few simple safety measures. To avoid spillage, use a high-sided pan specially designed for deep frying; fill the pan no more than half full.

Dry all utensils thoroughly before you use them; when water comes into contact with very hot fat, the water vaporizes instantaneously and makes the fat splatter. If you regulate the heat properly, there is little chance of the oil or fat catching fire; but as a simple precaution, keep a tight-fitting lid close to the frying pan so that flames can be quickly smothered.

1 Marinating the chicken. Cut up a chicken as shown on pages 16-19. Season the pieces or flavour them with a marinade—in this case, chopped onions, herbs, lemon juice and white wine. Instructions for preparing marinades appear on page 12.

2 Heating the oil or fat. Fill a deep pan with oil or fat to a depth of 8 to 10 cm (3 to 4 inches), and place it over a high heat. Drop a dab of batter into the fat to test the temperature; if the batter sizzles on contact, the fat has reached the right temperature (about 180°C or 350°F).

The Secrets of a Light Puffy Batter

Batter for coating deep-fried poultry should be prepared at least an hour in advance. If used immediately, the batter will be too elastic to cling properly to the poultry pieces, and it will shrink and split when it comes into contact with the hot fat. An hour's rest enables the batter literally to relax.

A simple batter can be made with water, flour, oil and eggs alone; replace water with milk or wine, for a more flavourful batter. To make a fluffier coating, blend the flour with beer, and fold beaten egg whites into the batter just before frying (*recipe, page 166*). The beer causes the mixture to ferment slightly and, together with the egg whites, gives the batter a light, airy texture. Pale ale was used here, but any other beer will serve equally well.

1 Mixing the batter. Put flour, salt and oil into a mixing bowl. Separate the eggs, add the yolks to the bowl and reserve the whites. Slowly pour in the beer, beating the ingredients together with a wire whisk. Cover the bowl with a towel and set aside for 1 hour at room temperature.

2 Folding in the whites. Beat the egg whites until they form soft peaks. With a wooden spoon or spatula, gently fold the whites into the batter mixture.

3 **Coating the pieces with batter.** Remove the chicken pieces from the marinade and pat them dry with a towel. Holding each piece by one corner, dip it into the batter, then slip it into the pan, using tongs. Handle the chicken carefully to avoid wiping off the batter. Do the same with each remaining piece, but do not crowd the pan; you may well need to deep fry the pieces in at least two batches.

4 **Cooking the pieces.** Adjust the heat during the 15 to 20 minutes it takes for the chicken to cook through, so the batter browns in the same time. The poultry pieces will float in the fat; turn them occasionally with a fork or a wire skimmer so they cook through evenly. When they are done, remove them with the skimmer. Place them on a towel, to drain off the excess fat. You can keep the pieces warm while you deep fry subsequent batches by arranging them on a heatproof platter and setting them in a warm oven.☐

Boned Chicken Breasts with a Surprise Filling

Presented in different guises, boned and stuffed chicken breasts are a delectable feature of many cuisines. Perhaps the most celebrated example is the Russian dish known as chicken Kiev (*recipe, page 100*), which calls for a flattened chicken breast that is rolled around a finger of butter, dipped in beaten egg and flour, coated with breadcrumbs and then deep fried. Italian versions of the dish substitute slices of *prosciutto* or cheese for the butter. Try creating your own simple stuffing mixtures, too—such as a combination of fresh herbs, butter, bread-crumbs and egg. The dish demonstrated here resembles a traditional chicken Kiev, except that instead of being rolled around the filling, the breast is slit to make a roomy "purse" in which the butter stuffing—or any other suitable filling—is lodged securely.

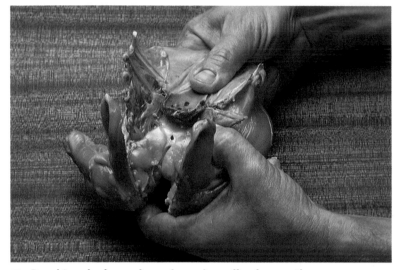

1 Breaking the breastbone from the collar-bones. If you start with whole chickens, cut them up by either of the methods shown on pages 16 to 19. But do not remove the wings; they will give the halved breast portion a neat cutlet shape. Skin the breast, turn it skinned side down and cut off the outer joint of each wing. Slit the membrane that covers the breastbone and the attached cartilage. Grasp the breast by its wide end and bend the breastbone back (*above*) to snap it from the collar-bones.

2 Removing the breastbone and cartilage. Snap the breastbone from the piece of white cartilage embedded in the narrow end of the breast. With your fingers, prize the breastbone from the flesh. Press the tips of your thumbs underneath the cartilage and ease it out of the flesh (*above*). If any ribs remain attached to the breast, carefully trim them away with a sharp knife.

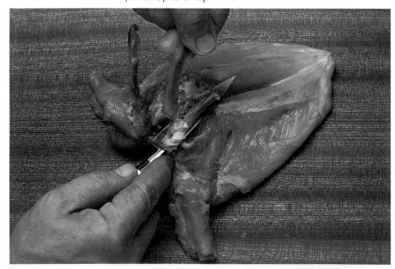

3 Removing the collar-bones. Twist back one wing to expose the shoulder joint. Cut through the connecting tendons. With the knife tip, cut through the flesh that covers the collar-bone to expose the joint it shares with the shoulder-blade and wishbone. Cut through the joint to free the collar-bone and shoulder-blade (*above*), and remove these bones. Repeat with the other wing.

4 Removing the wishbone. Turn the breast over. Feel the shape of the wishbone beneath the flesh, and carefully cut away the surrounding flesh with the knife tip (*above*). When the wishbone is uncovered, grasp it where the prongs meet and pull it out. Turn the breast over again and halve it along the cleft that held the breastbone. Each portion will now resemble a cutlet.

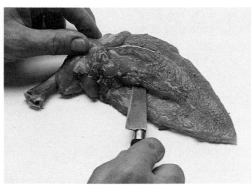

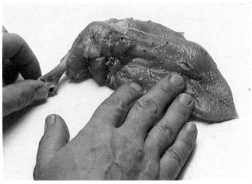

5 **Cutting a pocket for the stuffing.** With the knife tip, make a deep slit along the thick edge of each "cutlet". Be careful not to penetrate as far as the opposite side of the cutlet.

6 **Stuffing the cutlets.** Cut two pieces of plain or seasoned butter into finger shapes that can be slipped neatly into the pockets. It will be easier to shape the butter if it has been refrigerated for an hour or so beforehand.

7 **Sealing the stuffed cutlets.** With your fingertips, press the edges of the pockets together. You will find that the two surfaces of raw flesh cling together; no skewers are needed.

8 **Coating with breadcrumbs.** Place each cutlet on a plate covered with flour; sprinkle more flour over the cutlet (*far left*) to coat it completely. Dip both sides of the cutlet in beaten egg (*centre*). Place each cutlet in a mound of breadcrumbs and finish the coating by sprinkling with more crumbs to cover. Refrigerate the cutlets for an hour to set the coating.

9 **Deep frying the cutlets.** In order not to damage the breadcrumb coating, hold each cutlet by the wing bone and slip it into a pan of hot oil or fat. Use tongs if preferred. The cutlets will be done in 10 to 15 minutes: serve them immediately. □

3
Roasting and Grilling
Juicy Meat from Dry Heat

Stuffings to add flavour and moisture
Trussing birds two ways
How to judge roasting time
Testing for doneness
Three techniques for carving
Controlling the heat of your grill

Roast poultry seems made for feasting. Served golden-brown and glistening at the centre of the family table, a plump bird turns the simplest meal into a celebration—especially when appetites have already been whetted by the wonderful aroma wafting from the spit or oven.

Roasting is a method of cooking by intense, dry heat. When poultry is subjected to such heat, the skin and outermost layer of flesh are quickly cooked; then, beneath this protective barrier, the meat's own juices spread the heat inward to complete the cooking. Grilling is a kindred process, but the dry heat emanates from only one direction—above or below the meat in most cases—so that only one side seals and cooks at a time. Securing the meat to a spit that turns it as it cooks combines the effect of the direct heat from a grill with the even warmth of an oven. In the days when open fires were the only source of heat in the kitchen, all roasting was accomplished in this manner. Often, cooks burned fragrant woods that perfumed the meat as it cooked, using a primitive method to produce a result that is hard to equal with more sophisticated equipment.

Roasting in an oven, however, is not quite the same as roasting in front of a fire or on a grill over a bed of coals, since moisture evaporating from the meat in a confined space may prevent it sealing perfectly. But few kitchens today can accommodate an open fire, and the advantages of a modern oven—efficient insulation, with a safe and easily-regulated heat source—more than compensate for its limitations.

Although plain oven roasting is uncomplicated, it demands fine judgement from the cook. Anyone who has chewed the dried-out meat of a carelessly roasted bird knows that an elaborate oven is not in itself a guarantee of success. Choice of material is most important: only young birds should be roasted. Old fowl will become desiccated long before the cooking has had time to tenderize them. Many of the techniques demonstrated in this chapter—such as stuffing, trussing and basting—are designed to preserve and supplement the natural succulence of young poultry, as well as to enhance its flavour and appearance. Soundly understood and imaginatively applied, they will make it possible to produce good results when you roast any kind of bird, be it a majestic turkey for 10, a family chicken or a diminutive squab to serve one.

A plump turkey, basted with pan juices, develops an appetizing brown glaze outside. And inside, the meat beneath this protective shield of crisp skin retains its natural moisture and flavour while it cooks to succulence.

Five Ways to Fill a Bird with Goodness

One of the simplest ways to vary roast poultry is by resorting to different stuffings. The five panels on the right sketch different approaches to the creation of stuffings, and suggest ways of extending the better-known techniques to make more original use of ingredients.

Plain bread is the foundation for many stuffings, but the results can be varied as much by the method of preparation as by the choice of accompanying ingredients. One kind of stuffing is based on dry bread cubes that have been baked or fried in butter until crisp (*first panel*). Although no moisture is added before the bird is stuffed, this rough-textured stuffing is anything but dry after roasting; it absorbs meat juices and becomes moist and flavourful—yet retains its crispness.

A softer, more even-textured stuffing can be made by combining bread and other ingredients with a liquid (*second panel*). To give the stuffing extra flavour, substitute a simple stock for the usual water or milk by simmering for half an hour the bird's neck, gizzard and heart, together with a carrot and a small bunch of parsley. Strain and skim the stock before mixing it into the stuffing.

Vegetable-based stuffings (*third panel*) offer an interesting change from the familiar bread mixtures. Prepare and chop different vegetables according to their various needs (see panel) and mix them with a white curd cheese, such as Italian *ricotta,* for bulk and a smooth, binding texture.

Whatever kind of stuffing you make, you can enrich it economically by mixing with it the bird's giblets—its liver, heart and gizzard (*fourth panel*). Clean, chop and quickly sauté the giblets before adding them to the stuffing.

Chicken and turkey always benefit from being smeared with butter before roasting; but if you feel like trying something slightly more ambitious, stuff additional butter—seasoned with herbs or other flavourings—beneath the skin of the breast (*fifth panel*).

A Dry Bread Stuffing

Make the croûtons for a dry bread stuffing from a firm loaf about two days old. Choose other ingredients that will complement poultry: here, chopped celery, parsley and mixed herbs are combined to complete a stuffing for the roast turkey used in the demonstration on pages 40-42.

1 **Browning the croûtons.** Cut the bread into chunks. Melt the butter in a pan. Fry the bread over a low heat, stirring with a wooden spoon. Add more butter as it is absorbed, and continue frying until the croûtons are evenly browned. Or, cook the cut bread for half an hour in a buttered baking tin in a moderate oven.

2 **Mixing the stuffing.** Place the croûtons with the other ingredients in a bowl. The best way to mix any kind of stuffing is with your hands: this combines all elements thoroughly and produces a light, airy mixture.

A Moist Bread Stuffing

Although you can season moist bread stuffing in many ways, one of the oldest flavour combinations is sage and onion (*recipe, page 164*). The pungency of the herb and the sweetness of the pre-cooked onion give the stuffing an appetizing perfume that improves with roasting.

1 **Preparing the ingredients.** Parboil an onion for about 10 minutes. Chop it roughly (*above*). Use fresh sage if possible, but a half teaspoon of the dried herb will do. Mix the chopped sage and onion with fresh, coarse breadcrumbs, chopped parsley, salt, pepper, butter and an egg yolk for binding.

2 **Moistening and mixing.** Add just enough liquid—here, chicken stock—to completely moisten the ingredients. Mix the stuffing together gently but thoroughly, using a spoon, a fork or your fingers.

A Vegetable and Cheese Stuffing

Leaf vegetables such as spinach are prepared by parboiling them, pressing them dry and chopping them. Moist vegetables such as courgettes (*recipe, page 102*), turnips or swedes should have their high water content reduced (*below*) before they are combined with other ingredients.

1 **Drawing out moisture.** Coarsely shred courgettes with a flat or rotary grater. (Treat turnips and swedes the same way.) In a deep bowl, arrange the shreds in 2.5 cm (1 inch) layers, each liberally salted. Leave them for 30 minutes to allow the salt to draw out their water. Then squeeze out the salty water (*above*).

2 **Cooking the vegetables.** Sauté the courgettes in butter for 7 to 8 minutes over a moderate heat. Toss them regularly (*above*) with a flick of the wrist, or stir with a wooden spoon, so that they cook evenly. When they are dry and lightly coloured, take the pan off the heat. Let them cool before mixing the stuffing.

Preparing Giblets

Reserve the bird's gizzard, heart and liver to add to most bread-based stuffings. Wash them in cold water to rinse away any blood before you cut them up, and cut away any white connective tissue. Goose giblets are shown here; but treat those of other birds in the same way.

1 **Cutting up the giblets.** Pare away the dark red flesh from the thick hard membrane that lines the gizzard. Slice the gizzard, heart and liver.

2 **Cooking the giblets.** Melt butter in a saucepan and add the giblet pieces. Sauté them briefly over a moderate heat: when they have changed colour from red to a pinkish grey, add them to the other stuffing ingredients. They will cook through as the bird roasts.

Buttering Under the Skin

Flavourings and a generous quantity of butter placed underneath the breast skin will blend together to nourish the breast meat of a roasting bird. Anchovies and almonds are used below, but you could substitute pistachios and slivers of grilled, peeled sweet pepper.

1 **Inserting the flavourings.** Pull back the skin at one side of the neck to expose half the breast flesh. Still holding back the skin, use a small, sharp knife to cut little slits all over the breast; insert an almond into each pocket. Lay anchovy fillets on the surface (*above*). Repeat on the other side of the breast.

2 **Buttering the breast.** Soften the butter to room temperature. With your hand, spread it beneath the breast skin, generously covering the anchovies and almonds.

Removing the Wishbone and Trussing the Bird

Oven roasting is perhaps the simplest of all cooking methods: put the bird in the oven (see page 43 for temperatures and roasting times), baste it, turn the bird periodically so that it browns evenly and take it out ready to eat. But a few preliminaries will greatly improve the dish.

Removing the wishbone from the uncooked bird (*right*) will enable you to carve the breast easily and more neatly, after roasting. If the bird—here a turkey—has a high-arched breast that might colour too quickly, thump the ridge of the breast with your fist to flatten it a little.

Stuffing, of course, adds variety of flavour and of texture, and it helps prevent the bird from drying out in the oven (see previous pages for the preparation of stuffings, and page 164 for recipes).

The next step—trussing the bird—provides a tidy look for any kind of poultry. More important, by holding the legs and wings close to the bulk of the body, trussing gives a compact shape that will cook at about the same rate throughout.

The skin of a lean bird should be generously smeared with fat (*overleaf*), or barded—covered with strips of fat bacon—as a protection against the intense dry heat.

For the correct way to roast fat birds such as duck and goose, see page 46.

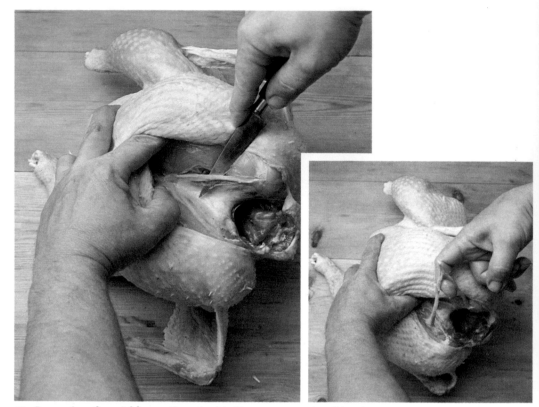

1 **Removing the wishbone.** Turn the bird breast-up and pull back the neck skin until you are able to locate the wishbone with your fingers. With the tip of a small knife, cut through the flesh under the contour of the bone on both sides just deeply enough to free it (*above, left*). When the bone is attached only at the ends, hook your finger under it (*inset*) and pull it out.

3 **Closing the tail vent.** Thread a trussing needle with butcher's twine or thin string. Starting at one end of the vent and leaving a tail of string about 10 cm (4 inches) long, sew up the vent by stitching to and fro through both edges of the flesh. Cut off the string, leaving a 10 cm (4 inch) length hanging loose. Omit this step if the tail vent is small and neat.

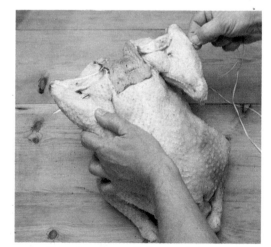

4 **Securing the neck flap and wings.** After threading the trussing needle again with twine or string—at least 60 cm (2 feet) is a convenient length for any bird—fold the wing tips as shown and fold the flap of neck skin on to the back. Pass the needle through one wing, the shoulder and the neck flap, and out through the other wing. Do not unthread the needle.

5 **Securing the drumsticks.** Turn the bird breast uppermost. Using the same string as in Step 4, pass the needle through the upper part of one drumstick and the body, and out through the same point in the opposite drumstick.

2 Stuffing the bird. Fill the turkey cavity partly through its tail vent (*above*) and partly through its neck opening. Do not pack the stuffing tightly; stuffing expands slightly as it cooks and the skin of an overstuffed bird may split.

Tying with a Single Length of String

Although a long trussing needle is essential for dealing with large, bulky birds such as turkey and goose, smaller birds can be trussed effectively using just one long piece of string, as shown here. You will need at least twice as much string as would be necessary to encircle the bird lengthwise; a generous length is easier to pull tight, and the excess can be cut off when the job has been completed.

Before you begin to truss the bird, pull down the flap of neck skin and fold it over to close the neck opening. If the bird has been stuffed, handle it carefully so that the stuffing does not spill out.

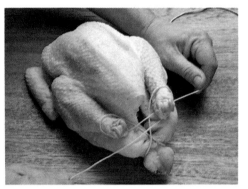

1 Securing the drumsticks. Place the bird on its back with the string underneath its tail. Cross the string ends and loop each end over and around the opposite drumstick. Pull both ends away from the bird (*above*) to draw the drumsticks and tail tightly together over the vent.

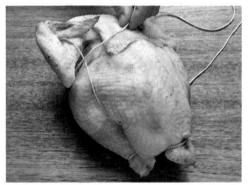

2 Completing the trussing. Turn the bird on its breast. Leaving one string end loose, bring the other end across the thigh, loop it around the upper wing, and pull it firmly across the neck flap (*above*). Still working with the same end, loop the string around the other wing, tie it securely with the loose end of string and cut off the excess string.

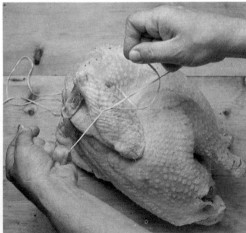

6 Tying the first knot. Remove the needle from the string. Turn the bird on its side, with the loose ends of string from leg and wing on top. Pull the string tight, tie a secure knot close to the wing (*above*) and cut off the excess string.

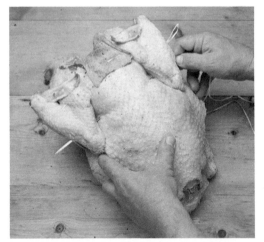

7 Securing the wing joints. Thread the needle with another length of twine or string 60 cm (2 feet) long. Turn the bird breast-down. Insert the needle through the wing near the middle joint, push it through the body and out through the other wing (*above*). Leave a length of string and do not unthread the needle.

8 Securing the lower drumsticks. Turn the bird breast-up. Draw the string through the lower part of one drumstick, through the body and out through the opposite drumstick (*above*). Remove the needle. To finish, turn the bird on its side, with the two string ends nearest to you. Pull them tight, tie a knot at the wing, and cut off the excess lengths. ▶

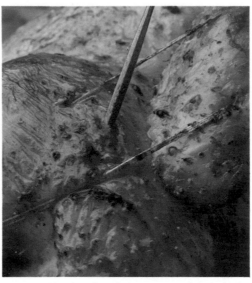

9 **Anointing the bird.** To allow the skin to brown crisply without becoming hard, smear the bird all over with butter (*above*), or oil. Use a pan that is just big enough to let you turn the bird and baste it easily with a spoon as it roasts.

10 **Testing for doneness.** At the end of the roasting time, push a skewer into the thickest part of a thigh. If the juices that run out are clear, the bird is done; if they are pink, roast it for up to 10 minutes more and test again.

11 **Removing the trussing strings.** Take the cooked bird out of the pan. Before carving it, let the bird rest in a warm place so that the flesh will relax and reabsorb some of its juices (allow 20 minutes for a turkey, less time for smaller birds). Cut each trussing string near the knot (*left*); grasp the knot and pull out the string. See page 44 for carving instructions.□

A Guide to Oven Temperatures and Roasting Times

The chart below suggests the times and temperatures for roasting whole unstuffed birds (add 20 to 25 minutes to the overall time if a bird is stuffed). Experience and familiarity with your own oven will soon enable you to improve on the brief approximations given here.

Two methods—quick and slow—are presented. In quick roasting the bird is started in a hot oven and the temperature is then reduced for the bird to cook until done. The initial period of high heat is essential for drawing off excess grease from fat birds such as duck and goose; and it will be enough to cook small lean birds such as guinea-fowl and pigeon completely. Larger lean birds may be roasted either by the quick method, or by the slow method—which needs less supervision—in an oven set at a constant moderate temperature.

Whichever method you follow, the bird will roast and brown more evenly if you change the way it lies in the pan several times while it roasts. Lay the bird on one side for about a third of the cooking time; then turn it on its other side for an equal time; and finally place it breast-up, until done.

To keep the flesh from drying and help the skin to brown, baste the bird regularly—about every 10 to 15 minutes—using the drippings in the bottom of the roasting pan. If you find that the breast is browning too quickly before the bird is cooked through, shield it by covering it with a loose sheet of aluminium foil; alternatively, reduce the oven temperature slightly.

TYPE OF BIRD		SIZE OF BIRD		QUICK ROASTING			SLOW ROASTING
				Cooking time at high temperature	Cooking time at reduced temperature		Cooking time at constant temperature
CHICKEN		2-3 lb 1-1.5 kg		30 min at {220°C 425°F Mark 7}	15-30 min at {170°C 325°F Mark 3}		1¼-2 hr at {170°C 325°F Mark 3}
		3-5 lb 1.5-2.5 kg			30 min-1 hr		
CAPON		5-8 lb 2.5-3.5 kg		45 min at {220°C 425°F Mark 7}	45 min-1¾ hr at {180°C 350°F Mark 4}		2½-3½ hr at {170°C 325°F Mark 3}
TURKEY		8-12 lb 3.5-5.5 kg		50 min at {220°C 425°F Mark 7}	1½-2 hr at {180°C 350°F Mark 4}		3½-4 hr at {170°C 325°F Mark 3}
		12-15 lb 5.5-7 kg			2-2½ hr		4-4½ hr
		15-20 lb 7-9 kg			2½-3 hr		4½-5 hr
DUCK		4-6 lb 2-3 kg		30 min at {220°C 425°F Mark 7}	1-1½ hr at {180°C 350°F Mark 4}		
GOOSE		8-10 lb 3.5-4.5 kg		45 min at {220°C 425°F Mark 7}	1¾-2 hr at {170°C 325°F Mark 3}		
		10-12 lb 4.5-5.5 kg			2-2½ hr		
GUINEA-FOWL		1½-3 lb 0.75-1.5 kg		30 min-1 hr at {220°C 425°F Mark 7}			
POUSSIN PIGEON SQUAB		1-1½ lb 0.5-0.75 kg		20-30 min at {220°C 425°F Mark 7}			

Learning to Carve with Skill and Confidence

Carving a turkey is easy, provided you use the right tools. Pick a pointed knife with a very keen edge and a long, flexible blade that can cut straight through a joint yet bend enough to follow the contours of the bird. And choose a large two-tined fork for holding the bird while you cut.

Carve the leg, wing and breast from one side of the turkey before you cut into the other side. Work with the back of the fork on the first side so that whenever possible the tines do not pierce the skin and flesh. Then stick the fork firmly into the carcass to hold it steady while you slice the other side. Carve only as much as you will serve at once so that the rest stays hot and moist. If there is stuffing, spoon it out through neck and vent.

Chickens and guinea-fowl are handled much like turkeys, but smaller birds are merely halved (see box). To carve duck and goose, which have a different shape, see the demonstration on page 46.

1 Removing the first leg. Lay the turkey breast-up on a carving board or a large platter. Steady the bird with the carving fork. Cut the skin between the thigh and breast. Bend the thigh outward to locate the hip joint, and slice down through the joint (*above*) to remove the whole leg.

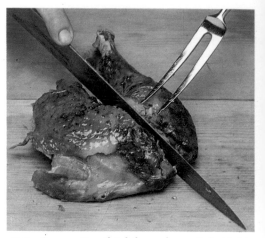

2 Separating thigh from drumstick. Hold the knife so that it bisects the angle between the thigh and drumstick bones, and cut down firmly through the joint to sever the leg into two portions.

How to Carve Small Birds

Roast chicken can be carved with the same long, flexible knife used for turkey—and by the same method except for its legs. If the chicken is large, separate the drumstick from the thigh and serve each half separately (but do not slice the meat off the bones). With small chickens, serve thigh and drumstick in one piece.

Carving poussins and other small birds requires a long but rigid knife and a different, far simpler, method. Half a bird is just the right amount for one serving. All you need do is split the bird in two by cutting straight down along the centre of the breastbone and backbone.

A heavy, rigid blade halves a small bird neatly.

A slender, flexible blade curves as it cuts across a chicken breast.

3 **Slicing the drumstick.** Cut a thick slice of meat and skin from one side of the drumstick, parallel and close to the bone (*above*). Rolling the leg over, cut three more slices in the same way, one from each side of the bone.

4 **Slicing the thigh.** Keeping the knife blade parallel to the bone and steadying with the back of the fork, cut down through the thigh (*above*) to slice it into four or more pieces, according to its size.

5 **Removing the first wing.** Slice down through the corner of the breast towards the wing. Move the wing to find the joint; cut through the joint (*above*). Remove the wing with the piece of breast attached. This will provide a single serving.

6 **Carving the breast.** Hold the back of the carving fork against the side of the breast-bone on the side you are going to carve and slice down diagonally through the meat. Lift each slice off between the fork and the knife (*left*). If you removed the wishbone before roasting the bird (*page 40*), you can cut the breast cleanly into large slices as shown. □

Special Techniques for Roasting and Carving Fatty Birds

Because the thick skin of goose and duck includes a great deal of fat, these birds should not be roasted in the same way as lean poultry such as turkey or chicken. There is no need to protect the breast meat by barding or smearing with fat; on the contrary, fat must be drawn off during roasting so that the cooked bird—a goose in this instance—will not be too greasy.

To start this process, lightly pierce the skin all over with a trussing needle (or similar, sharp-pointed instrument) before the stuffed and trussed bird is placed in a hot oven. During cooking baste the bird every 15 to 20 minutes with its own plentiful fat, thus melting out more fat and helping to crisp the skin as well.

Carving, too, requires a slightly different technique. The bodies of goose and duck are narrower than those of other birds, and their leg and wing ligaments are tighter and tougher. A heavy, rigid knife is needed to deal with their close-set, sinewy structure, although the tender breast meat should be carved with the same slender, flexible carving knife used for lean birds.

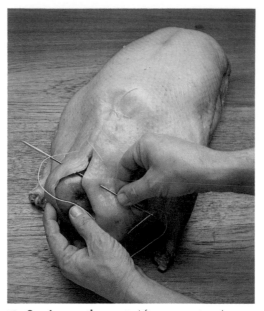

1 Sewing up the vent. After removing the wishbone, as demonstrated on page 40, fill the goose loosely with a suitable stuffing—here apples and onions, although any number of other stuffings will do. Sew up the vent, and truss the goose as shown on page 40.

2 Roasting the goose. Place the goose in a shallow pan in a hot oven: a little water in the pan will keep the fat from burning during the rather long cooking (for times and temperatures, see page 43). Lay the bird first on one side, then on the other to ensure even cooking and rich browning, and baste it regularly as soon as its copious fat begins to flow.

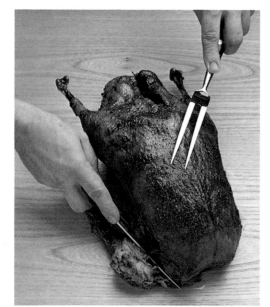

3 Removing the wing. When the goose is ready to serve, locate the joint by gently moving the wing bone. Using a heavy-bladed knife, cut down firmly through the joint, severing the strong tendons (*above*) to separate the wing.

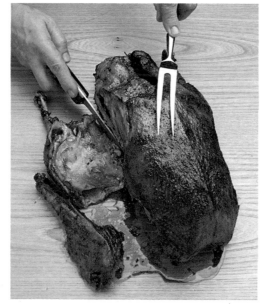

4 Removing and dividing the leg. With the heavy-bladed knife, cut through the skin in an arc around the leg. Press the knife down between the thigh and the body. The leg will fall away from the body (*above*) and the joint will be exposed. Cut through the joint to free the leg. Separate it into thigh and drumstick.

5 Carving the breast. Using a long knife with a slender blade, carve the breast into slices (*above*). Work from the front of the bird, with the knife blade close to horizontal. Lift the slices by holding them between the knife and the fork to avoid piercing the meat unnecessarily.□

An Extraordinary Method for Stuffing Under the Skin

Stuffing, traditionally confined to the body cavity of the bird, can turn a plain roast into elegant party fare if it is inserted between the skin and flesh instead. This unorthodox method is shown here with a chicken and a moist courgette and *ricotta* cheese stuffing (*demonstration, page 39; recipe, page 102*), but the technique can be used with a large variety of stuffings and applied to guinea-fowl and capon, as well.

Supple and strong, poultry skin is firmly attached to the body in four places: the backbone, the end of each drumstick and the crest of the breastbone. Elsewhere, only thin membranes join skin to flesh,

and these membranes can be detached easily by working your fingers under the skin. If the bird's skeletal structure is first collapsed by splitting it along the backbone then flattening it with a sharp blow (*below*), the pockets between the skin and the flesh will accommodate a layer of filling up to 5 cm (2 inches) thick.

If the skin has been torn—either by the butcher or while being loosened and stuffed—use a large sewing needle and thread to make good the damage. Even a small tear may enlarge drastically during the stuffing process.

Although the technique may look fanciful at first, it has several very practical advantages. Because the bird is flattened,

it cooks quickly and evenly. The tender breast meat is protected from drying out by a thick coat of stuffing that keeps it moist while the whole bird cooks through. And the skin, capacious and flexible, can conceal an unusually generous amount of stuffing. As the stuffing swells slightly during cooking, the skin expands smoothly to match the contours beneath. Basted from the outside by the cook and from the inside by the stuffing, the bird turns a rich, crisp brown.

At table, the promise of the exterior is more than fulfilled when the bird is carved to reveal an unexpected and quite delicious interior.

1 **Cutting through the backbone.** Place the chicken on its breast. Using poultry shears, cut along the entire length of the backbone, as near as possible to the centre of the bone so that the skin remains firmly attached to each side of the back. If you work without shears, lay the bird on its back, insert the blade of a long, heavy knife through the body cavity, and press down hard with a rocking motion to cut through the backbone.

2 **Flattening the bird.** Open the bird out as much as possible and place it on a flat surface with the breast uppermost and the legs turned inwards. Using the heel of your hand or the flat side of a wooden mallet, strike the bird firmly on the breast. Do not be gentle; the object is to break the breastbone, the collar-bones, the ribcage and the wishbone. There will be more room inside the skin if the underlying bone structure is not rigid.▶

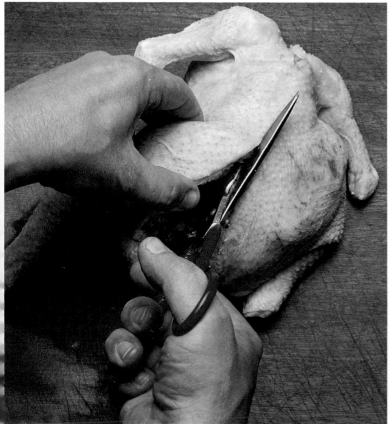

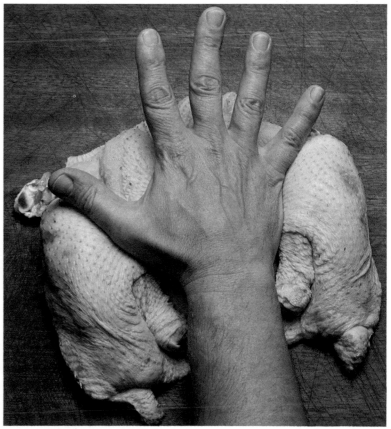

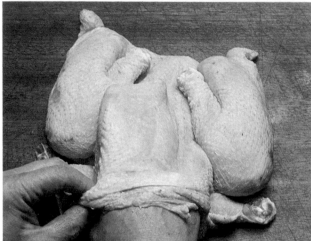

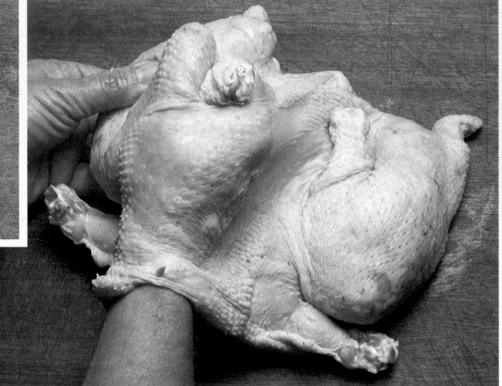

3 **Loosening the skin.** Starting at the neck, slip your fingers between the skin and flesh and work them towards the tail to loosen the skin over one side of the breast (*above*). With your entire hand underneath, free the skin by degrees from the leg, leaving the skin attached only at the tip of the drumstick (*right*). Do the same to the other side of the breast.

4 **Stuffing the bird.** From the neck, push the filling under the skin with one hand, using the other hand to settle the stuffing into place from the outside (*right*). After stuffing the thighs and drumsticks, push a thick coating over the breast. Finally, pull the neck flap over the opening and tuck it under the bird. If there is no neck flap, put less stuffing towards the neck.

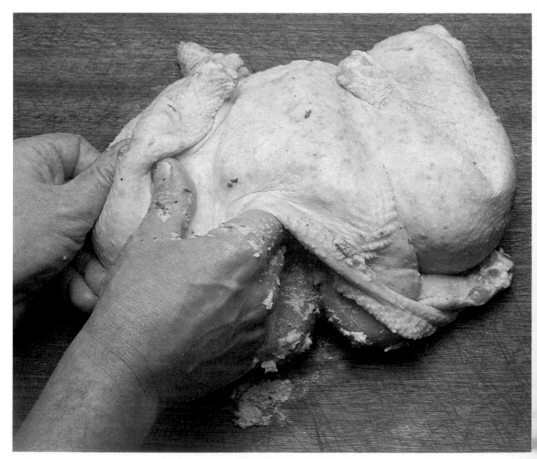

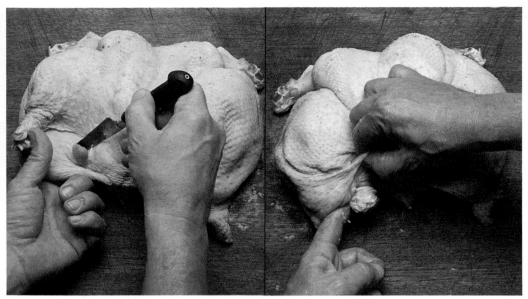

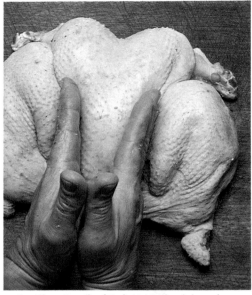

5 **Pinning the drumsticks.** To keep the drumsticks from spreading outwards during cooking, pin them under a flap of skin. Make a small slit with the point of a knife between the thigh and the breast (*above, left*). Push the end of the leg through the slit (*above, right*): the knob of bone on the drumstick will hold it in place. Follow the same procedure with the other drumstick.

6 **Shaping the bird.** Using both hands, smooth the skin so the stuffing layer conforms to the bird's natural shape. Place the bird in a roasting pan and set it in a hot oven. Lower the heat after 10 minutes, and baste frequently with roasting juices after half an hour. The chicken will cook in 50 to 60 minutes.

7 **Carving the bird.** Split the bird in two, using a very sharp knife and cutting gently through skin and stuffing. Because you broke bones to flatten the bird, you will meet with little resistance as you slice through the breast. To remove the legs, cut along the curved creases between the thighs and the body (*left*).□

Grilling: The Benefits of Extra Care

As a method for bringing out the true taste of poultry, undisguised by sauces or stuffings, grilling has no rival. A gas or electric grill is the most convenient kind to use, but charcoal ashes or—best of all—the embers of a wood fire will give poultry a delectable savour. And a few pear, apple or grapevine twigs added to the coals will impart a finer aroma and taste.

Whatever the source of the heat, grilling demands more finesse than oven roasting. Too much heat applied too close to the poultry will char it on the outside before it is cooked within, while too little heat will dry up the meat before it is cooked. On gas or electric grills equipped with automatic temperature controls, the cook must watch the grill constantly and adjust the heat control to prevent the meat from burning or drying. On barbecues, the cook must adjust the position of the grid to increase or decrease the heat.

As a general rule, grill poultry under or over a moderate heat, and position the meat at least 10 cm (4 inches) from the heat source. Whole birds—such as chicken and guinea-fowl—should be flattened (*page 47*) to produce compact shapes that cook evenly. Two-thirds to three-quarters of the cooking time should be applied to the underside of poultry pieces or a whole bird to avoid charring the skin.

To preserve the natural moisture—and flavour—of grilled birds, marinate them beforehand in an oil-based marinade (*page 12*), and baste them as they cook, preferably with the marinade. Chicken breasts are particularly difficult to keep moist; it is wiser to use them for kebabs or brochettes. Cut the breast meat into small pieces, steep them in a marinade, and put them on a skewer with vegetables (sweet green peppers, mushrooms and onions are natural choices), a few bay leaves for flavour, and some rolled-up bacon rashers for extra fat. Baste the vegetables often as they grill so that they do not char before the meat is done.

To test grilled poultry pieces for doneness, pinch the meat between your thumb and forefinger: if the meat is firm and springy, it is cooked; if it is soft and yielding, it is underdone. The "skewer test" used for roasting (*page 42*) is not suitable for grilled poultry pieces because it tends to waste the meat juices.

An array of poultry on a charcoal grill shows the variety of ways in which birds can be prepared for grilling. The chicken and guinea-fowl (*below, left*) are whole but flattened. Above them are chicken wings, skewered so that they can easily be turned. Chicken brochettes and two chicken quarters occupy the rest of the grill.

1 **Marinating.** Liberally smear the poultry with an oil-based marinade. Here, chicken quarters are being rubbed with a marinade of olive oil, dried mixed herbs, salt and pepper. For extra flavour, steep the poultry in the marinade for at least an hour or two before cooking.

2 **Preparing a charcoal grill.** Lay the charcoal pieces loosely to allow ventilation. About 45 minutes after they are lit, the burning coals will be covered with grey ash: this indicates that the fire is ready. If you like, put some fruitwood twigs on the coals (*above*). After the twigs have reduced to embers, arrange the poultry on a grid above the heat.

3 **Basting the poultry.** To keep the chicken pieces from drying out, baste them often with fat or a marinade. Additional flavour can be added at the same time by applying the marinade with a brush of rosemary twigs (*right*), an alternative to using this attractive, but sometimes overpowering, herb directly.

4 **Cooking to doneness.** Grill large pieces or whole, flattened poultry for about 40 minutes. Brochettes and smaller pieces, such as the chicken wings, will cook through in a total time of 10 to 15 minutes. Just before removing the poultry from the grill, you can add a sprig of rosemary to the fire, to lend an extra fillip of flavour to the meat. □

4
Braising
Creating an Assemblage of Flavours

An all-purpose veal stock
Garnishes for braises
Cleansing a sauce
Adding wines and spirits
Stuffing boned poultry
Sauce thickened with eggs and cream

During the preparation of a simple braise, red wine is added to chicken legs, carrots and onions that have been lightly fried. The wine will draw savoury juices from the chicken and vegetables while contributing its own distinctive bouquet.

Like many other cooking terms, "braise" is French in origin: it comes from the word for a bed of live coals, such as those in a nightwatchman's brazier. Its earliest usage in the field of cookery referred to the ancient practice of embedding a tightly closed vessel in hot ashes, usually overnight, to achieve a long, slow stewing process. Old copper braising pans often had a depression in the lid so that hot coals could be heaped on top and the food cooked by heat from above as well as below. Today, braising is a general term for a cooking process in which meats, vegetables and a relatively small amount of liquid are enclosed in a pan or casserole and simmered very gently, either in a slow oven or over the lowest possible heat. Stews, daubes, ragouts and fricassées are all braises; and although the preparation of these dishes may vary considerably in detail, the basic techniques are common to all of them.

Braising is one of the most gratifying and versatile of all cooking methods, and it yields delectable results with poultry. The process is often started by browning poultry pieces in fat or oil to produce coagulated meat residues that will contribute to the flavour, body and colour of the braising liquid. Next, the meat is removed, and aromatic vegetables—usually onions and carrots—are coloured in the fat that remains in the pan. The liquid—water, stock or a decent, drinkable wine—is then poured in and stirred to incorporate all the rich pan deposits. Lastly, the meat is returned to the enriched liquid, and the pan is covered with a close-fitting lid. With the surface of the liquid barely trembling, the meat is simmered until it is done. It should not be allowed to boil: too high a temperature toughens the flesh without shortening the cooking time, while the turbulence of boiling liquid interferes with the delicate merging of flavours.

The cook's work is not over when the meat is done. The sauce in the pan or casserole will contain an emulsion of cooked fats that are difficult to digest and would give the food a muddy taste. The emulsion must be drawn to the surface and removed by a careful process of skimming (*page 57*) that leaves the braising juices lightened and purified. After cleansing, it may still be necessary to concentrate the flavour and improve the body of the braising liquid by reducing it, or perhaps by straining it through a sieve and adding a purée of some of the vegetables. The balanced flavours of the finished dish will be the reward of such scrupulous care.

Composing a Classic Chicken Braise

Chicken braised in wine is a classic dish—or rather, many classic dishes; scores of recipes develop the theme with variations that depend on the country of origin and the imagination of the creator. One of the most celebrated is *coq au vin* (*recipe, page 110*), a speciality of France's Burgundy region that combines chicken with the full-bodied red wine of that province. Cooked with care and attention, the dish is not only a superb example of French provincial cuisine; it is also a model of braising techniques.

Given the choice, a Burgundy cook will prepare *coq au vin* with a farmyard rooster about one year old. Such a bird, too tough for roasting or frying, has more flavour than its young relations, and its flesh, tendons and sinews yield gelatine to thicken and enrich the braising liquid. Since, in all probability, you will have to use a commercially reared chicken, choose a large roasting chicken. And to give extra body to the sauce, supplement the wine with veal stock (see box).

Like most fine braises, *coq au vin* is an assembly of ingredients that are first prepared individually to bring out their flavours. Different recipes may call for variations in the choice of ingredients and the order of working, but *coq au vin* is usually started by frying unsmoked bacon or fat pork pieces, cooking aromatic vegetables in the bacon fat, then browning the chicken pieces in the same pan. Only then is the braising liquid added.

While the chicken is simmering on the stove or in the oven, the garnish vegetables—in this case, small white onions and mushrooms—are partly cooked and then set aside. To prevent them from losing their shape, texture and flavour, they are not added to the braising vessel until the last few minutes of cooking.

When the chicken is done, the liquid is cleansed of fat and impurities to produce a rich, yet pure and digestible sauce.

1 Preparing the aromatics. Melt down pieces of unsmoked streaky bacon or fat pork by frying them in a little oil (strongly cured bacon should first be parboiled, to rid it of excess salt, and then dried). When the pieces are golden-brown, remove them and set them aside to drain: they will form part of the garnish for the finished dish. In the same pan, gently fry chopped onions and carrot pieces (*above, right*). Cook the onions and carrots for about 20 minutes, stirring frequently to prevent them from burning. Remove them from the pan and reserve.

The Multiple Blessings of Veal Stock

A good stock forms the basis of literally thousands of dishes, from delicate sauces to hearty stews. Such dishes can only be as good as their foundation, and there is no substitute for a stock made from fresh, natural ingredients. Since stock should contribute body and flavour to a dish without overwhelming the taste of other ingredients, veal—which is rich yet mild in flavour—is the best choice for a general-purpose stock, suitable for all poultry dishes.

To make a veal stock (*recipe, page 166*), you will need a cracked veal knuckle to furnish gelatine, and some inexpensive veal cuts—rib tips or a shank bone with plenty of meat left on—for flavour. These are gently simmered with aromatic vegetables—carrots, onions and a bouquet garni—for about four hours before straining the liquid and removing the surface fat. Although the bones require the full 4 hours to give up their gelatine, the meat will have surrendered much of its goodness after half that time. If you remove it at this point you can take advantage of the flavour that remains. Left to cool and served with coarse salt, pickles and a salad, the veal pieces will make a meal in themselves.

Although veal stock is by no means difficult to make, it does require lengthy cooking. For this reason, it is best to prepare a large quantity at one time—enough for a week or two of use. The finished stock will keep for at least a fortnight in a sterilized, sealed container in the refrigerator, provided it is brought to the boil for a few minutes every three or four days to prevent the growth of bacteria. Better still, as the stock loses nothing by being frozen, it can be divided into convenient ½ litre (1 pint) batches and stored in a freezer.

2 **Colouring the chicken.** Season the chicken pieces with salt. Add more fat or oil to the pan if necessary, and cook the pieces over a moderate heat, turning them until they are lightly browned all over. Sprinkle flour on the chicken (*above, right*) and turn the pieces until the flour is lightly coloured. The flour will help thicken the braising liquid. Return the onions and carrots to the pan.

3 **Flaming with brandy.** Brandy is not an essential ingredient, but it can be added even when recipes do not specify it. Flaming burns off the alcohol so that only the flavourful essence remains to enrich the finished dish. Pour over a little brandy (too much will drown the other flavours), carefully set it alight and stir the contents of the pan until the flames die. ▶

1 **Skimming the liquid.** Put the veal bones and meat in a saucepan and add cold water to cover. Heat slowly, taking about an hour to reach the boil. As the water comes to the simmer, a scum will rise to the surface. Remove it with a spoon. Keep skimming until no more scum forms. A dash of cold water added after each skimming helps bring the scum to the surface.

2 **Adding the vegetables.** To the gently simmering pot, add whole carrots, onions (one of them stuck with two or three dried cloves), and a bouquet garni. If you like, include a whole bulb of garlic, unpeeled; peeled garlic cloves will cook to a purée that cannot be removed from the stock.

3 **Straining the stock.** After the stock has simmered for about 4 hours, it should be carefully strained. Pour out the contents into a bowl or clean pot.

4 **Deglazing with wine.** Pour the wine (perhaps the same wine that you plan to serve with the meal, but any good red wine will do) into the pan and bring to a boil. Scrape the bottom of the pan (*above, right*) with a wooden spoon to loosen all the residues—they are important flavouring elements. The next stage—the slow braising—can be done in the same pan or in an earthenware or metal casserole. (Earthenware can be used on top of the stove if protected from direct heat by a fireproof mat.)

5 **Adding stock and simmering.** Pour in sufficient hot veal stock to cover the chicken. Add a bouquet garni (*page 15*). Whether you braise in the oven or on top of the stove, regulate the heat so the liquid barely trembles. If the bird is old, simmer for about 1½ hours; a young chicken will cook in 45 minutes or so.

6 **Preparing the garnish.** While the chicken is cooking, peel the small onions. Drop the onions into butter, cover the pan, turn the heat low, and cook for 20 to 30 minutes. Stir or shake the onions frequently to prevent them from colouring unevenly. Wash and dry the mushrooms and trim their stems. When the onions are done, remove and set them aside. Using the same pan, toss the mushrooms in butter for a few minutes—over a high heat so that the moisture they exude evaporates quickly (*above, right*), thus preventing the mushrooms from stewing.

7 **Straining the braising liquid.** When the chicken pieces are tender, remove them to a warm dish. Pour the braising liquid through a strainer into a saucepan. Discard the remains of the bouquet garni and return the carrots and the chicken to the braising vessel. The onions, unlike the carrots, will have lost most of their texture, but do not discard them: press them through the strainer with a pestle (*above, right*) or a wooden spoon to give more body to the sauce. Skim the surface fat off the sauce, using first a spoon and then absorbent paper.

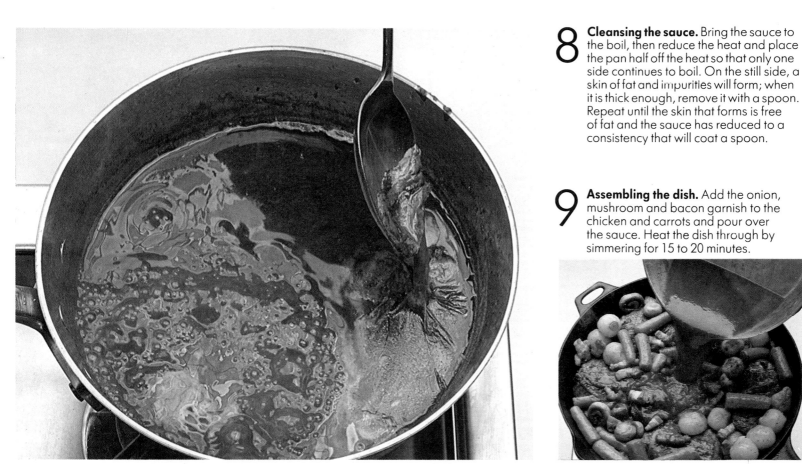

8 **Cleansing the sauce.** Bring the sauce to the boil, then reduce the heat and place the pan half off the heat so that only one side continues to boil. On the still side, a skin of fat and impurities will form; when it is thick enough, remove it with a spoon. Repeat until the skin that forms is free of fat and the sauce has reduced to a consistency that will coat a spoon.

9 **Assembling the dish.** Add the onion, mushroom and bacon garnish to the chicken and carrots and pour over the sauce. Heat the dish through by simmering for 15 to 20 minutes.

10 **Finishing the dish.** Gently fry cubes of bread—croûtons—in butter until they are golden-brown. Use slightly stale bread, with crusts removed, and plenty of butter. Sprinkle the croûtons with a little chopped parsley or with a *persillade,* made by mixing chopped parsley and pounded raw garlic (*above*). Cook the parsley or *persillade* with the croûtons for a minute, then scatter the garnish over the finished dish (*right*).□

Changing a Braise into a Fricassée

When egg yolks—sometimes with fresh cream—are mixed with warm braising liquid, they form an emulsion that binds and thickens the liquid and transforms it into a smooth, rich sauce. Finishing a chicken braise with the enriched sauce turns the dish into a classic chicken fricassée (*recipes, page 120*).

Up to the point when the egg-and-cream mixture is added, the preparation could be almost identical to that of the *coq au vin* shown on the preceding pages. To avoid masking the delicate flavour of the sauce, however, it is best to omit the bacon from the braise and use white wine in place of red wine.

The secret of success lies in preventing the blended egg yolks from cooking completely. Too much heat applied too rapidly will cause the proteins in the yolks to coagulate, curdling the sauce. After the cream has been blended with the eggs, the mixture should be diluted by the addition of some of the warm braising juices before it is poured into the pan; this will reduce the danger of coagulation. Thereafter, you must guard against overheating the sauce. It should be only gently warmed—never allow it to reach even a light simmer—if the sauce is to remain creamy and smooth.

1 **The initial blending.** In a bowl, blend the egg yolks and cream smoothly with a fork. Continue to stir until both ingredients are thoroughly amalgamated.

2 **Diluting the mixture.** Pour some of the warm—not boiling—liquid from the braised chicken into the blended egg-and-cream mixture, stirring the mixture briskly as you pour.

3 **Thickening the sauce.** Set the pan containing the chicken over a very gentle heat. Add the egg-and-cream mixture to the braising liquid left in the pan. Stir, moving the pieces around, until the sauce is blended throughout. You may have to lift the pan off the heat, or even dip its base in cold water, to prevent overheating. Stir until the sauce thickens and coats the spoon.

Wines and Spirits in Cooking

Wine is not only the perfect accompaniment to good food, it is also a valuable cooking ingredient in countless dishes. Used in a marinade (*page 12*), it will not only flavour young poultry, but help tenderize older fowl. In a braise, red or white wine can provide all or part of the cooking liquid. And a little added to a pan after sautéing will dissolve the coagulated juices and furnish the liquid for a quick and convenient sauce.

But wine in cooking should be regarded as a raw material and, like other raw materials, it must be cooked; alcohol that is perfectly acceptable in a drink is harsh and aggressive in food. In addition, wine contains acids, tannin and other complex organic compounds that, uncooked, would give a sauce an overpowering and unpleasant winey taste. Alcohol itself evaporates at only 80°C (176°F), well below the boiling point of water: even the slow simmer of a braise will dispose of it eventually. But in preparations where the cooking time is less than 45 minutes, the wine must be boiled vigorously to eliminate the alcohol and smooth the rough edges of its other constituents. After boiling, only the essences of the wine remain to contribute mellowness and depth of flavour to the finished dish.

It is a wise rule to use only wine that is good enough to drink, for there is no such thing as a cooking wine. The finest of wines, however, lose far more of their unique qualities through heating than they will contribute to the food: cooking with the great wines is therefore wasteful. The ends of bottles that you have drunk at table may be stored for a few days for later use in the kitchen. Take the precaution of storing the wine in a narrow-necked, tightly corked bottle to minimize contact with the air; different wines may be mixed as long as they are of the same colour. Wine that becomes acid through contact with the air should be reserved for making vinegar.

Whether you choose red or white wine is largely a matter of personal preference. Red wine gives more body and a deeper colour to a sauce; white wine is usually more acidic and more delicately flavoured. Poultry is often cooked with white wine—but there are many exceptions, the most famous of which is *coq au vin,* demonstrated on pages 54-57.

Madeira wine—poured into the pan in which chicken breasts and mushrooms have been sautéed—produces a mellow, semi-sweet sauce. Rapid boiling will thicken the sauce and evaporate the alcohol in the wine.

Because of their powerful flavours, fortified wines such as sherry, port and madeira have comparatively few uses in poultry cooking—to enhance an aspic for glazing cold birds (*page 86*), for example, or added when a chicken is almost cooked—as in the recipe on page 114—to form the basis of a sauce. But duck, more than most other birds, is splendidly complemented by the sweetness and heaviness of port, which is used as a marinade and braising liquid in recipes such as duck with figs (*page 156*).

Spirits—whisky, rum, gin, brandy and liqueurs—have flavours that are even more concentrated. Most spirits can be used with poultry, but brandy is by far the most common. Because brandy—or any other spirit—has a strong taste and high alcohol content, few recipes call for more than half a glass. As with wine, only a good-quality brandy should be used in cooking. Again, good does not mean best: a very old and expensive cognac or armagnac should be saved for an after-dinner drink, not for the cooking pot. Brandy is usually added early in the cooking process, heated rapidly, and set alight to eliminate its alcohol. Flaming is not strictly necessary, since the alcohol will evaporate without being set on fire, but many cooks believe that flaming sears the brandy's flavour into every part of the food. To ignite brandy, you need only tilt the pan slightly towards a gas burner, or pass a match close to the bubbling liquid. The alcohol burns with a relatively cool flame—but keep your head out of the way.

Beer and cider also have much to offer an enterprising cook. Like wine, they are products of complex fermentation, and they are rich with the taste and aroma of hops and barley or apple. Naturally brewed, light-bodied beers are often chosen for cooking poultry, although in some cases brown ale is called for (*recipe, page 116*). Dry cider (flat, non-aerated cider is best) makes an excellent braising liquid, with a delicate flavour especially suited to chicken. Good cider may even be suggested as an alternative to white wine in some recipes, such as chicken with mutton (*page 115*), with different but not inferior results.

A Slow-Cooking Braise for Goose and Turkey

An old farmhouse braising method that develops a meltingly delicious flavour is cooking *en daube*—simmering meat and vegetables with a little liquid in a covered vessel for several hours. Duck, boiling fowl, turkey (*recipes, page 145*), and goose are especially suitable for treating in this way, since they can tolerate the long, slow cooking without losing their integrity of flavour and of texture. Goose is used in the daube demonstrated on these pages.

Any daube benefits from the addition of fresh pork rinds. These butchers' trimmings are a generous source of natural gelatine, and the long cooking time allows them to contribute their inimitable richness to the sauce. For extra body, add two calf's feet to the rinds (*Step 2, below*).

To make a daube, the poultry pieces, the rinds, the calf's feet and a mixture of chopped vegetables are arranged in layers: the vegetable juices provide most of the cooking liquid. Traditionally, the dish is prepared in the deep, bulbous *daubière* used here. This earthenware vessel has a narrow neck that cuts down on evaporation and allows the fat to collect on top for easy removal. But any pot deep enough to hold all of the ingredients in several layers will be equally suitable for this braise.

1 Preparing the bird. Cut up the goose, or other suitable bird, by the method illustrated on page 16. If you use goose or turkey, divide the breast—as is being done here—into 6 pieces. To draw out excess fat from goose or duck, grill the pieces skin side up for 20 minutes.

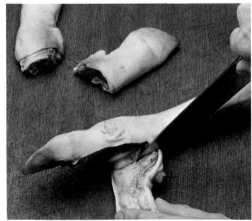

2 Preparing calf's feet and rind. Split the calf's feet lengthwise so that they will render their gelatine readily. Cut the pork rind into 5 cm (2 inch) square pieces. To cleanse the feet and rind of impurities that would muddy the cooking liquid, put them in a pan of cold water and bring the pan to a boil. After 5 minutes, drain them and rinse thoroughly in cold water.

3 Packing the daubière. Finely chop a mixture of vegetables: onions, shallots and carrots are obvious choices, while tomatoes and mushrooms may also be included, as in this recipe. Line the bottom of the *daubière* with the pork rinds and the calf's feet. Add the goose pieces, then vegetables and pork rinds, in alternating layers, sprinkling each layer lightly with salt. When the pot is half full, add a large bouquet garni, including a twist of dried orange peel (*above*). Continue adding the ingredients, finishing with a layer of vegetables and pork rinds.

4 **Adding wine.** Add enough wine—red or white—to cover the other ingredients. Cover the *daubière* and bring to a simmer on top of the stove—protecting the earthenware pot with a fireproof mat—or place the pot in an oven. Cook at the lowest heat for 5 hours: turkey or fowl will require from 2 to 4 hours, depending on the age and size of the bird.

5 **Removing fat.** If you wish to serve the daube the same day, the fat can be spooned off while it is still liquid. But if the dish is left to cool overnight, the fat will be semi-solid and easy to remove. Cooling and reheating has another advantage— it improves the flavour of the dish.

6 **A perfect daube.** Reheat the daube very gently so as to prevent the meat from disintegrating—1½ hours is about right. If the juices are too thin, drain them into a small saucepan, reduce and skim. Serve the finished dish from the *daubière*.□

Boneless Duck, Plumply Stuffed

The wonderful flavour of duck has been appreciated by generations of diners, but finding a way to extend the number of servings is a problem. Duck is seldom inexpensive, and its long body holds proportionately less flesh and more bone than do most other types of poultry: after carving, even a large duck furnishes significantly less meat than, say, a chicken of the same weight.

One solution is to bone the duck (*page 20*) and replace the skeleton with stuffing. Prepared this way, the stuffing itself becomes a major part of the finished dish, and a bird that would normally feed two now provides generous portions for six. With its bones removed, the duck can be sliced as neatly as a loaf, which makes serving and carving it at the table both elegant and impressive.

It is important to choose a stuffing that marries well with the rich taste of the duck. A forcemeat stuffing might be too heavy. A stuffing based on vegetables—such as chard or spinach (*page 39*)—is a good choice: its clean, simple flavour will not be overwhelmed by the duck itself. *Ricotta* cheese gives the stuffing a creamy texture, while eggs will bind it together

and ensure that the cooked bird will slice cleanly, without crumbling.

When the duck has been boned and stuffed, it can either be braised or roasted—or else cooked by a combination of the two methods, as demonstrated here. Superb results are obtained by first roasting the bird for a short time and then simmering it in stock. Partial roasting draws off fat and turns the skin an appetizing brown, while subsequent braising allows you to make use of the bones that have been removed. Simmered for several hours in veal stock (*page 54*) or water to which flavouring vegetables have been added, the bones surrender flavour and gelatine to furnish a braising liquid that can be reduced to a sumptuous sauce. The stock, however, must be prepared in advance of the main cooking—so be sure to leave yourself plenty of time.

Although this is a complex dish that requires care and planning, none of the techniques used—boning, stuffing, trussing—is difficult in itself. Only the combination is novel—one of the enormous number of possible variations on simple themes that makes cooking such an inexhaustible source of pleasure.

Basting in a Tight Space

A baster with a rubber bulb and a fine nozzle, which uses suction to draw up the pan juices is a handy way to baste a bird—especially if it is in a close-fitting pan. Do not use the baster if a liquid contains solid matter, or the nozzle will block.

1 Stuffing the duck. Fill the boned duck until it has regained its normal shape and is about two-thirds its former size. During cooking the bird will shrink slightly, while the stuffing will expand; if the duck is packed too full, its skin will split.

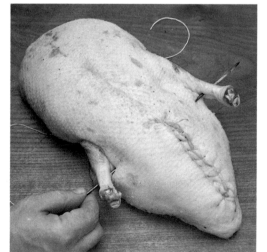

2 Trussing the duck. So that the duck retains its shape during cooking, truss the bird by the method demonstrated with a turkey on page 40, making sure that you secure the neck flap to prevent the stuffing from escaping.

3 Preparing for roasting. Pierce the skin all over the bird to allow the release of fat. Place the duck on its side in a pan and roast it in a hot oven for about 45 minutes, turning the bird from side to side at 15-minute intervals and finishing with the breast uppermost. Baste frequently with hot fat from the pan to draw more fat from the bird.

4 **Braising in stock.** Remove the bird from the roasting pan and pour off the excess fat. Deglaze the pan with a little wine. Place the bird in a close-fitting vessel and fill the pan to a depth of about 7.5 cm (3 inches) with hot stock. Add the roasting juices, cover the pan and put it in a hot oven. Braise for 20 minutes, basting often. Uncover and continue basting for about 30 minutes (*left*); as the stock reduces, the basting juices will glaze the skin.

5 **Carving the duck.** Turn off the oven. Pour off the braising liquid into a small saucepan, cover the braising pan and return the duck to the warm oven. Prepare a sauce by reducing the braising liquid and cleansing it (*page 57*). Transfer the bird to a platter or cutting board and remove the trussing strings. If you carve at the table your guests will be astonished by the ease with which you slice through the unresisting, boned duck. ☐

5
Poaching
Simple and Delicious

A plump chicken is lifted, glistening, from its bath of poaching liquid. The various vegetables bobbing on the surface have supplied richness to the broth and, full of mingled flavours, may serve as an accompaniment to the cooked bird.

At the beginning of the 17th century, when chicken was such a luxury that its presence on the table could serve as a yardstick of prosperity, King Henry IV of France declared: "I want there to be no peasant in my kingdom so poor that he cannot have a chicken in his pot every Sunday." The king was referring to poached chicken—*poule au pot* (see following pages)—made by cooking a fowl in water with fresh vegetables. The dish is still popular—deservedly so, for it exemplifies all of the virtues of the poaching method: simplicity, flavour and economy.

Poaching differs from braising in degree rather than principle. In braising, the bird is simmered to succulence in relatively little liquid. For poaching, a greater amount of liquid is used, and the liquid is rarely more extravagant than plain water or stock. Poaching liquid is seldom reduced, as braising liquid is; a portion can be set aside and thickened with flour to make a simple sauce, and the rest may be served as an appetizing broth to start the meal. In addition, any leftover broth can provide a stock which may be used in preparing other meals later in the week.

Most poaching recipes call for chicken—stuffed and cooked whole—and vegetables such as carrots, onions and turnips, either left whole or cut into pieces large enough to retain their texture during the long cooking. Other types of poultry may be used, however, including capon, duck and—provided you have a large enough pot—turkey or goose (*recipe, page 162*). You can also vary the vegetables according to personal preference and what is available in the shops or your garden.

Whichever combination of poultry and vegetables you choose, and whatever the poaching liquid, the art of successful poaching lies in regulating the temperature of the liquid throughout the cooking process. The bird should be immersed in a pot of cold or warm water and brought slowly to a simmer; if it were put directly into boiling liquid, the skin might split. During cooking, the poaching liquid should be kept just below the boiling point to prevent the bird from drying out and becoming stringy. The great French chef Escoffier considered this so important that he was moved to write: "However nonsensical it may sound, the best possible definition of a poaching is a boiling that does not boil."

Creating a Meal from a Single Dish

A whole chicken poached with vegetables is a complete meal in itself. The chicken and vegetables provide a satisfying main course, and the long cooking transforms the poaching liquid into a delicious clear broth; it can be served as a first course with a slice of bread and, if you like, a generous sprinkling of Parmesan cheese grated over the soup.

This poaching method was evolved to prepare a tough old hen for a peasant's dinner table, but you can substitute a large roasting chicken (*recipe, page 126*). Such a bird will be cooked in about an hour—approximately half the time required for an older boiling fowl. And although the gelatine-rich meat of the older bird produces a more savoury broth, it cannot match the younger roasting chicken for juicy tenderness.

All types of poultry benefit from being stuffed before poaching. The stuffing flavours the bird and is a delicious accompaniment in its own right. Most stuffings recommended for roasting are suitable (*recipes, pages 126 and 164*), but remember: the bird's vent must be sewn up to prevent liquid from seeping in—or stuffing from creeping out. To make an economical meal go even further, prepare more stuffing than you need; wrap the surplus in parboiled cabbage leaves and simmer them for about 30 minutes in a little of the poaching liquid. Serve the stuffed cabbage with the chicken.

After the bird is trussed, placed in just enough water to cover and brought slowly to a boil, the liquid must be skimmed. Only then is it time to add the vegetables and flavourings—in this case, leeks, carrots, onions, a bouquet garni and a whole head of garlic. Usually, the vegetables are served with the chicken; but if you are poaching an old bird, the 2 or more hours needed to render the meat tender will leave the vegetables limp and tasteless, with their flavour transferred to the broth. For a garnish that retains its taste and texture, replace the tired old vegetables with fresh ones about 30 minutes before the chicken is ready.

1 Immersing the chicken. Stuff and truss the chicken as you would for roasting (*page 40*). Place it in a pot containing enough water to cover the bird. Add salt and bring slowly to the boil, spooning off any scum that comes to the surface.

2 Adding vegetables. When no more scum forms, reduce the heat so that the liquid barely trembles. Add vegetables and a bouquet garni—and, if you like, a whole head of garlic. If you add leeks, as shown here, trim off the tough leaves and tie the stems in a bundle to prevent them from falling apart.

3 Poaching the chicken. Regulate the heat so that hardly a bubble breaks the surface of the liquid. Test a young bird for doneness after about an hour of cooking by pushing a skewer into the thickest part of a thigh; if the juices run clear the bird is cooked. Older birds would show clear juices after the same cooking time but will require up to 2 hours more to reach tenderness.

4 **Serving the broth.** When the bird is done, skim off any surface fat. Put a slice of bread in each soup plate, garnish with a slice of cooked carrot, and ladle the broth on top. Grate cheese over the soup. Leave a little poaching liquid in the pot with the chicken and vegetables to keep them warm and moist. Cover the pot until the chicken is ready to serve.

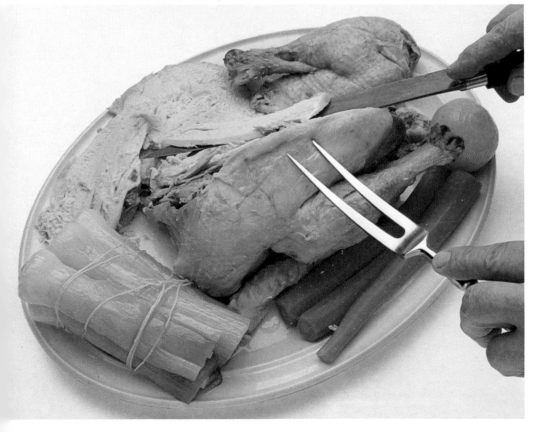

5 **Serving the chicken.** Remove the bird from the pot and cut the trussing strings as shown on page 42. Place the chicken on a warm serving platter and surround it with the vegetables before carving (*page 44*). Traditionally, *poule au pot* is accompanied by pickles, such as dill and gherkins, and coarse salt. Fresh creamed horseradish may also be served.□

Keeping Young Fowl from Falling Apart

A young chicken poached in chicken or veal stock will absorb flavour from the cooking liquid and emerge as rich-tasting as a mature boiling fowl. But, because it is young, it will be meltingly tender.

Unlike the broth of a *poule au pot*, the cooking liquid is not served as a soup; instead it is thickened with flour and butter to make a smooth *velouté*—velvety—sauce. To ensure that the sauce has body and a concentrated flavour, use a minimum of stock for cooking the chicken. Since the bird ought to be almost covered by the liquid, a closely fitting poaching vessel is essential.

Before being placed in the pot, the chicken should be wrapped in cloth to keep the flesh from falling apart as it cooks. The cloth also absorbs liquid and thus keeps the breast moist. Cheesecloth is traditionally used for the wrapper, but the stockinette shown here is more convenient. Sold in tubular rolls, it is easily cut to length and the stretchable fabric fits snugly around the bird.

Making the basic velouté sauce (*recipe, page 167*) is simple: after the chicken is done the broth is combined with a butter-and-flour *roux*. Cream may be added to the mixture to transform it into a *sauce suprême*; or—for a more sumptuous result—add both cream and egg yolks (*recipe, page 128*). Two more variations on the velouté are presented opposite.

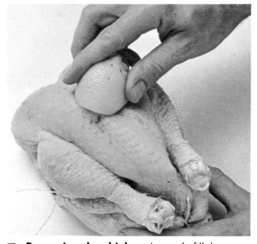

1 Preparing the chicken. Loosely fill the cavity with a stuffing (*recipes, pages 164-165*). Sew up the vent and truss the bird (*page 40*). To keep the chicken's skin white during cooking, rub the bird all over with a halved lemon or lemon juice.

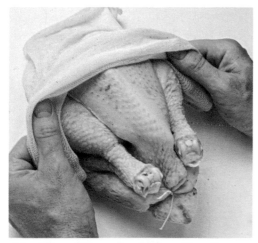

2 Wrapping up the chicken. Cut off a suitable length of stockinette (see text, above). Ease the chicken into the stockinette and tie both ends with string. If cheesecloth is used, wrap it around the bird tightly and tie up both ends.

3 Cooking in stock. Place the chicken in a close-fitting poaching vessel, with the breast uppermost. Add cold stock until the bird is almost submerged. Slowly bring to a very gentle simmer, spooning off the scum as the liquid comes to the boil. Cook for about an hour, or until the chicken is done.

4 **Making a velouté.** Pour most of the stock into a bowl; leave some in the poaching vessel to keep the bird warm. Make a *roux* by mixing butter and flour over a low heat. Pour in all the stock at once, whisking until it comes to the boil. Position the pan half off the heat and simmer for at least 30 minutes, whisking occasionally, to eliminate the taste of flour from the sauce.

5 **Cleansing and completing the sauce.** As the velouté simmers, a skin containing fat and impurities will form at the side of the pan that is off the heat. Skim it off at intervals, until the sauce is free of fat. You can serve the sauce at this point or transform it into a *sauce suprême* by the addition of cream (*above*).

6 **Coating the bird with sauce.** Lift the cooked chicken from the poaching vessel and unwrap it by untying and slitting the fabric covering. Cut away the trussing strings, place the bird on a warm platter and spoon a little of the sauce over it. Carve the bird and serve the pieces with the rest of the sauce.□

Variations on a basic sauce

The basic velouté is the foundation for a variety of sauces that are all excellent accompaniments to poached chicken.

The refreshing acidity of sorrel goes well with chicken. To make sorrel sauce (*right*), stem the sorrel leaves and, if they are not young and tender, blanch them quickly in boiling water. Next stew the leaves gently in butter until they melt into a purée. Whisk the purée into the velouté and add cream. (A word of advice: any pan used to cook sorrel must be made of stainless steel, tinned copper or enamelware. The plant's acid reacts with aluminium and cast iron to spoil the flavour and colour of the sauce.)

Alternatively, add peeled and seeded tomatoes, reduced to purée consistency in a small pan. Stirred into a velouté sauce and with cream blended in, the tomato purée forms a *sauce aurore* (*far right*)—named after its warm, rosy hue.

Sorrel sauce

Sauce aurore

6
Miscellaneous Cooking Methods

As a spoon breaks through the golden crust of a chicken pie, the delectable interior is revealed—chicken pieces baked with quartered artichokes and onions, moistened with rich veal stock. Pie fillings may include any type of poultry.

The previous chapters in this book—devoted to frying, roasting, braising and poaching—are lessons in the foundation skills of poultry cookery. These methods can provide you with a repertoire of hundreds of dishes; but they are not, of course, the only ways of preparing chicken, turkey, duck and goose. Good food does not always fit into tidy categories, and often the most interesting techniques are the hardest to classify. Some of the many other possibilities for preparing poultry are explored in this chapter, which also teaches ancillary skills required by the good cook.

Certain of the poultry preparations described here involve variations of the basic culinary methods: for example, the casserole on page 72 is a type of braise that can produce a complete meal from a single pot. Other methods have an identity all their own: a whole bird baked in a clay vessel, in foil or ovenproof paper, steams in its own juices in the oven (*page 74*). Preserving is not a method usually associated with poultry, but the demonstration on page 84 offers a traditional and effective way of storing cooked goose or duck without the aid of a deep freeze.

Several of the approaches to poultry cooking explained on the following pages rely on subsidiary skills. For instance, once you have learned how to make a creamy white sauce (*page 78*), you will be able to cook a superb gratin. In such a dish, poultry pieces are smothered in the sauce and browned in a hot oven or beneath a grill; a sprinkling of grated cheese or breadcrumbs—or both—helps a rich crust to form.

The white sauce can also be combined with poultry meat to make a delicious filling for pancakes and bread cases (the techniques for making wafer-thin pancakes and carving neat cases from loaves are given on page 80). Pastry-making is an art in itself, but by learning how to make a rough-puff pastry (*page 76*), you can create a whole range of substantial, nourishing pies with any kind of poultry.

Many of the methods in this chapter lend themselves well to leftovers—and demonstrate that these need not be a dull substitute for a meal prepared with fresh ingredients. But you need not wait until leftovers are available. Gratins, pancakes—and the pilaff on page 82—are so good that it is well worth cooking a chicken especially to make them.

Cooking a Whole Bird in a Casserole

Packed into a covered casserole with aromatic vegetables, a whole chicken cooks slowly to become a meal in itself. Both the chicken and the vegetables—typically, a mixture that includes onions and carrots—give up their moisture; thus only a minimum of additional liquid is necessary to prevent scorching. And when the chicken is done, the same vegetables provide a hearty accompaniment.

This sort of preparation is variously described as casseroled chicken, chicken *en cocotte*, or pot-roasted chicken. But the latter term is misleading, since dry, searing heat—the prerequisite of true roasting—plays no part in the cooking. Also, the casseroling can be done on top of the stove as well as in the oven. Strictly speaking, pot-roasting is a form of braising, and the roast appearance of the finished casseroled chicken is due mainly to a preliminary browning in oil or fat. The browned meat also helps colour and enrich the juices in the pot. In the simple version of casseroling demonstrated here, bacon pieces add more flavour to the dish.

When cooking is complete, the concentrated liquid that remains in the casserole may be served as a sauce without further reduction or embellishment, although many recipes do call for additional treatment of the sauce. Chicken casseroles can also be varied by introducing different vegetables, by stuffing the bird, or by employing wine or stock as the moistening agent, instead of the water used here (*recipes, pages 122-125*).

As to the choice of a vessel for the casserole, earthenware is probably the best material: it distributes heat evenly and well, and it usually looks attractive enough to be brought to the dinner table. Protected by a fireproof mat, such a pot can be used on top of the stove. But whatever the material, select a vessel that holds the chicken and vegetables snugly and has a tight-fitting lid, to ensure that the moist cooking atmosphere will work to maximum effect.

1 **Preparing the bacon.** Dice a few rashers of bacon. If you use strongly salted bacon, blanch it in boiling water for 2 minutes. Then put the pieces in a pan containing a little butter and stir frequently over medium heat until they are lightly coloured. Remove the bacon, reserve it and save the fat for browning the bird.

2 **Browning the chicken.** Wipe a young chicken clean and season it with salt and pepper. Place a bouquet garni in the cavity, or choose a stuffing from the recipes on pages 164-165. Brown the bird on all sides over low heat (*below*).

3 **Draining excess fat.** Transfer the chicken to the casserole and place it, covered, in a hot oven. After 10 minutes' cooking, remove the chicken from the oven and pour off the fat that has collected in the casserole (*above*).

4 **Adding liquid.** Surround the chicken with the bacon and the vegetables—here new potatoes, small onions and carrots —that have first been lightly coloured in fat. Add just a few tablespoons of liquid—water in this case (*above*).

5 **Completing the dish.** Place the covered casserole in a moderate oven for about 1 hour; or cook over a low heat on top of the stove, protected by a fireproof mat. Turn the bird occasionally. Towards the end of the cooking time you can use a skewer to test for doneness by the method shown in Step 10, page 42. Serve directly from the casserole, or else turn the chicken on to a dish, surround it with the vegetables, and spoon the juices over it. Serve the vegetables before you carve the bird.□

Cooking with the Bird's Own Juices

Baking poultry in a close-fitting covering has long been an effective way of achieving moist, tender results without having to baste the bird or supplement its juices. For example, various peoples completely cover a bird with wet clay and bury it in the embers of a fire. When the cooking is done, the clay, which hardens into a brittle shell, is cracked open and pulled off.

A simplified version of this method, suitable for the ordinary kitchen, makes use of an unglazed clay "brick"—a lidded pot designed to surround the natural contours of the bird (*right*). Before the bird is added, the pot is soaked in water; the liquid absorbed by the porous clay will keep the bird from drying out. As the cooking proceeds, the bird's natural juices are released and provide extra moisture.

Other ways to cook poultry include wrapping the bird in aluminium foil or transparent ovenproof sheets and steaming it in the oven. To prevent juices spilling as the bird cooks, the wrapping should be folded carefully (*below, right*), but not so snugly that steam is prevented from circulating around the bird. In the case of foil, the poultry must be cooked at a higher temperature than for conventional oven roasting, since aluminium's reflectivity makes it an efficient insulator.

Seasoning Unglazed Vessels

If food is cooked in a new unglazed clay vessel it will acquire an earthy taste, and its own flavours will permeate the clay. Cooks who are familiar with unglazed clay vessels swear by two simple techniques devised to deal with these problems.

First, the vessel is rubbed, inside and out, with peeled garlic cloves. The oil from the garlic acts as a barrier against unwanted flavours. Secondly, to eliminate the taste of clay, the vessel is filled with water, then celery leaves, onion skins, leek greens and some chopped carrots are added. The vessel is placed on a fireproof mat and the mixture simmered for at least two hours.

Obviously, a vessel treated in this way should only be used for savoury dishes.

Baking in a Clay Pot

1 **Preparing for the oven.** Submerge the cooking vessel in water for about 30 minutes. While it is soaking, truss the chicken (*page 40*). The bird can be stuffed or, as here, simply rubbed with lemon, olive oil, salt, pepper and garlic. Season the bird's cavity with salt and pepper; and, if you like, insert a bouquet garni, some coarsely chopped onion and chopped garlic. Drain the vessel. For added flavour, make a bed of lemon slices (*above, left*) and arrange olives around the bird (*above, right*).

Baking in Aluminium

1 **Preparing the bird.** Lay a doubled sheet of aluminium foil lengthwise in a roasting pan or an ovenproof dish. Next, place the chicken on the foil and rub the bird with butter or oil to keep the flesh moist and prevent the skin sticking to the foil. Add a little liquid—water or wine—and, if you like, cover the breast with chopped and sautéed carrots, onions and celery.

2 **Wrapping the bird.** Draw the two long sides of the doubled sheet together across the top of the bird. Neaten each edge by folding it back. Holding the two edges together, fold them over, and then fold again. Pinch along the length of the double fold to form a tight seal.

2 **Cooking and serving.** Put the lid on the pot and place the vessel in a cold oven; unglazed clay may crack if it is put directly into a hot oven. Set the oven at 230°C (450°F or Mark 8) and let the chicken cook for about 1½ hours.☐

3 **Completing the parcel.** At each end of the sheet, repeat the folding and pinching technique to make a fairly loose but well-sealed parcel. To compensate for the insulating properties of foil, cook the bird at a temperature 15°C (30°F) higher than that recommended in the roasting chart on page 43.

4 **Unwrapping after cooking.** To remove the foil, first make a long slit lengthwise and allow the steam to escape. Pull the foil apart, lift the bird on to a serving platter and spoon the cooking juices over it.☐

Creating a Light Flaky Crust

The flaky crust of a butter-rich pastry perfectly complements poultry. Making puff pastry takes no special skill, but it does require special techniques. First, sizeable lumps of butter are mixed into the flour; water is added before the lumps break down. The dough is then repeatedly rolled out and folded until the butter is distributed through the pastry in thin leaves. Then, in the hot oven, the steam released by both the butter and the dough puffs up the layers.

Keep the dough very cold until it is cooked, so that the butter does not melt—use chilled butter, and work rapidly. If possible, roll the dough on a marble slab. If you make plenty of pastry you can freeze some for later use.

1 Combining the butter and flour. Put roughly equal amounts of flour and unsalted butter pieces in a chilled bowl. Use two table knives to cut the butter into the flour, rather than risking melting the butter by mixing it in with your fingers.

2 Binding the dough with water. When the butter pieces are well coated with flour, but only slightly reduced in size, pour in just enough ice-cold water to bind the mixture together. Stir quickly with a fork, trying not to mash the butter.

3 Gathering the dough. Work the dough quickly with your fingertips until it can be gathered into a firm ball. Wrap the ball in waxed paper or plastic film to keep it moist and chill it in the refrigerator for 2 to 3 hours, or in the freezer for 20 minutes.

4 Flattening the dough. Place the stiff, chilled dough on a cool, liberally floured surface. Flatten it a little, first with the heel of your hand, then with the rolling pin, until it feels workable. Turn it over so that it is floured on both sides.

5 Rolling out the dough. Pressing lightly and evenly, roll out the dough into a long strip. Turn the strip over frequently to keep it floured on both sides—but always roll in the same direction.

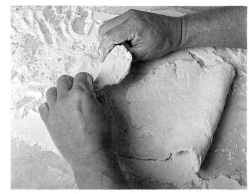

6 Making the first fold in the dough. Fold in both ends of the dough towards the middle of the strip. The ends should meet or overlap by an inch or two.

7 Making the second fold. Fold the dough in half again to align the first two folded edges with each other. You will now have a rectangle of dough four layers thick.

8 Rolling the layered dough. Chill the dough for about 30 minutes, then repeat Steps 5 to 7 two or three times. Chill the dough after each repetition.

Morsels Baked in a Pie

A pie offers a golden opportunity to combine poultry with virtually any ingredients—vegetables, eggs, seasonings, or even other meats. In this demonstration, chicken pieces are cooked with raw, cured ham, artichoke hearts, hard-boiled eggs and a little stock. The recipes on pages 140-141 suggest other combinations; the choice is limited only by what your imagination tells you will be complementary. For the crust that seals in the ingredients and juices, you could use any pastry, but the rough-puff pastry shown here (see box, opposite) is particularly light, crisp and satisfying.

The poultry in the pie can be pre-cooked or raw, boned or unboned. If you use raw, unboned chicken, as here, allow a longer cooking time and—after an initial period at fairly high heat to set the crust—bake the pie at a moderate heat so that crust and contents will be ready together. The poultry pieces should be small enough to fit snugly into the dish without wasting space; the jointing method shown on page 16 yields convenient sizes.

Be generous with the filling so that the pastry will not sag, and do not be afraid of a few bulges in the finished crust: they give a hint of the riches beneath.

1 Packing the dish. Line the dish neatly with slices of ham. Fit in the chicken pieces and use the artichoke hearts and quartered hard-boiled eggs to fill all the gaps. Add only a little liquid—stock (*above*), wine or even water; the ingredients will yield some moisture of their own, and the liquid level must not approach the crust to make it soggy. Sprinkle salt, chopped onion, mixed herbs and freshly chopped parsley over the other ingredients.

2 Covering the dish. On a floured work surface, roll out enough chilled dough to form a pie top about an inch larger all around than the rim of the dish. Turn the dough often as you roll, to keep it well floured on both sides. Moisten the rim of the dish, roll the dough loosely around the pin and unroll the dough over the dish.

3 Sealing the crust. Tuck under the excess dough to make a double thickness at the edge. Pinch and press the dough against the moistened rim. With floured thumbs, crimp the edge. To glaze the pastry, brush the top of the pie with beaten egg mixed with a little water.

4 Baking the pie. Start the pie in a hot oven. In 10 or 15 minutes, when the crust has puffed and firmed, reduce the heat until the poultry is cooked. If you are using cooked poultry, reduce the heat in the same way, and serve the pie as soon as the crust has turned golden-brown —about 40 minutes.□

A Gratin Sauce with Many Uses

A white sauce made from butter, flour and milk (*recipe, page 166*) is a versatile resource for enhancing poultry, particularly chicken and turkey. The simple version demonstrated here may appear in many guises—from a creamy blanket for a chicken gratin (*opposite page*) to a smooth basis for a pancake or bread case filling made from leftovers (*page 80*).

Every white sauce begins with a *roux*—a mixture of butter and flour that is gently cooked for a few minutes in a heavy pan. When milk is added, the flour thickens the mixture slightly.

The sauce is gently simmered for at least 40 minutes to eliminate the taste of flour and to reduce it to the desired consistency. Although it is possible to produce a white sauce with substantial body more quickly, by increasing the quantity of flour, it will not have either the refined texture or the purity of flavour of a sauce that has been only lightly bound and cooked thoroughly.

It is not critical whether the milk is added warm or cold, away from the heat or over it. The simplest method is to add the milk cold, all at once. If you whisk briskly, the sauce will be free of lumps. If lumps should form, simply strain the sauce through a sieve.

To make enough white sauce to coat a chicken for a gratin, add about ½ litre (18 fl oz) of milk to a *roux* made from 30 g (1 oz) of butter and 2 tablespoons of flour. If the sauce thickens too much, correct it by stirring in a little more milk. And if you have to keep the sauce warm before you are ready to use it, place a knob of butter on the surface to prevent a skin from forming; stir or whisk in the butter before you use the sauce.

1 Making a roux. Melt the butter in a heavy saucepan over a low heat. Add the flour and cook gently for 2 to 5 minutes—stirring constantly—until the mixture separates slightly and assumes a granular look. The brief cooking and heavy pan ensure a delicately pale final sauce; longer cooking would darken it.

2 Adding the milk. With the pan still on a gentle heat, pour the milk all at once into the *roux*, whisking briskly to blend the *roux* and milk smoothly. Raise the heat and continue whisking all the time while the sauce is coming to the boil.

3 Simmering the sauce. When the sauce has reached the boil, turn the heat very low and simmer gently for at least 40 minutes, stirring occasionally. Test the consistency: the sauce is thick enough for a chicken gratin when it will coat a spoon. Season to taste with salt, pepper and, if you like, with nutmeg. Add the pepper only at the last minute so as not to destroy its fragrance.

Putting a Golden Crust on a Smooth Sauce

One of the simplest ways of dressing up plain cooked chicken—or any lean poultry—is by cloaking it in a smooth white sauce (*opposite page*) and then crisping the top to a golden-brown gratin, or crust, under a grill or in the oven. The resulting dish is a generous one that flatters both the texture and the flavour of the meat.

The cooked poultry should be arranged in a shallow baking dish, if possible without overlapping, so that the pieces present a reasonably flat and regular surface; otherwise the coating sauce will not brown evenly. Pan-fried or grilled chicken or turkey pieces suit the method perfectly, as do any poultry leftovers, on or off the bone. You can also use a whole small chicken, as shown below, if you split and flatten the uncooked bird by the method on page 47. The bird can then be grilled or roasted, unstuffed, before being covered with a liberal coating of sauce.

1 Coating the poultry. Prepare a white sauce of the required consistency, following the instructions on the opposite page. Arrange the cooked poultry in a shallow, heatproof dish. Spoon the sauce over the poultry until it is completely covered.

2 Adding breadcrumbs and cheese. To form a crisper, browner crust, generously sprinkle breadcrumbs or grated, dry cheese—or both—over the sauce. The breadcrumbs and cheese can be mixed in any proportions you like: here a mixture of crumbs and freshly grated Parmesan, in equal quantities, is added.

3 Browning the gratin. If the poultry you use is already hot from cooking, brown the dish under a medium-hot grill. If you are using pre-cooked poultry that must be warmed through, place the dish in a fairly hot oven (190°C, 375°F or Mark 5). After about 20 minutes the meat will be hot and the crust will be brown.□

Presenting Leftovers with Flair

Transforming leftover chicken and turkey in creative ways is a skill in itself. Small scraps need to be boned and cut into bite-sized chunks. Then, to counteract the cooked bird's tendency to dryness, the chunks must be warmed in a moistening sauce, as shown below. To make chicken scraps look appetizing and attractive, the mixture can be used as pancake filling or presented in bread cases.

A pancake batter should have the consistency of single cream. You can vary it, by adding some brandy or by substituting beer for the milk or water called for in the recipe (*page 167*). Or you can give the batter colour as well as flavour by adding a pinch of powdered saffron—for a delightful yellow tint—or a teaspoon of finely chopped herbs, for flecks of green.

When serving the chicken filling in bread cases, allow one case for each person. Make the cases from a large, stale loaf. Firm-crumbed bread can be shaped readily; if you must use a light-textured loaf, freeze it for a few hours before attempting to cut it into hollow cubes.

Wafer-Thin Pancake Wrappings

1 Mixing the batter. In a mixing bowl, beginning at the centre and then working outwards, whisk together the ingredients for the batter. Melt one or two tablespoons of butter in the crêpe pan that will be used for making the pancakes, and add the butter to the mixing bowl. Whisk the mixture gently until all the butter is well blended.

2 Pouring the batter. With a cloth or paper towel, lightly wipe the pan to remove the excess butter (if there is too much butter the pancakes will cook unevenly). Starting near the rim of the pan, pour in the batter and spread it by tilting the pan until the base is covered with a thin layer. Cook the pancake until the edges begin to curl and turn golden.

Dressing up a White Sauce

Used as the basis of a chicken filling for pancakes and bread cases, a white sauce (*recipe, page 166*) lends itself to all sorts of variations. The addition of sautéed mushrooms and parsley is a traditional enhancement. Alternatively, add pieces of sweet red pepper to introduce a new taste and texture; or colour the sauce with saffron or puréed sorrel.

Fashioning Bread Cases

1 Cutting the bread case. Trim the crust from a firm loaf, cut out a 7.5 cm (3 inch) cube of bread and, with a pointed knife, carve the centre of the cube, allowing about 1 cm (½ inch) for the walls and cutting down to within 1 cm (½ inch) of the base. Insert the knife horizontally 1 cm (½ inch) above the base (*above*). Swivel the knife to free the centre section.

2 Completing the bread case. Lift out the centre section. If it cannot easily be lifted, slice along the original cuts again until the centre is completely detached. Shake out any crumbs remaining in the case.

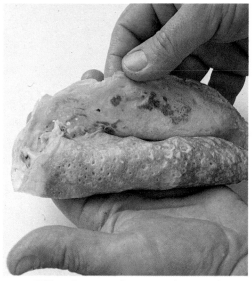

3 **Turning the pancake.** Slide a round-tipped knife under the pancake and flip it over. Cook the other side for about half a minute until it is a pale golden colour. Remove the pan from the heat and slide the pancake on to a warmed dish. Cook the rest of the pancakes similarly. Do not add more butter to the pan: the butter in the batter will keep the pan greased.

4 **Filling the pancake.** As each pancake is cooked, stack it neatly on top of the others. When the batch is complete, take each pancake in turn and, holding it across the palm of one hand, spoon in the prepared filling. Cup your hand to prevent the filling from running. Roll up the pancake around the filling.

5 **Handling the filled pancakes.** Arrange the filled pancakes in a buttered ovenproof dish, flap side underneath. If desired, sprinkle them with grated cheese. Dot with butter and heat them in a hot oven. To serve, slip a spoon under each pancake and, lightly pressing down on the top with a fork, lift up. □

3 **Preparing the case for the oven.** With a pastry brush, spread melted butter on all the surfaces of the case, inside and out. Put all the cases on a rack, place the rack in a tray to catch any butter that drips, and place in an oven preheated to 170°C (325°F or Mark 3).

4 **Flavouring with garlic.** Bake the cases for 25 to 30 minutes, turning them until all the outside surfaces are crisp and golden. Remove the cases from the oven and lightly rub all the surfaces with a peeled clove of garlic.

5 **Serving the bread cases.** Spoon the prepared filling into the case. To finish, sprinkle a pinch of chopped parsley over the filling, or garnish with equal quantities of chopped parsley, chervil and chives, together with a few leaves of finely chopped tarragon. □

Poultry Pieces Bedded in Fluffy Rice

A bed of hot, fragrant rice transforms leftover chicken or turkey into a new and succulent main dish. Rice and poultry are natural complements—as proved by a world-wide range of dishes, from Turkish *pilaff* and Indian *pilau* to Spanish *arroz con pollo*. The flavourings vary, as do the types of rice used and the details of preparation; but the underlying principles of the partnership between poultry and rice remain the same. As the poultry simmers and the grains of rice swell with cooking liquid, they absorb the flavours of all the seasonings, vegetables, herbs and spices. The result is a harmonious dish that stretches a relatively small quantity of meat into a meal of generous proportions. Moreover, if there are no leftovers to hand, it fully justifies sautéing or roasting poultry expressly for the purpose (*recipe, page 97*).

The pilaff demonstrated here uses just a few simple ingredients: roast chicken pieces, onion and sweet pepper, a pinch of saffron for its aroma and rich colour, and plain water—but its preparation could stand as the pattern for any number of elaborations. The rice is prepared first, by a few minutes of gentle sautéing with flavourings; the liquid is then poured on; finally the poultry is added to simmer until the rice is done.

There is no mystery in cooking the rice successfully. Choose a good-quality, long-grain rice. For a cleaner flavour, wash it well before use to rinse away any traces of powdery rice flour left over from the milling process. Allow the rice to drain thoroughly: it should be as dry as possible when you add it to the oil, pepper and onion in the pan.

Some cuisines traditionally use more liquid to simmer the rice, some less; but a good rule of thumb is to use twice as much liquid as rice, measured by volume not weight. While the rice is cooking, the pan should be tightly covered and left undisturbed over a very low heat until all the liquid is absorbed. The grains should be tender, but not soft or mushy.

1 **Sautéing the vegetables.** Halve a green pepper, then remove the seeds and the white ribs. Slice, chop, and place the pepper, together with chopped onion, in a pan containing a little hot olive oil. Fry over low heat until the onion is translucent—about 10 minutes.

2 **Adding the rice.** Rinse and drain the rice. Add it to the pan with a little salt, stirring continuously as the grains turn first translucent, then milky and opaque. The oil they absorb will help to keep them separate during cooking. If you are using saffron, stir it in at this point so that its colour is evenly spread.

3 **Adding the liquid.** Bring the cooking liquid—in this case, water—to the boil in another pan before adding it slowly to the sautéed rice and vegetables (*below*); by adding the liquid hot you avoid checking the cooking process even briefly. Stock can be substituted for water to add an extra element of flavour.

4 **Adding the poultry pieces.** Add the prepared poultry pieces to the vigorously bubbling liquid. Cover the pan with a tight-fitting lid and simmer as gently as possible for about 20 minutes. Take the pan off the heat and allow it to stand for 10 minutes with the lid on. In this way the rice can absorb any remaining liquid without overcooking.

5 **Fluffing the rice.** At the last minute add some butter, cut in small pieces, and mix it into the hot rice by tossing lightly with two forks: a spoon could crush the grains together and spoil the texture of the dish. Taste for seasoning, and scatter freshly chopped parsley on top before serving—direct from the pan, if you like.□

A Time-Honoured Method for Preserving Goose

Goose will keep for months if it is salted and sealed under a layer of its own fat; and although freezing makes such methods of storage unnecessary today, the pungent, briny flavour of the meat—quite unlike fresh goose—is ample reason for turning your hand to this rustic skill.

The method was developed by the farmers of south-west France in order to preserve the meat of geese bred and then slaughtered for their livers—their *foie gras*. The essence of the technique is to salt the meat and then, after cooking it, to cover it completely with its own rendered fat, creating an airproof seal that keeps out bacteria and protects the meat from contamination. Only the force-fed *foie gras* geese yield enough fat for the whole preserving process, but smaller geese, and duck too, are suitable if their fat is supplemented with lard.

Preserved goose is delicious in a cassoulet or simply heated through and served with lentils or sautéed potatoes.

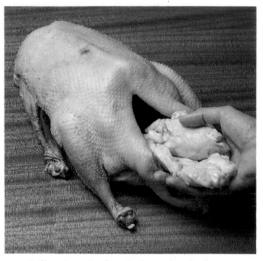

1 Collecting the fat. Pull out the thick cluster of fat from the bird's cavity, and trim the fat from the gizzard. Cut up the goose by the method shown on page 16, divide the breast into four, and trim off excess skin—another bountiful source of fat. Refrigerate the fat until you are ready to render it.

2 Salting the goose. The goose pieces must be salted for at least 24 hours before being stored. Sprinkle a thick layer of coarse salt over the bottom of a non-porous pot just large enough to hold all the pieces. Fill with alternate layers of goose and of salt seasoned with mixed dried herbs. Finish with a layer of salt. Cover and leave in a cool place.

Rendering Goose and Duck Fat

The body cavity and skin of goose and duck—and of older chicken—contain large quantities of fat that can be used for frying (*page 24*) or for preserving poultry. But it has first to be refined—or rendered—by melting out the pure fat from the tissues that run through it. The melting must be done in water; if it is cooked over direct heat, the tissues around the fatty globules would burn and impart an acrid taste to the fat. After the water evaporates, the fat is strained to remove the crisp tissues, or cracklings. The identical method can be used to refine suet for frying.

1 Melting out the fat. Cut up the fat and skin (from Step 1, above) and place them in a pan with a cup or two of water. Bring the water to a simmer over low heat and skim off any impurities that rise to the surface. During the early stage of cooking, the surface of the liquid will be broken by a few large bubbles (*above, left*); but as the fat melts and the water evaporates, more and smaller bubbles will rise (*above, right*). Cook, stirring, until the tissues darken into cracklings.

2 Straining the fat. Drape a double layer of muslin or cheesecloth over a sieve and strain the rendered fat into a heatproof container. Do not throw the cracklings away; they make a delicious snack or soup garnish.

3 **Removing salt and herbs.** When you remove the pieces of goose a day later, brush off all loose particles of salt and herbs from the meat and wipe each piece clean with a cloth. The salt will have drawn off some of the moisture from the goose and it will have begun to penetrate the flesh to act as a preservative.

4 **Cooking the goose.** Melt the rendered goose fat (see box, opposite) in a heavy saucepan over a low heat. Add the pieces of goose. If there is not enough fat to cover all the pieces, supplement it with melted lard. Simmer very slowly, turning the pieces occasionally, until the meat is so tender that it can be cut with a spoon; that will take from 1 to 2½ hours, depending on the age of the bird. Remove the meat but continue to simmer the fat until any spitting stops, indicating that all moisture has evaporated. Strain the fat through a cheesecloth-covered sieve.

5 **Preparing the preserving pot.** Wash out the salting pot and sterilize it by filling it with boiling water. Turn the pot upside-down to drain and let it air-dry. When it is quite dry, pour in a little strained fat. Swirl and tilt the pot so that the fat sets in a thick layer on the sides and bottom as it cools. This lining will form an airtight seal between the sides of the pot and its contents. Put in a layer of goose, skin side down to avoid trapping air beneath the concave inner surfaces. Cover with melted fat. Repeat until all the pieces are used, covering each layer with fat.

6 **Filling the pot.** Finish by pouring a 2.5 cm (1 inch) layer of fat over the contents and allow to cool. Refrigerate unused fat. By next day, the top layer of fat will have shrunk and exposed some meat: melt the reserved fat and add enough to seal the goose. Cover the pot and store it: a cellar or a cool larder is traditional, but a refrigerator will, of course, do. The preserved goose will develop its full flavour in three to four weeks. To serve, warm the pot enough to melt the fat, and remove the desired number of pieces. Re-seal the pot with melted fat and return it to storage.□

A Gleaming Centrepiece for the Cold Table

Set in the place of honour at a cold buffet, a whole cooked chicken or duck glazed with aspic excites the eye as well as the palate. In addition to making the dish appetizing to look at, the aspic serves to keep the bird moist and it contributes its own subtle flavour; it is to cold food what a sauce or gravy is to hot dishes.

In the 19th-century heyday of *haute cuisine*, chefs took great pains to make aspic of crystal clarity. To achieve the desired effect, they simmered a meat stock with a paste of egg whites and finely minced lean beef. The egg-and-beef mixture absorbed any particles that clouded the stock and was then removed by straining the liquid through muslin.

For an informal meal, there is no need to go to such lengths. The preparation described on this page requires nothing more elaborate than a basic veal stock (*recipe, page 166*) enriched by the addition of a glass of Madeira or sherry. The gelatine in the veal bones is a natural setting agent and the stock should readily jell in a refrigerator to give a translucent amber-coloured aspic.

Any bird, whether it is roasted or poached, can be coated with aspic after it has been well chilled. Cool the stock until it is just on the point of setting: when cool stock is spooned over a cold bird it forms a thin glaze almost on contact. Continue applying the stock to build up the coating to the desired thickness. Return the bird to the refrigerator for a short time before the application of each new layer in order to set the aspic. When the glazing has been completed, put the bird back in the refrigerator until it is needed.

1 Cooling stock. Fill a bowl with crushed ice and set a smaller, thin-walled glass or metal bowl in the ice. Pour a ladleful of veal stock into the small bowl and stir with a spoon. As soon as the stock begins to congeal, it is ready for use. If it congeals too much, warm it for a moment over low heat until it liquefies again.

2 Coating the bird. Put the chilled bird on a rack above a dish. Spoon stock over the bird until the skin is evenly covered with a thin glaze of aspic. Let excess stock drip into the dish; you can warm it and re-use it for subsequent layers. Refrigerate the bird for about 10 minutes between coats and before decorating.

3 Decorating the bird. To make an eye-catching presentation, dip sliced, peeled olives and blanched tarragon leaves in aspic and lay them in a pattern on the glaze. Continue applying layers of stock until you have reached the desired thickness.

Anthology of Recipes

Drawing upon the cooking traditions and literature of more than 20 countries, the Editors and consultants for this volume have selected 201 published poultry recipes for the Anthology that follows.

The selections range from the simple to the unusual—from poached chicken delicately flavoured with tarragon to a mouth-watering dish of stuffed guinea-fowl with raspberries. The Anthology also spans nearly 2,000 years and includes recipes by 107 writers—from the Roman gastronome Apicius to such distinguished exponents of the classic culinary art as Escoffier and Curnonsky, as well as modern cookery writers such as Elizabeth David and James Beard. Many of the recipes are by little-known authors of now rare and out-of-print books held in private collections. A large number of these recipes have never before been published in English.

Not surprisingly, the cooking of France is well-represented. Some of the world's greatest poultry dishes, including duck braised with orange, chicken fricassée and *coq au vin* are French inspirations. Absent from the Anthology, however, are elaborate and extravagant recipes from *haute cuisine*. Throughout this book, the emphasis is on authentic dishes meticulously prepared with fresh, natural ingredients that blend harmoniously.

Since many early recipe writers did not specify amounts of ingredients, these have been judiciously added; and where appropriate, introductory notes in italics have been added by the Editors. Modern terms have been substituted for archaic language, but to preserve the character of the original, and to create a true anthology, the authors' texts have been changed as little as possible. Some instructions have been expanded, but in cases where cooking instructions may seem somewhat abrupt, all the reader has to do is refer to the appropriate demonstration in the front of the book to find the technique explained in words and pictures. Cooking terms and ingredients that may be unfamiliar are explained in the combined Index and Glossary at the end of the book.

For ease of use, the Anthology is organized by poultry type. Recipes for standard preparations—stock, pastry, batter and a white sauce—appear at the end of the Anthology. The serving suggestions included in some recipes are, of course, optional.

All recipe ingredients are listed in order of use, with both metric and imperial weights for each ingredient in separate columns. The two sets of figures are not exact equivalents, but are consistent for each recipe. Working from either metric or imperial weights and measures will produce equally good results, but the two systems should not be mixed. All spoon measures are level.

Chicken

Chicken Sauté with the Herbs of Provence

Poulet Sauté aux Aromates de Provence

To serve 4

2 kg	chicken, cut up into serving pieces	4 lb
4 tbsp	olive oil	4 tbsp
	salt and pepper	
20 cl	dry white wine	7 fl oz
500 g	ripe tomatoes, skinned, seeded and roughly chopped	1 lb
2	garlic cloves, finely chopped	2
1	anchovy fillet, washed and drained	1
	dried savory and marjoram	
	powdered bay leaf	
1	large sprig fresh basil	1
90 g	black olives, stoned	3 oz

Sauté the chicken in the olive oil. Season with salt and pepper. Remove the chicken pieces. Deglaze the pan with the wine. Add the tomatoes, garlic, anchovy, a pinch each of savory, marjoram and bay leaf, and the sprig of basil. Allow this scented mixture to simmer and reduce. Add the olives. Return the chicken to the pan to warm in the sauce, and serve.

JEAN-NOËL ESCUDIER
LA VÉRITABLE CUISINE PROVENÇALE ET NIÇOISE

Chicken Sauté with Garlic or Peppers

Sauté Dauphinois

To serve 6 to 8

Two 1 kg	chickens, cut up into small serving pieces	Two 2 to 2½ lb
	salt and pepper	
10 cl	olive oil or half olive oil and half butter	4 fl oz
24	garlic cloves, unpeeled	24
1	bouquet garni	1
4 tbsp	finely chopped parsley	4 tbsp

Season the chicken pieces with salt and pepper and place them in a large sauté pan containing the hot oil (or butter and oil). Cook over a high heat, turning the pieces for 5 to 6 minutes. Reduce the heat to low, cover the pan and cook for 15 minutes. Remove the lid occasionally to turn the pieces.

Add the garlic cloves and bouquet garni. Cook for another 20 minutes or so, remove the bouquet garni, then transfer the contents of the pan to a hot serving dish and sprinkle with chopped parsley.

The garlic (which becomes as soft as butter) is squeezed from its skin on to the guests' plates.

Another excellent *sauté dauphinois* can be prepared by replacing the garlic with 500 g (1 lb) of quartered sweet green peppers. In this case the peppers should be cooked for about 30 minutes.

CURNONSKY
CUISINE ET VINS DE FRANCE

Chicken Sauté Cacciatora

Pollo Sauté alla Cacciatora

To serve 6

1.5 kg	chicken, cut up into serving pieces	3 lb
3 tbsp	oil	3 tbsp
60 g	butter	2 oz
	salt and freshly ground pepper	
250 g	mushrooms, sliced	8 oz
1	onion, chopped	1
10 cl	dry white wine	4 fl oz
1 tbsp	flour	1 tbsp
¼ litre	chicken or veal stock, boiling	8 fl oz
2 tbsp	brandy	2 tbsp
4	ripe tomatoes, skinned, seeded and chopped	4
1 tbsp	chopped parsley	1 tbsp
1 tbsp	chopped fresh tarragon or 1 tsp dried tarragon	1 tbsp

Dry the chicken pieces thoroughly on paper towels. Heat the oil and half of the butter in a very large frying pan over fairly high heat and brown the chicken, a few pieces at a time, for about 2 minutes on each side. As the pieces brown, remove them from the pan and add fresh pieces.

When all are browned, return only the thighs and drumsticks to the pan, cover tightly, reduce the heat to low, and simmer for 10 minutes. Add the breasts and wings, and simmer for 15 minutes longer, or until all of the pieces are tender. Remove them from the pan to a hot platter, season them with salt and pepper, and keep them warm. Sauté the mushrooms in the remaining butter in a covered frying pan for about 8 minutes; remove from the heat and reserve.

Drain off most of the fat from the pan in which the chicken cooked, add the onion, cook over medium heat until the onion is golden; add the wine, raise the heat and cook until it has evaporated. Stir in the flour, cook for 1 minute, add the boiling stock, and cook until thickened. Heat the brandy in a ladle over medium heat, ignite it, and add it to the pan. When the flame dies, add the tomatoes and herbs to the pan, season with salt and pepper, and simmer for 10 minutes.

Return the pieces of chicken to the pan, add the mushrooms, simmer for 3 minutes, and turn the chicken and sauce out on to a hot serving platter.

LUIGI CARNACINA
GREAT ITALIAN COOKING

Chicken Sauté Normandy-Style
Poulet Sauté d'Yvetot

To serve 4

1.5 kg	chicken, cut up into serving pieces	3 lb
60 g	butter	2 oz
500 g	russet apples, peeled, cored and sliced	1 lb
4 tbsp	Calvados	4 tbsp
	salt and pepper	

Sauté the chicken pieces in butter in a frying pan; meanwhile, arrange the sliced apples in a casserole. After 20 minutes, or when the chicken is half cooked, remove it from the pan and lay it on top of the apples. Deglaze the frying pan with Calvados. Taste the juices for seasoning, and add them to the casserole.

Cover the casserole and put it in a moderate oven, 180°C (350°F or Mark 4) for a further 20 to 30 minutes.

MICHEL BARBEROUSSE
CUISINE NORMANDE

Chicken Sauté with Cream
Poulet à la Crème

To serve 4

1.5 to 2 kg	chicken	3 to 4 lb
90 g	butter	3 oz
	salt and pepper	
250 g	mushrooms, sliced	8 oz
2 tbsp	flour	2 tbsp
½ litre	double cream	18 fl oz

Put half the butter into a casserole, sauté the chicken until golden and season with salt. Cover and cook gently for barely an hour. Add the mushrooms.

Separately, prepare a *roux* with the remaining butter and the flour. Let it cook for 10 minutes and whisk it with the cream. Season with salt and pepper. Cut the chicken into pieces. Combine the chicken pieces and sauce with the cooking juices and mushrooms in the casserole. Serve at once so that it will remain hot.

CURNONSKY
À L'INFORTUNE DU POT

Chicken Sauté Forestière
Poulet Sauté à la Forestière

To serve 8

2 kg	chicken, cut up into serving pieces	4 lb
150 g	green bacon, rind removed, coarsely chopped	5 oz
150 g	butter	5 oz
200 g	morels, stems removed, carefully washed to remove sand, and halved	7 oz
3	shallots, chopped	3
	salt and pepper	
4	large potatoes, peeled, washed and cut into 1 cm (½ inch) cubes	4
4 tbsp	dry white wine	4 tbsp
4 tbsp	veal stock	4 tbsp
1 tbsp	chopped parsley	1 tbsp

Blanch the bacon by immersing it in boiling water for 5 minutes, then drain it, dab it dry and put it in a casserole with 50 g (2 oz) of the butter. Let it cook over a low heat for a few minutes, turning it periodically, until lightly coloured. Remove the bacon and put in the chicken, leaving it to cook for 4 to 5 minutes. Take out the wings and the breast pieces, but leave the legs to cook for another 7 to 8 minutes.

When all the chicken pieces are golden, put the chicken wings and breast, and the bacon, back into the casserole. Add the morels and sprinkle with shallots. Season with salt and pepper, cover the casserole and cook in an oven preheated to 200°C (400°F or Mark 6) for 30 to 40 minutes.

While the chicken is cooking, prepare the potato garnish. Dry the potato cubes thoroughly. Melt 75 g (2½ oz) butter in a frying pan and turn the potatoes in it until they are coloured.

When the chicken is cooked, arrange the pieces on a platter and keep them warm.

Add the wine to the casserole, reduce it rapidly, add the veal stock and let it boil for 2 minutes. Then remove the casserole from the heat. Add the rest of the butter and mix well. This sauce should be poured over the chicken, and the whole sprinkled with parsley. Arrange the potato cubes around the outside of the dish.

ODETTE KAHN
LA PETITE ET LA GRANDE CUISINE

Sautéed Chicken with Parmesan

Poulet Sauté au Parmesan

To serve 3

1.5 kg	chicken, cut up into serving pieces	3 lb
125 g	butter	4 oz
½ tsp	salt	½ tsp
2 tbsp	flour	2 tbsp
15 cl	single cream	¼ pint
60 g	Parmesan cheese, grated	2 oz
3	egg yolks	3
	fresh breadcrumbs	

Brown the chicken pieces for 20 minutes in 20 g (½ to 1 oz) of butter and sprinkle on a little salt. In another pan cook the flour in the rest of the butter, without browning. Stir in the cream, 2 teaspoons of Parmesan and salt to taste, and stir these together over a low heat. Remove the pan from the heat and finish thickening the sauce with the egg yolks.

Sprinkle 6 teaspoons of the Parmesan on the bottom of a fireproof dish, arrange the chicken pieces on it, coat with the sauce, and put in the oven for 5 minutes. Sprinkle on the remaining Parmesan, along with the breadcrumbs, and brown for another minute or two in the oven, then serve.

ALI-BAB
ENCYCLOPEDIA OF PRACTICAL GASTRONOMY

Chicken Sauté with Morels

Poulet Sauté aux Morilles

This method of sautéing, in which the butter is not heated before the addition of the chicken pieces, is often used when a particularly pale, delicate sauce is required.

To serve 4 to 6

2 to 2.5 kg	chicken, cut up into serving pieces	4 to 5 lb
30 g	butter	1 oz
	salt and pepper	
10 cl	white wine	4 fl oz
125 g	morels, carefully cleaned	4 oz
1	truffle, finely chopped	1
20 cl	double cream	7 fl oz

Butter a sauté pan, put in the chicken pieces and season with a pinch each of salt and pepper. Place the pan on a moderate heat: the chicken will soon become golden. Cook for about 30 minutes, then add the wine. When the wine has reduced a little, add the morels and the truffle, incorporate the cream and cover the pan. Simmer for 10 to 15 minutes and serve.

A. ESCOFFIER
LE CARNET D'ÉPICURE

Poussins with Sweet Red Peppers

Poussins aux Piments Doux

To skin peppers easily, follow the instructions on page 11.

To serve 2 to 4

Two 750 g	poussins, halved	Two 1½ lb
60 g	butter	2 oz
	salt	
	ground allspice	
	dried marjoram	
6	large sweet red peppers, roasted or grilled, skinned, seeded and finely shredded	6
20 cl	dry white wine	7 fl oz

In a large sauté pan, sauté the chickens in the butter until coloured. Season with salt, allspice and marjoram.

Add the peppers to the chickens, pour in the wine, and cook with the pan covered for about 25 to 30 minutes. Place the chickens on a serving dish and arrange the garnish of peppers on top of them.

LÉON ISNARD
LA CUISINE FRANÇAISE ET AFRICAINE

Chicken Sauté with Tomatoes

Sauté de Poulets aux Tomates

The preparation of tomatoes called for in this recipe is designed to eliminate excess liquid and acidity, and is rarely described in cookery books. Skin the tomatoes, halve them horizontally and remove the seeds. Salt them generously and leave them to drain for about 2 hours in a sieve. This gives a result that no squeezing by hand can produce and is essential to the quality of the finished dish.

To serve 8 to 10

Three 1.5 kg	chickens, cut up into serving pieces	Three 3 lb
4 tbsp	olive oil	4 tbsp
60 g	butter	2 oz
	salt and pepper	
	chicken or veal stock	
6	large ripe tomatoes, skinned, halved, seeded and drained	6
1	garlic clove	1
	cayenne pepper	
1 tbsp	finely chopped parsley	1 tbsp

Place the chicken legs in a sauté pan with the butter and oil; cover and cook for approximately 25 minutes until they are three-quarters done. Add the breasts; season with salt and pepper, and finish cooking together with the legs. Drain the chicken pieces, leaving the fat in the pan. Arrange the pieces in a casserole and moisten with a little stock; keep them warm.

Cut each halved tomato in two. Place the tomatoes in a frying pan with some of the fat in which the chicken was cooked; season and add the garlic clove; sauté over a high heat, without breaking up the tomato pieces. As soon as the excess moisture has evaporated from the tomatoes, remove the garlic clove, dust the tomatoes with a pinch of cayenne pepper and add the chopped parsley.

Place the chicken pieces in a pyramid on a plate, surround them with the tomatoes, and moisten with their own juice.

URBAN DUBOIS AND ÉMILE BERNARD
LA CUISINE CLASSIQUE

Chicken Sauté Archduke

Poulet Sauté Archiduc

There are numerous ways of cooking Chicken Archduke but the basic recipe is more or less invariable: the chicken must be sautéed without allowing it to colour, and onion and cream must always be added. The method of diluting the juices can be varied by using brandy or Madeira; the sauce can be finished off with whisky or port; the garnish can be of cucumbers, mushrooms, quartered artichokes or truffles.

To serve 1 to 6

2 to 2.5 kg	chicken, cut up into serving pieces	4 to 5 lb
100 g	butter	3½ oz
2 tbsp	chopped onion	2 tbsp
	paprika	
10 cl	white wine	4 fl oz
15 cl	cream	¼ pint
1 tsp	lemon juice	1 tsp
2	cucumbers, peeled, cut into chunks and simmered in butter	2

Sauté the chicken in 60 g (2 oz) of the butter without colouring it. When it is half cooked, after about 30 minutes, add the onion that has been lightly cooked in 15 g (½ oz) of the butter and a good pinch of paprika. Continue cooking for another 20 to 30 minutes until the chicken is done. Remove the chicken from the pan and keep it hot.

Dilute the cooking juices with the white wine, boil down by half, pour in the cream and cook at boiling point for a few moments. Incorporate the rest of the butter, add the lemon juice, and strain. Arrange the chicken on a hot dish, garnish with the cucumber chunks and coat with the sauce.

PROSPER MONTAGNÉ
LAROUSSE GASTRONOMIQUE

Chicken Sauté with Cream

Poulet Sauté à la Crème

The butter used to enrich the sauce for this sauté should be cut into small pieces and swirled into the pan juices off the heat. Instructions for making chicken velouté appear on page 167.

To serve 4

1.5 to 2 kg	chicken, cut up into serving pieces	3 to 4 lb
100 g	butter	3½ oz
¼ litre	double cream	8 fl oz
1 to 2 tbsp	chicken velouté (optional)	1 to 2 tbsp

Sauté the chicken, without browning it, in 60 g (2 oz) of the butter. Deglaze the pan juices with the cream, and add the chicken velouté. Boil down the sauce by half. At the last moment add 40 g (1½ oz) butter.

Place the chicken on a dish and coat it with the sauce.

PROSPER MONTAGNÉ
LAROUSSE GASTRONOMIQUE

Chicken Sauté with Lime Flowers

Poularde au Tilleul

This recipe was created by M. René Lasserre, the proprietor of Chez Lasserre, in Paris, in honour of Les Floralies, a flower show. Dried lime flowers are obtainable from pharmacies.

To serve 4

2 kg	chicken, cut up into 8 serving pieces	4 lb
	salt and pepper	
60 g	butter	2 oz
1 tbsp	dried lime flowers	1 tbsp
10 cl	dry white wine	4 fl oz
4 tbsp	chicken stock	4 tbsp
½ tsp	ground lime flowers	½ tsp
3 tbsp	double cream	3 tbsp
10 cl	strong lime-flower tea, made with 1 tbsp lime flowers	4 fl oz

Season the chicken pieces with salt and pepper, and sauté them in butter in a casserole. Cover and continue cooking over low heat for 20 minutes. Sprinkle with the lime flowers 5 minutes before the end of the cooking time.

Remove the chicken pieces and keep them warm. Deglaze the pan with the white wine and reduce. Add the chicken stock and the ground lime flowers. Bind the sauce with the cream and leave to simmer, without reaching the boil, for 10 minutes. Finally, add the lime-flower tea. Arrange the chicken pieces on a platter and cover with the sauce. Serve with rice.

ROBERT COURTINE
MON BOUQUET DE RECETTES

Brittany Chicken Sauté

Poulet Sauté Bretonne

To serve 4 or 5

2 kg	chicken, cut up into serving pieces	4 lb
60 g	butter	2 oz
100 g	leeks, white part only, sliced and stewed in butter	3½ oz
1	small onion, sliced and stewed in butter	1
100 g	mushrooms, finely sliced and sautéed in butter	3½ oz
10 cl	cream	4 fl oz
10 cl	*roux*-thickened chicken stock or sauce suprême	4 fl oz

Stiffen the chicken pieces in hot butter for a few minutes without colouring them. Add the leeks and onion. Cover the pan and set it in a moderate oven, 180°C (350°F or Mark 4), for 20 minutes. About 5 minutes before the chicken is quite cooked, add the mushrooms.

Arrange the chicken on a serving dish. Add the cream and the *roux*-thickened stock to the vegetables. Reduce to half the volume, then pour the sauce and the vegetables over the chicken.

A. ESCOFFIER
A GUIDE TO MODERN COOKERY

Chicken Sauté with Tomatoes

Le Poulet Sauté aux Tomates

To serve 4

1.5 kg	chicken, cut up into 10 serving pieces	3 lb
	salt and pepper	
15 cl	olive oil	¼ pint
6	medium-sized onions, quartered	6
1	shallot, chopped	1
	dried thyme	
10	sprigs parsley	10
2	garlic cloves, crushed	2
6	ripe tomatoes, skinned, seeded and coarsely chopped	6
20 cl	white wine	7 fl oz
60 g	black olives	2 oz
	lemon juice	

Season the chicken pieces with salt and pepper. In a large frying pan, heat 5 tablespoons of olive oil. Add the onions, the shallot, a pinch of thyme and the parsley. Allow the onion to cook until golden and then put these ingredients aside.

In the same frying pan, heat the remaining olive oil and fry the chicken pieces until golden-brown. Then add the garlic, the tomatoes, the reserved onion mixture and the white wine. Reduce the liquid to half by vigorous boiling for 10 to 15 minutes, stirring frequently.

About 3 minutes before serving, throw in a handful of black olives and add a dash of lemon juice.

A quicker variation calls for reducing the tomatoes in a separate pan, moistening the pan in which the chicken has just cooked with a glass of white wine or stock, and adding the tomatoes, olives and a slice of lemon just before serving.

Another variation is to add a few button mushrooms cooked in their own juice, or dried ceps that have been soaked and drained, 10 minutes before serving.

JACQUES MÉDECIN
LA CUISINE DU COMTÉ DE NICE

Chicken Greater than the Sum of its Parts

Murgi ka Kima

To serve 2 or 3

300 g	chicken meat, finely chopped	10 oz
60 g	clarified butter	2 oz
12	cloves	12
1	large onion, halved lengthwise and thinly sliced crosswise	1
	salt	
1 tsp	ground turmeric	1 tsp
3 tbsp	fresh lime juice	3 tbsp
	Spicy paste	
1 tsp	finely chopped garlic	1 tsp
2 tsp	chopped onion	2 tsp
1 tsp	finely chopped ginger root	1 tsp

To make the spicy paste, whirl the garlic, onion and ginger in a blender, using only as much water as is necessary to facilitate grinding to a fine paste. Reserve.

In a heavy, medium-sized saucepan, heat the butter almost to smoking. Keep the lid of the pot close by. Drop in the cloves, close the pot immediately, and shake it over the heat for 1 minute. Take off the lid, remove the cloves with a slotted spoon, and discard them. Fry the onion in the same butter. When the onion is just golden, add the chicken. Salt to taste. Stir and turn with a spatula for 5 minutes. Add the turmeric. Continue stirring for 10 minutes. Do not add any water. Add the spicy paste and cook, uncovered, until tender (never add water). Add the lime juice to the pan, stir, and serve very hot.

SHIVA JI RAO AND SHALINI DEVI HOLKAR
COOKING OF THE MAHARAJAS

Chicken Sauté with Vinegar

Volaille de Bresse Sautée au Vinaigre

To serve 4

1.5 kg	chicken, cut up into 8 serving pieces	3 lb
150 g	butter	5 oz
	salt and pepper	
4	shallots, chopped	4
¼ litre	wine vinegar	8 fl oz

Heat 100 g (3½ oz) butter in a skillet big enough to hold the pieces of chicken. Season the pieces with salt and pepper, and brown them lightly. The butter should remain light in colour. Cover, and continue cooking in a fairly hot oven, 190°C (375°F or Mark 5), for about 20 minutes.

When cooked, place the pieces of chicken on a platter, cover, and keep them warm.

Sauté the shallots without letting them brown in the butter left in the skillet. Deglaze with the wine vinegar. Boil to reduce it by half and whisk the remaining butter into the sauce. Pour the sauce on the pieces of chicken, carefully coating them.

PAUL BOCUSE
LA CUISINE DU MARCHÉ

Sautéed Chicken Breasts with Cheese from the Jura

Suprêmes de Volaille Jurassienne

To serve 4

2	whole chicken breasts, skinned, boned and halved	2
60 g	flour	2 oz
¼ tsp	grated nutmeg	¼ tsp
	salt and freshly ground black pepper	
2	eggs, lightly beaten	2
60 g	dry breadcrumbs	2 oz
30 g	Gruyère cheese, grated	1 oz
90 g	butter, melted	3 oz
1	lemon, cut into 4 wedges	1

Season the flour with nutmeg, salt and pepper. Dredge the chicken breasts lightly in the flour mixture, then in the eggs, then in a mixture of breadcrumbs and grated cheese. In a large skillet, brown the chicken breasts on all sides in the melted butter. Cook for about 15 minutes. When done, serve hot with lemon wedges.

NIKA STANDEN HAZELTON
THE SWISS COOKBOOK

Chicken Breasts Sautéed in Butter, with White Wine and Almonds

Suprêmes de Volaille Amandine

To serve 6

3	whole chicken breasts, halved	3
	flour	
	salt and freshly ground white pepper	
125 g	butter	4 oz
2 tbsp	lemon juice	2 tbsp
75 g	split blanched almonds	2½ oz
1 tsp	finely chopped garlic	1 tsp
1 tbsp	finely chopped onion	1 tbsp
4 tbsp	dry white wine	4 tbsp
2 tsp	finely chopped parsley	2 tsp

Bring a pan of salted water to the boil and put in the chicken breasts. Boil them for 2 minutes and drain. Remove all the skin and breastbone, but leave attached the tiny tip of wing bone, if there is one, on each half breast. Dry the half breasts thoroughly with paper towels.

Mix some flour with a little salt and pepper and dust the chicken breasts with it. Heat half the butter in a heavy pan. Put in the chicken breasts and brown them very slowly on each side. Add the lemon juice and season with salt and pepper. Cover the pan and sauté gently, over low heat, until the chicken is tender. Then remove the chicken, set it aside, and add to the pan the almonds, garlic, onion and another 30 g (1 oz) of butter. Shake the pan over medium heat until the almonds are nicely browned. Then stir in the rest of the butter alternately with the wine.

Return the chicken to the pan, and reheat. Arrange the pieces in a shallow serving dish. Spoon the almonds and sauce over the pieces, and sprinkle with chopped parsley.

DIONE LUCAS AND MARION GORMAN
THE DIONE LUCAS BOOK OF FRENCH COOKING

Spezzatino of Chicken in Vinegar

Spezzatino di Pollo all'Aceto

To serve 6

1.5 kg	chicken, cut up into serving pieces	3 lb
4	anchovy fillets, rinsed and drained	4
2	garlic cloves	2
10 cl	white wine vinegar	4 fl oz
	salt and freshly ground pepper	
	flour	
10 cl	oil	4 fl oz
3	sprigs rosemary (or 1 tsp dried rosemary)	3

Pound the anchovy fillets and the garlic to a paste in a mortar. Add the vinegar and blend until smooth. Season the chicken with salt and pepper and dust with flour.

Heat the oil with the rosemary until smoking and brown the chicken a few pieces at a time, on all sides. As the pieces become brown, remove them from the pan and add fresh ones. When all are browned, return only the legs and thighs to the pan, cover tightly, reduce the heat and simmer for 10 minutes. Add the breasts and wings and simmer for another 15 minutes. When the chicken is fully cooked, transfer it to a hot platter and keep it warm.

Drain off all but 2 tablespoons of the fat in the pan, add the vinegar mixture, and reduce over a high heat to half its quantity. Return the pieces of chicken to the pan, cover tightly, and simmer over a very low heat for 5 minutes. Transfer the chicken to a hot serving platter and spoon the sauce over it.

LUIGI CARNACINA
GREAT ITALIAN COOKING

Pan-Fried Chicken with Mustard

To serve 4

1.5 to 2 kg	frying chicken, cut up into 8 serving pieces	3½ lb
2 tbsp	German mustard	2 tbsp
1 tbsp	Dijon mustard	1 tbsp
2	egg yolks	2
2 tbsp	double cream	2 tbsp
150 g	stale white breadcrumbs	5 oz
	flour	
	salt and freshly ground black pepper	
	corn oil	

Skin the chicken pieces, using a piece of absorbent paper to give you a better grip, and pat each piece dry.

In a medium-sized bowl or deep soup plate, blend the mustards smoothly with the egg yolks and cream.

Have the breadcrumbs spread out on one sheet of grease-proof paper, and a little flour on another.

Season each chicken piece with salt and freshly ground black pepper. Dust it with flour. Dip it in the mustard mixture, turning it over to make sure it is entirely coated, and roll it in breadcrumbs, patting them on firmly.

Place the pieces on a plate and chill for 3 to 4 hours to firm up the coating and allow the mustard flavour to penetrate the chicken.

When ready to fry the chicken, select a large, deep frying pan (or two smaller ones) that will take all the pieces comfortably in one layer. Pour in corn oil to a depth of about 2.5 cm (1 inch) and place the pan(s) over a moderate heat.

When the oil is hot enough to make a bread cube froth on contact, add the chicken pieces; the oil should not quite cover them. Fry them over a moderate heat for 15 to 20 minutes or until the chicken is cooked through, crusty and golden-brown, turning the pieces occasionally. (Use a pair of tongs or two spoons to avoid piercing the chicken.)

Drain the chicken pieces on absorbent paper and serve immediately.

Note: If you have to fry the chicken in two batches—or if it is not to be served immediately—you can keep it hot in an oven at the lowest setting for 15 to 20 minutes.

ROBERT CARRIER
THE ROBERT CARRIER COOKERY COURSE

Marinated Fried Chicken

Chicharrones de Pollo

A recipe from the Dominican Republic.

To serve 4

1.5 to 2 kg	chicken, chopped into 16 small pieces by dividing the wings, thighs, drumsticks and breasts into halves	3 to 4 lb
4 tbsp	dark rum	4 tbsp
4 tbsp	soy sauce, preferably the Japanese type	4 tbsp
4 tbsp	strained fresh lime juice	4 tbsp
45 cl	vegetable oil	16 fl oz
½ tsp	salt	½ tsp
	freshly ground black pepper	
125 g	flour	4 oz

Warm the rum in a small pan over a low heat. Off the heat, ignite the rum with a match and gently shake the pan back and forth until the flame dies. Add the soy sauce and lime juice to the rum.

Place the chicken in a deep bowl and add the rum mixture, turning the pieces with a spoon to coat them evenly. Marinate at room temperature for about 2 hours, or in the refrigerator for at least 4 hours, turning the chicken pieces occasionally.

Preheat the oven to the lowest setting and line a large shallow baking dish with a double thickness of paper towels. Pat the pieces of chicken completely dry with paper towels and season them with the salt and a few grindings of pepper. Dip them in the flour and shake vigorously to remove the excess. In a heavy 25 to 30 cm (10 to 12 inch) skillet, heat the oil over a high heat until it is very hot but not smoking.

Fry 5 or 6 pieces of chicken at a time for about 6 minutes on each side, turning them with tongs or a slotted spoon and regulating the heat so they colour richly and evenly without burning. As they brown, transfer the pieces to the lined baking dish and keep them warm in the oven.

Serve the chicken as soon as all the pieces are cooked, accompanied if you like with hot boiled rice.

THE EDITORS OF TIME-LIFE BOOKS
FOODS OF THE WORLD—THE COOKING OF THE CARIBBEAN ISLANDS

Marinated Fried Chicken

Kotopoulo Tiganito Marinato

To serve 4 or 5

1 to 1.5 kg	chicken, washed, dried, and cut up into serving pieces	2 to 3 lb
	salt and freshly ground pepper	
90 g	flour	3 oz
30 cl	olive, corn, or peanut oil	½ pint
	small tomatoes, or tomato wedges	
	watercress and parsley sprigs	
	Marinade	
4 tbsp	olive oil	4 tbsp
4 tbsp	white wine vinegar	4 tbsp
4 tbsp	lemon juice	4 tbsp
2	garlic cloves, chopped	2
1	small onion, sliced	1
1	bay leaf, crushed	1
1 tsp	dried thyme or marjoram, or oregano	1 tsp
2	peppercorns, crushed	2
2 or 3	juniper berries	2 or 3
4	coriander seeds, cracked	4

Combine all the marinade ingredients in a bowl. Dip the chicken in the marinade, coating the pieces on all sides. Cover and refrigerate for at least 2 hours, or overnight if desired. Drain the chicken, then season lightly with salt and pepper. Put the flour in a paper bag, add the chicken pieces and shake lightly until they are coated with flour.

Put the oil in a heavy frying pan to the depth of 1 cm (½ inch) and heat almost to the smoking point. Slip the chicken into the hot oil and fry to a light chestnut colour, turning on all sides. Using tongs, remove the chicken to a roasting pan, discarding the remaining oil in the frying pan.

Bake the chicken in a moderate oven at 180°C (350°F or Mark 4) for 50 minutes or until tender, pouring off the oil as it collects in the pan. (The chicken will be crisp and a rich chestnut colour.) Arrange the chicken on a platter, alternating tomatoes, watercress and parsley round the edge.

VILMA LIACOURAS CHANTILES
THE FOOD OF GREECE

Tangerine Peel Quick-Fried Chicken in Hot Sauce

Instructions for chopping a chicken into 16 to 20 pieces are given in the recipe for crackling fried chicken on page 100.

To serve 4

1 kg	spring chicken, chopped through the bone into 16 to 20 pieces	2 to 2½ lb
3	slices fresh ginger root	3
1	onion, sliced	1
	salt	
3 tbsp	soy sauce	3 tbsp
3 tbsp	dry sherry	3 tbsp
6 tbsp	vegetable oil	6 tbsp
2	chili peppers, seeded and chopped	2
1 tbsp	dried tangerine peel, or peel from 1 large fresh tangerine, broken into small pieces	1 tbsp
2 tsp	wine vinegar	2 tsp
2 tsp	sugar	2 tsp
	black pepper	
1 tsp	sesame oil	1 tsp

Place the chicken pieces in a deep bowl. Add the ginger and onion, sprinkle with salt and 1 tablespoon each of the soy sauce and sherry. With your fingers, work this marinade into the chicken and leave to marinate for half an hour; then remove the ginger and onion.

Heat the oil in a large frying pan. When hot, add the marinated chicken. Turn and fry for 3½ minutes. Remove and drain the chicken and pour away any excess oil from the pan.

Add the chili peppers and tangerine peel to the remaining oil in the pan. After 15 seconds stir-frying over high heat, return the chicken to the pan. Turn the chicken completely over once. Mix the rest of the sherry and soy sauce with the vinegar, sugar, and pepper; pour evenly over the chicken. Stir-fry for a further ½ minute and sprinkle with sesame oil.

KENNETH LO
CHINESE FOOD

Deep-Fried Marinated Chicken

Toriniku No Tatsuta-age

To serve 4

350 g	chicken breast, skinned and boned	12 oz
1	1 cm (½ inch) cube fresh ginger root, peeled and finely grated	1
10 cl	soy sauce	4 fl oz
3 tbsp	*sake* (Japanese rice wine)	3 tbsp
	katakuriko or cornflour	
	vegetable oil for deep frying	
2	spring onions, trimmed, using white and green parts	2

Cut the chicken into bite-sized pieces and place them in a bowl. Mix the ginger with the chicken. Pour on the soy sauce and *sake* and mix. Marinate for 30 minutes. Lift out the chicken pieces and roll them in the *katakuriko* or cornflour, shaking to remove the excess.

Heat 5 to 7 cm (2 to 3 inches) of oil in a *tempura* pan or a saucepan to about 175°C (340°F) on a frying thermometer, or until bubbles form on wooden chopsticks stirred in the oil. The heat should be a little lower than moderate.

Fry the chicken pieces, a few at a time, until golden-brown. Drain them on the rack of the *tempura* pan or on paper towels. Arrange the pieces on a platter.

Cut the spring onions crosswise into 2.5 cm (1 inch) pieces, then cut them lengthwise into fine strips. Crisp them for a few minutes in cold water, then squeeze them dry in a kitchen cloth. Add to the platter with the chicken and serve.

ELISABETH LAMBERT ORTIZ WITH MITSUKO ENDO
THE COMPLETE BOOK OF JAPANESE COOKING

Fried Chicken

To serve 4 to 6

1.5 kg	chicken, cut up into serving pieces	3 lb
60 g	flour	2 oz
1 tsp	salt	1 tsp
¼ tsp	pepper	¼ tsp
½ tsp	curry powder (optional)	½ tsp
10 cl	milk, or as needed	4 fl oz
90 g	butter	3 oz

Preheat the oven to 180°C (350°F or Mark 4).

Pat the chicken dry. Mix the flour, salt, pepper and curry powder in a bag. Dip the chicken pieces in the milk, then shake them in the bag, a few pieces at a time, until coated.

Melt enough butter to lightly coat the bottom of a heavy frying pan and quickly brown the chicken pieces in it. Melt additional butter—about 60g (2 oz)—in a small pan.

Use a flat baking pan large enough to hold all the chicken without piling it up. Place the chicken pieces skin side down in the pan, pour over the melted butter and bake them on the lower rack of the oven for about 25 minutes. Baste and turn the pieces. Bake them for another 35 minutes, or until browned and done.

To cook on top of the stove, flour the chicken following the same preparation methods as above. Then place the chicken pieces in the heavy, greased skillet and brown them over a low heat. Cover the pan and steam until the pieces are almost done—about 1 hour and 10 minutes. Remove the cover, raise the heat and let the chicken pieces crisp for 10 minutes.

JANE MOSS SNOW
A FAMILY HARVEST

Fried Chicken with Cream Gravy and Mush

To serve 6 to 8

Two 1 to 1.5 kg	young chickens, cut up into serving pieces	Two 2 to 3 lb
	salt and pepper	
	flour	
100 g	lard	3½ oz
	Mush	
150 g	white cornmeal	5 oz
1 litre	boiling water	1¾ pints
1 tsp	salt	1 tsp
1	egg yolk	1
	Cream gravy	
15 g	butter	½ oz
½ tbsp	flour	½ tbsp
¼ litre	single cream	8 fl oz
	salt and black pepper	

To make the mush, dribble the cornmeal into rapidly boiling salted water, stirring constantly, then let boil over direct heat for 2 to 3 minutes and continue cooking for 1 hour in a double boiler. Let it cool slightly, add the egg yolk, beat well and set it aside to get cold.

Meanwhile, sprinkle the chicken pieces with salt and pepper, cover them with a towel and let them stand for 30 minutes. Dry each piece carefully and roll it in flour. Heat the lard in a heavy iron skillet; when the fat is very hot, but not smoking, put in the chicken (frying only a few pieces at a time). Turn them to brown on both sides, keeping the heat at an even temperature so that the chicken will not brown before it cooks through. As the pieces are cooked, drain them on absorbent paper, place them in the middle of a hot platter and keep them in a warm part of the stove until ready to serve.

Drop the mush, a tablespoonful at a time, into the remainder of the hot fat in which the chicken was fried, turning to fry on both sides. The cakes should be about 1 cm ($\frac{1}{2}$ inch) thick and should have the circumference of a water glass. Fry each cake a golden-brown on each side and arrange in a border round the chicken pieces.

Use the same frying pan to make the gravy. Melt the butter and sift in the flour; when well mixed with the butter and remaining grease and bits left from frying the mush, add the cream, a little salt and a little black pepper. Let it thicken then pour it into a sauceboat and serve.

SHEILA HIBBEN
AMERICAN REGIONAL COOKERY

Southern Fried Chicken with Cream Gravy

To serve 4

1 to 1.5 kg	chicken, cut up into serving pieces	2 to 3 lb
	salt	
125 g	flour	4 oz
250 g	lard, or 125 g (4 oz) vegetable shortening combined with 125 g (4 oz) lard	8 oz
	Cream gravy	
2 tbsp	flour	2 tbsp
15 to 20 cl	chicken stock	6 fl oz
15 cl	single cream	$\frac{1}{4}$ pint
	salt and white pepper	

Wash the chicken pieces under cold running water and pat them thoroughly dry with paper towels. Sprinkle the pieces with salt on all sides. Put the flour in a sturdy paper bag. Drop the chicken into the bag a few pieces at a time and shake the bag until each piece is thoroughly coated with flour. Remove the chicken pieces from the bag and vigorously shake them free of all excess flour. Lay them side by side on a sheet of greaseproof paper.

Preheat the oven to 95°C (200°F or Mark $\frac{1}{4}$) and in the middle of the oven place a shallow baking dish.

Over a high heat melt the lard or combined lard and shortening in a heavy 25 cm (10 inch) frying pan. The fat should be 0.5 cm ($\frac{1}{4}$ inch) deep. If it is not, add a little more. When a light haze forms above the fat, add the chicken pieces, starting them skin side down. Since the legs and thighs will take longer to cook than the breasts and wings, put them into the pan first.

Cover the pan and fry the chicken over a moderate heat for about 6 to 8 minutes, checking every now and then to make sure the chicken does not burn. When the pieces are deep brown on one side, turn them over and cover the pan again. Continue frying until all the pieces are cooked. Transfer the finished chicken to the baking dish in the oven and keep the chicken warm in the oven while you make the gravy.

Pour off all but 2 tablespoons of fat from the frying pan. Add the flour, and stir until the fat and flour are well combined. Pour in the chicken stock and about two-thirds of the single cream. Cook over a moderate heat, beating with a whisk until the gravy is smooth and thick. If the gravy is too thick for your taste, stir in the remaining cream to thin it. Strain it through a fine sieve if you wish. Taste for seasoning, then pour into a heated sauceboat and serve with the fried chicken arranged attractively on a heated serving dish.

THE EDITORS OF TIME-LIFE BOOKS
FOODS OF THE WORLD—AMERICAN COOKING

Spanish Chicken Sauté with Rice

Poulet au Riz à l'Espagnole

For instructions on preparing artichokes, see page 11.

To serve 4

1.5 kg	chicken, cut up into serving pieces	3 lb
4 tbsp	olive oil	4 tbsp
2	onions, chopped	2
2	garlic cloves, finely chopped	2
4	tomatoes, skinned, seeded and roughly chopped	4
4	tender artichoke hearts	4
4	sweet red peppers, seeded and quartered	4
60 g	freshly shelled peas	2 oz
	ground saffron	
	salt and pepper	
300 g	rice	10 oz
$\frac{1}{2}$ litre	water	18 fl oz

In a fireproof casserole, sauté the chicken pieces in the olive oil. As soon as they are brown, add the onions, garlic, tomatoes, artichoke hearts, red peppers, peas and a good pinch of saffron. Season with salt and pepper, add the rice, and lightly brown everything together.

Add the water and bring to a fast boil; then complete the cooking by placing the covered casserole in a moderate oven for 20 minutes.

Note: This recipe is a good one for ensuring that the grains of rice remain separate, providing the dish is removed from the oven 2 minutes before the rice is completely cooked. Serve immediately.

LÉON ISNARD
LA CUISINE FRANÇAISE ET AFRICAINE

Deep-Fried Eight-Piece Chicken

This dish is said to date back to A.D.600. Some cooks prepare it by removing the legs and wings, then chopping the breast and back each in half for a total of 8 pieces. The breast and wings need less cooking than the drumsticks and should be removed from the hot oil first.

To serve 8

1.5 to 2 kg	chicken, cut up into 8 serving pieces	3 to 4 lb
2	slices fresh ginger root, finely chopped	2
1	spring onion, finely chopped	1
1	egg, lightly beaten	1
30 g	flour	1 oz
2 tbsp	sherry	2 tbsp
	oil for deep frying	

Add the ginger and spring onion to the beaten egg, along with the flour and sherry. Blend to a smooth batter.

Dip the chicken pieces in the batter to coat. Meanwhile, heat the oil. Add the chicken, a few pieces at a time, and deep fry until golden. Drain on paper towels and serve.

GLORIA BLEY MILLER
THE THOUSAND RECIPE CHINESE COOKBOOK

Garlic-Fried Chicken

Spezzatino di Pollo Fritto

To serve 4

1.5 kg	chicken	3 lb
1	egg, lightly beaten	1
100 g	flour	3½ oz
2 tsp	salt	2 tsp
½ tsp	black pepper	½ tsp
5	garlic cloves, 3 pressed or mashed to a paste	5
10 cl	vegetable oil	4 fl oz
10 cl	olive oil	4 fl oz
1 or 2	lemons, cut into wedges	1 or 2

Have the butcher chop the chicken, bones and all, into 2.5 cm (1 inch) pieces. Wash and dry the pieces. Dip them in the egg, then in a mixture of the flour, salt, pepper and mashed garlic. Let the pieces stand a few minutes to dry.

Heat the oils in a skillet; add the whole cloves of garlic. When they are browned, remove them. Add the chicken pieces. Fry them until browned and tender. Serve garnished with lemon wedges.

ROMEO SALTA
THE PLEASURES OF ITALIAN COOKING

Erskine Caldwell's Genuine Southern Fried Chicken

To serve 6

Two 1.5 to 2 kg	chickens, cut up into serving pieces	Two 3 to 4 lb
1.25 litres	milk	2 pints
3 or 4	eggs, beaten	3 or 4
	salt	
	Tabasco sauce	
	flour	
	breadcrumbs	
	oil or fat for deep frying	

Soak the chicken pieces overnight in the milk, to which the eggs, some salt, and a good dollop of Tabasco have been added. Drain and dry the chicken pieces, roll them in a mixture of half flour and half breadcrumbs, and fry them in deep fat until they are brown. Finish the cooking in a moderate oven, approximately 180°C (350°F or Mark 4), for 10 to 15 minutes but do not allow the chicken to dry out.

Serve with baked yams, grilled tomatoes and green salad.

BERYL BARR AND BARBARA TURNER SACHS (EDITORS)
THE ARTISTS' AND WRITERS' COOKBOOK

Deep-Fried Small Chickens

Petits Poulets Frits

To serve 8

Two 1 kg	chickens, quartered and wing tips removed	Two 2 to 2½ lb
	salt and pepper	
1 to 2 tbsp	chopped parsley	1 to 2 tbsp
5 tbsp	lemon juice	5 tbsp
	flour	
3	eggs, beaten	3
	breadcrumbs	
	oil for deep frying	
2	large bunches parsley (optional)	2

Season the chicken quarters with salt and pepper, and sprinkle them with chopped parsley and then with the lemon juice. Marinate for at least 1 hour, turning the pieces occasionally. Drain and flour each piece separately. Roll the pieces in the beaten eggs and cover them with breadcrumbs.

Twelve to 15 minutes before serving, immerse the legs, which take longest to cook, in hot deep fat; 5 minutes later, add the breasts. When the pieces are done and nicely coloured, drain them, salt them lightly and arrange them on a folded napkin or a bed of parsley that has been deep fried for a few seconds.

URBAIN DUBOIS
L'ÉCOLE DES CUISINIÈRES

Fried Chicken Florentine

To serve 4

1.5 kg	chicken, cut up into serving pieces	3 lb
250 g	flour	8 oz
1	egg, lightly beaten	1
35 cl	olive oil	12 fl oz
	Marinade	
3 tbsp	olive oil	3 tbsp
4 tbsp	lemon juice	4 tbsp
	salt and pepper	
2 tsp	chopped parsley	2 tsp

Make a marinade of oil, lemon juice, salt, pepper and parsley. Pour it over the chicken pieces in a casserole and let stand for about 2 hours, turning the pieces occasionally. Take the chicken out of the marinade, dry the pieces well, flour them thoroughly, dip them into the beaten egg and fry them in deep olive oil for about 15 minutes.

ADA BONI
THE TALISMAN ITALIAN COOK BOOK

Chicken with Walnuts, Peking-Style

To serve 6

1	whole chicken breast, skinned, boned and diced	1
1 tsp	salt	1 tsp
1 tbsp	cornflour	1 tbsp
1	egg white	1
125 g	blanched walnuts	4 oz
	vegetable oil for deep frying	
2 tbsp	vegetable oil	2 tbsp
1	sweet green pepper, diced	1
1	sweet red pepper, diced	1
2 tbsp	soy bean paste	2 tbsp
2 tbsp	sugar	2 tbsp
1 tbsp	dry white wine	1 tbsp
4 tbsp	chicken stock, as needed	4 tbsp

Mix the chicken with the salt, cornflour and egg white, tossing well. Put the walnuts into a strainer and deep fry them in oil heated to 150°C (300°F) until light brown and crispy. Dip them up and down in the oil to get them as brown as you like. They are easy to burn, so be careful. Drain the walnuts well and set them aside. Sauté the peppers in 1 tablespoon of oil for 1 minute. Drain them. Add the other tablespoon of oil and sauté the bean paste for 3 minutes, stirring constantly. Add the sugar. Deep fry the chicken pieces in oil heated to 190°C (375°F) for 1 minute. Drain the pieces and put them into the bean paste. Add the wine. If the sauce is too thick, add stock. Toss furiously. Add the peppers and walnuts and allow to heat through, stirring constantly.

YU WEN MEI AND CHARLOTTE ADAMS
100 MOST HONORABLE CHINESE RECIPES

Marinated Fried Whole Chicken

Marinade de Poulet

The oranges for both the marinade and the sauce in this recipe should be bitter Seville oranges. However, if bitter oranges are not available, the juice of blood oranges mixed with a little lemon juice can be substituted. The chickens should be split and flattened by the method shown on page 47.

To serve 4

Two 1 kg	chickens, split down the back and flattened	Two 2 lb
250 g	lard	8 oz
	flour, or thin batter (page 166)	
	Seville orange juice (optional)	
	Marinade	
10 cl	dry white wine	4 fl oz
10 cl	wine vinegar	4 fl oz
10 cl	Seville orange juice	4 fl oz
	allspice and cayenne pepper	
	salt	
1	large onion, finely sliced, or 3 or 4 Welsh or spring onions, finely sliced	1
1 tbsp	*fines herbes*	1 tbsp

Place the flattened chickens in a dish with the marinade liquid, and season with the spices and salt. Add the onion and *fines herbes* and marinate for 2 to 3 hours. Turn the chickens in the marinade several times so that they are thoroughly flavoured, then drain them.

Flour the chickens, or soak them in very thin batter, and fry them in the lard until they turn an attractive golden-brown. The authentic sauce to serve with this is orange juice; or you can boil up the marinade, strain it, and serve that as the sauce.

NICOLAS DE BONNEFONS
LES DÉLICES DE LA CAMPAGNE

Chicken Kiev

To serve 6

3	chicken breasts, skinned, boned and halved	3
	salt	
¼ tsp	pepper	¼ tsp
2 tbsp	chopped chives	2 tbsp
90 g	unsalted butter, cut into 6 finger-sized pieces and frozen hard	3 oz
75 g	flour	2½ oz
2	eggs, lightly beaten	2
90 g	fresh breadcrumbs	3 oz
	vegetable oil for deep frying	

Flatten the breasts to a thickness of about 0.5 cm (¼ inch) by placing them between 2 pieces of waxed paper and pounding them lightly with a mallet or rolling pin. Discard the paper and lay out the flattened breasts, boned side uppermost. Salt to taste, and sprinkle with the pepper and chives. Place a finger of frozen butter on each breast half. Roll up the butter in the breast meat as you would wrap a package, tucking in the ends at the beginning of the roll. Dip the rolls in flour, then in beaten egg, and finally roll them in the breadcrumbs. Chill in the refrigerator for 3 hours or more. Heat the oil to 185°C (365°F) in a saucepan or deep frying pan—the oil should be deep enough to cover the rolled breasts. Deep fry the breasts for 4 to 5 minutes, until golden-brown. Drain them on paper towels and serve immediately.

CARL LYREN
365 WAYS TO COOK CHICKEN

Crackling Fried Chicken

This crisp crackling dish, one of the best regional Chinese recipes of its type, is a good contrast to versions that are more soft and moist. The meat may be removed from the bones using fingers or chopsticks.

To serve 4

1.5 kg	chicken	3 lb
2 tsp	salt	2 tsp
4	slices fresh ginger root, finely chopped	4
½ tbsp	malt sugar, or ordinary sugar	½ tbsp
5 tsp each	white vinegar and light soy sauce	5 tsp each
2 tbsp	water	2 tbsp
1½ tbsp	sherry	1½ tbsp
3 tbsp	cornflour	3 tbsp
	vegetable oil for deep frying	

Mix the salt and ginger together and rub the chicken thoroughly inside and out. Marinate for 3 hours in an airy place.

Chop the chicken into 16 to 20 pieces the Chinese way. To do so, you will need a very sharp, heavy cleaver (or a razor-sharp Chinese chopper, which is available from Chinese provision shops). Chopping through the bones is made much easier if you work on a very thick chopping board, as the action requires a very firm base.

Divide the chicken into 4 pieces by splitting it in half lengthwise and cutting off each leg. Chop each of the legs crosswise into 3 pieces, and each wing into 2 pieces, giving 10 pieces. Then chop each of the 2 body pieces into 3 across and right through the breastbone, producing 6 pieces. Split 1 or 2 of the larger pieces in half, to obtain 16 to 20 pieces.

Mix the sugar, vinegar, soy sauce, water, sherry and cornflour into a paste. Rub the pieces of chicken with half of this paste, and leave them to dry in an airy place for 2 hours. Rub in the remainder of the paste, and leave to dry for 1 more hour.

Heat the oil in a deep-fryer until very hot. Deep fry the chicken in two lots for 3 to 3½ minutes each, when the pieces should be very crisp. Serve hot.

KENNETH LO
CHINESE FOOD

Basic Roast Chicken with Stuffing

To serve 4

1.5 kg	roasting chicken	3 lb
	salt and freshly ground black pepper	
30 g	softened butter	1 oz
	Bread stuffing	
30 g	butter	1 oz
2 or 3	rashers lightly smoked bacon	2 or 3
1	Spanish onion, finely chopped	1
100 g	dry white bread, trimmed and cut into 1cm (⅓ inch) cubes	3 to 3½ oz
3 tbsp	finely chopped parsley	3 tbsp
	thyme and rosemary leaves, crumbled	
1	egg	1
4 tbsp	milk, or chicken stock	4 tbsp
	salt and freshly ground black pepper	

Preheat the oven to 180°C (350°F or Mark 4).

To make stuffing: in a large frying pan, fry the bacon in half of the butter until it is crisp. Remove the bacon; add the chopped onion to the pan and sauté over a moderate heat until it turns soft and golden. Remove the onion from the pan with a slotted spoon.

Add the remaining butter to the frying pan. When it has melted, add the bread cubes and toss over a moderate heat until they have taken up all the fat and turned a light golden colour.

Crumble the bacon rashers into a mixing bowl. Add the

sautéed onion, bread cubes, parsley and a generous pinch each of thyme and rosemary, and toss lightly with a fork until well mixed.

In another, smaller bowl, beat the egg with the milk or stock. Pour this over the bread mixture, tossing with the fork to distribute the liquid evenly. Season the stuffing with salt and pepper.

Wipe the chicken clean both inside and out.

Fill the cavity of the chicken with the bread stuffing. Skewer or sew up the vent with a few stitches of thread.

Lay the chicken in a roasting pan. Rub the bird with salt and pepper, and spread with the softened butter.

Roast the chicken for about $1\frac{1}{4}$ hours, basting it frequently with its own juices (supplemented if necessary with a tablespoon or two of boiling water).

To serve: transfer the chicken to a heated serving dish. Discard the skewers or thread, and keep the bird hot.

Pour 2 or 3 tablespoons of water into the roasting pan and bring to the boil over a moderate heat, stirring and scraping the base and sides with a wooden spoon to dislodge crusty bits stuck there. Simmer for a minute, stirring. Taste for seasoning; pour into a heated sauceboat and serve with the chicken.

ROBERT CARRIER
THE ROBERT CARRIER COOKERY COURSE

Chicken with Anchovies

Poulet aux Anchois

This 19th-century recipe, originally for a spit-roasted chicken, has been adapted for oven roasting. The salted anchovies called for in the recipe must be filleted, washed and patted dry before use. If you substitute filleted canned anchovies, which are saltier, soak them in water for 10 minutes before you use them. The techniques required for stuffing a chicken under the skin are demonstrated on pages 47-49.

To serve 4

1.5 kg	chicken	3 lb
8	anchovy fillets, washed, dried and chopped	8
90 g	green streaky bacon, chopped	3 oz
2 tbsp	chopped parsley	2 tbsp
4 or 5	Welsh or spring onions, chopped	4 or 5
	pepper	
	grated nutmeg	
4 or 5	thin strips pork fat	4 or 5
10 cl	veal or ham stock	4 fl oz

Mix together three-quarters of the anchovies with the other chopped ingredients. Season with pepper and nutmeg, and spread the stuffing mixture under the skin of the chicken. Bard the breast of the chicken with the pork fat. Truss the bird and roast it for 30 minutes at 220°C (425°F or Mark 7). Lower the heat to 170°C (325°F or Mark 3) and cook for about 30 minutes more. Remove the pork fat for the last 15 minutes. Degrease the roasting pan before deglazing with the stock, to which the remaining chopped anchovies have been added.

OFFRAY AINÉ
LE CUISINIER MÉRIDIONAL

Chicken with Olives

Entrée de Poularde aux Olives

The original recipe (1691) calls for Champagne, which at this period could have been either a sparkling white wine or a non-sparkling red wine. The latter makes more sense in the context of this recipe.

To serve 4

1.5 to 2 kg	roasting chicken	3 to 4 lb
1	slice pork fat	1
3 tbsp	Seville orange juice	3 tbsp
	Sauce	
1 tbsp	chopped parsley	1 tbsp
3 tbsp	chopped Welsh or spring onion	3 tbsp
30 g	green bacon, chopped	1 oz
1 tbsp	flour	1 tbsp
4 tbsp	chicken or meat roasting juices or chicken or veal stock	4 tbsp
15 cl	red wine	$\frac{1}{4}$ pint
1 tbsp	capers, chopped	1 tbsp
2	anchovy fillets, chopped	2
100 g	olives, stoned and crushed	$3\frac{1}{2}$ oz
1 tbsp	olive oil	1 tbsp
1	bouquet garni of parsley, chervil, tarragon, chives, thyme and a bay leaf	1
$\frac{1}{4}$ litre	*roux*-thickened veal stock	8 fl oz

Choose a very tender, plump chicken; bard its breast with a generous slice of pork fat and roast it. While the chicken is roasting, make the sauce by cooking the chopped parsley and onion for a moment or two with the chopped bacon and flour. Add the roasting juices or stock, the wine, capers, anchovies, olives, olive oil and bouquet garni. Bind the sauce with the thickened stock, season well and degrease.

Remove the roasted chicken from the pan, cut off the legs at the joints, and make slits in the thighs, wings and breast. Crush all sections slightly with the flat of a large knife blade, then put them in a casserole with the sauce and all their juices. Cover the casserole and keep them warm, basting them regularly. To serve, arrange the chicken on a dish, cover it with the sauce, and sprinkle over the orange juice.

MASSIOLOT
LE CUISINIER ROIAL ET BOURGEOIS

Split, Stuffed Baked Chicken

Poulet Fendu Farci au Four

Carving presents no problem when this chicken is split and stuffed as shown on pages 47-49.

To serve 4		
1.5 kg	chicken	3 lb
1 tsp	crumbled, mixed dried herbs (thyme, oregano, savory)	1 tsp
3 tbsp	olive oil	3 tbsp
	Stuffing	
90 g	fresh white cheese (*ricotta* or cream cheese)	3 oz
60 g	fresh white breadcrumbs	2 oz
60 g	butter	2 oz
	salt and pepper	
1 tbsp	finely chopped fresh marjoram leaves and flowers (if unavailable, substitute *fines herbes*)	1 tbsp
1	large egg	1
1	medium-sized onion, finely chopped, stewed gently in 15 g (½ oz) butter for 15 minutes, without colouring, and cooled	1
500 g	small firm courgettes, cut into a *julienne*, salted, squeezed, sautéed in 30 g (1 oz) butter, and cooled	1 lb
	freshly grated Parmesan cheese	

Split the chicken the entire length of the back, flatten it out, and loosen the skin.

Sprinkle the chicken on both sides (but not beneath the skin) with the herbs, pat and rub generously with olive oil, and leave to marinate for an hour or two.

Mash the white cheese, breadcrumbs and butter together with the salt and pepper and herbs, using a fork; add the egg, mashing; then mix in the onion and the courgettes, and, finally, the Parmesan, adding enough to bring the stuffing to a firm, stiff consistency.

Stuff the chicken, taking a handful of stuffing at a time and forcing it into place, pushing with the fingers of one hand beneath the skin while moulding and forcing with the other from the outside. Coat the drumsticks and thighs well first before worrying about the breast. When all of the stuffing is in place, fold the neck-skin flap (if there is any) over the throat orifice and tuck it beneath the bird.

With a small, sharply pointed knife, pierce the web of skin and thin flesh between the inside of the thigh and the tip of the breast, making a slit just large enough to receive the drumstick tip. Then force the drumstick gently up and push its tip through the slit to the underside. Repeat on the other side.

Place the bird in a roasting pan and mould the surface with your hands to force the skin and stuffing into a plump version of the natural form. Salt and pepper the bird and roast it in a preheated oven, starting at 230°C (450°F or Mark 8) and turning the oven down to about 190°C (375°F or Mark 5) some 10 minutes later. Start basting regularly after 30 minutes. Count 50 minutes to 1 hour roasting time, depending on the size of the chicken, and if, after about 40 minutes, it seems to be colouring too rapidly, turn the oven down further, placing a sheet of aluminium foil loosely over the bird.

Transfer the bird to a round, heated serving platter; don't attempt to serve the juices—they are too fat and the dish needs no sauce (chill the scrapings and juices, discard the fat, and use them for flavouring a dish of leftovers).

RICHARD OLNEY
SIMPLE FRENCH FOOD

Chicken Stuffed with Figs

Le Poulet Farci aux Figues

To serve 4		
1 to 1.5 kg	chicken, giblets reserved	2 to 3 lb
75 g	butter	2½ oz
2	medium-sized onions, finely sliced	2
10	fresh black figs, peeled and cut lengthwise into 8 pieces	10
250 g	rice, washed in a sieve under running water and drained	8 oz
½ litre	water	18 fl oz
	salt and pepper	
	olive oil	
	cayenne pepper	

In a large flameproof casserole, heat 60 g (2 oz) of the butter over a medium heat and cook the onions gently in this until they are transparent. Do not allow them to brown.

Chop the chicken giblets coarsely. Add the figs and the giblets to the onions, and leave to cook until the giblets lose their pink colour. Then add the rice and stir until the grains are well coated with butter.

Add the water, salt to taste, and a little pepper and bring to the boil. Reduce the heat and simmer gently for 25 to 30 minutes, or until all the liquid has been absorbed. Remove the casserole from the heat and add the remaining butter.

Preheat the oven to 200°C (400°F or Mark 6). Dry the inside of the chicken well and stuff it with about two-thirds of the fig mixture, reserving the rest. Sew up the chicken.

Place the chicken, back uppermost, in a fairly deep roasting pan. Smear the bird with oil, sprinkle with salt and cayenne pepper, and place the pan on the middle shelf of the oven. Leave the bird to cook for about 45 minutes. To test whether the chicken is cooked, pierce one of the thighs with a skewer. The juice released should be pale yellow. If it is pink, cook for a further 5 to 10 minutes.

Take the chicken from the oven. Remove the sewing thread. Leave the bird to cool for 5 minutes, as this will make it easier to carve. Stir the reserved fig and rice mixture with a fork, reheat it over a low heat and serve it separately.

JACQUES MÉDECIN
LA CUISINE DU COMTÉ DE NICE

Stuffed Chicken, Cyprus-Style

Kotopoulo Yemisto Kypriotiko

The stuffing for this is crunchy and flavourful, and may be used with turkey by doubling the quantities.

To serve 5 or 6

1 to 1.5 kg	chicken, liver reserved	2 to 3 lb
3 tbsp	vegetable oil or butter (plus extra for roasting)	3 tbsp
60 g	almonds, blanched and quartered lengthwise	2 oz
150 g	long-grain rice	5 oz
10 cl	dry white wine	4 fl oz
30 cl	water	½ pint
	salt	
1 tsp	ground cinnamon	1 tsp
	granulated sugar	
75 g	currants	2½ oz

Wash and dry the chicken, and set it aside. In a medium-sized saucepan, heat the oil or butter and sauté the almonds and liver, then remove them with a slotted spoon. Chop the liver and set it aside with the nuts. Add the rice to the fat in the pan and sauté over medium heat, stirring constantly. Then pour in the wine and water, and add the salt, cinnamon, and a pinch of sugar. Cover and cook for 12 minutes, or until the rice is almost tender. Stir in the almonds, liver and currants and remove the pan from the heat.

Spoon the stuffing into the cavity of the chicken and close tightly with skewers. Truss the chicken and brush the surface lightly with melted butter or oil. Set the bird in a roasting pan, breast side up, and roast it for 1¼ hours, or until tender, in a moderate oven at 180°C (350°F or Mark 4)—turning it with 2 wooden spoons every 20 minutes and basting frequently with the drippings. Remove the stuffing from the cavity and transfer it to the centre of a warm platter. Carve the chicken and arrange the pieces around the stuffing. Serve warm.

Note: For a popular mainland version, instead of the almonds, cinnamon, and rice, substitute pine nuts, nutmeg, and a little chopped celery and parsley, and soaked bread.

VILMA LIACOURAS CHANTILES
THE FOOD OF GREECE

Chicken Stuffed with Brains

Poulet à la Franc-Comtoise

To serve 4

1 kg	chicken	2 to 2½ lb
	salt and pepper	
1	calf's brain	1
	truffles, sliced	
60 g	butter	2 oz

Season the chicken inside with salt and pepper. Wash the brain under running water; then soak it for a few minutes in cold water. Remove the surface membrane, and season with salt and pepper. Tuck the truffle slices into the brain, and ease it into the chicken cavity. Sew up the opening with strong thread, coat the top of the chicken with butter and place the bird in a roasting dish. Cook in a moderate oven, 180°C (350°F or Mark 4), for about 1¼ hours. When the chicken is golden-brown, cover it with buttered paper. To serve, carve the chicken, arrange it on a warm dish, and pour over the juices from which the fat has been skimmed.

EDITIONS GUTENBERG
LA CUISINE LYONNAISE

Roast Chicken Oregano, Peloponnesos Style

Kota Fournou Ladorigani

To serve 4 or 5

1 to 1.5 kg	chicken, washed and dried	2 to 3 lb
	salt and freshly ground pepper	
4 tbsp	olive oil	4 tbsp
3 tbsp	lemon juice	3 tbsp
1½ tsp	oregano	1½ tsp
	sliced tomatoes and cucumber	

Season the chicken, inside and out, with salt and pepper, then truss it. Whisk the olive oil, lemon juice and 1 teaspoon of the oregano in a small bowl and brush over the chicken. Place the chicken in a roasting pan and roast in a moderate oven at 180°C (350°F or Mark 4) for 1¼ hours, turning every 20 minutes and basting with the remaining marinade. Sprinkle the remaining oregano on the chicken and serve warm, garnished with slices of tomato and cucumber.

VILMA LIACOURAS CHANTILES
THE FOOD OF GREECE

Elizabeth Frink's Roast Lemon Chicken

To serve 4

1.5 kg	chicken	3 lb
2	lemons	2
1	small garlic head	1
	salt and pepper	
2 tbsp	olive oil	2 tbsp
30 g	butter	1 oz
	chopped parsley	

Rub the outside of the chicken with the rind of 1 lemon. Chop up the lemon and put it inside the chicken with the garlic. Season with salt and pepper, and roast for 1½ hours at 170°C (325°F or Mark 3), with a mixture half of olive oil and half of butter poured on top of and inside of the chicken. Half an hour before taking the chicken out of the oven, pour freshly squeezed lemon juice and chopped parsley over the top.

BERYL BARR AND BARBARA TURNER SACHS (EDITORS)
THE ARTISTS' AND WRITERS' COOKBOOK

Chicken à l'Oignon

This recipe has been adapted from a 19th-century original version by the French chef Louis Eustache Ude. An easy way to flavour a chicken under the skin is shown on pages 47-49.

To serve 4

1.5 kg	tender young chicken	3 lb
	salt and pepper	
1	medium-sized onion, thinly sliced	1
125 g	softened butter	4 oz
	chicken stock (optional)	

Season the inside of the chicken with salt and pepper. With your fingers, carefully loosen the skin over the breast meat, poking down towards the legs as far as you can go without tearing the skin. Insert the onion slices under the loosened skin so that they form a layer between it and the flesh. Fasten down any loose ends of skin with toothpicks to keep the onion snugly lodged as the chicken roasts.

Before placing the chicken in an oven preheated to 190°C (375°F or Mark 5), spread the softened butter over the skin that covers the onions. Salt and pepper the entire bird, to taste. Place it in a shallow earthenware dish or open roasting pan, and don't give it another thought for 45 minutes. Then baste it with the fat and juices that have collected in the pan. Repeat twice, and roast the bird for a total of 1½ hours. Serve it hot out of the oven, as soon as possible, to savour the crackling golden skin with the tender slices of onion oozing juice underneath. (Add a small quantity of chicken stock or bouillon if more sauce is wanted.)

For an accompaniment, parboil potato balls for 2 minutes. Sprinkle them with paprika and roast them along with the chicken, basting at the same time you attend to the chicken.

ESTHER B. ARESTY
THE DELECTABLE PAST

Parslied Chicken

Volaille "Truffée" au Persil

The fromage blanc *called for in this recipe is a fresh cheese made from skimmed milk and containing no fat solids. To prepare a home-made substitute, thoroughly blend roughly equal quantities of low-fat cottage cheese and plain yogurt with a dash of lemon juice until the mixture is smooth and shiny and has the consistency of lightly whipped cream.*

To serve 4

1 kg	chicken	2 to 2½ lb
5 tbsp	chopped parsley	5 tbsp
1 tbsp each	chopped chives and tarragon	1 tbsp each
2	shallots, chopped	2
50 g	button mushrooms, chopped	2 oz
1 tbsp	*fromage blanc*	1 tbsp
	salt and pepper	
1 tsp	peanut oil	1 tsp
	Gravy	
1	garlic clove, unpeeled but flattened	1
1 tbsp	chopped parsley	1 tbsp
20 cl	chicken stock	7 fl oz

Preheat the oven to 240°C (475°F or Mark 9).

Put the parsley, chives, tarragon, shallots, mushrooms, *fromage blanc*, salt and pepper into a bowl and work them into a smooth paste. Lift the skin away from the breast and thighs of the chicken (by sliding your fingers between the skin and the flesh) so that you can insert the parsley mixture, patting it into an even layer over the breast and thighs.

Season the chicken inside with salt and pepper and roast it for 40 minutes, having brushed the outside with peanut oil.

When it is cooked, remove the chicken from the roasting pan and keep it hot. To prepare the gravy, put the garlic and the parsley into the hot juices in the roasting pan. Add the chicken stock and bring to the boil, scraping the bottom of the pan thoroughly with a fork to detach the caramelized juices. Reduce this gravy by one-third and taste for seasoning.

Carve the chicken into 4 serving pieces, put them on a large hot dish, and carefully moisten each piece with some of the gravy poured through a conical strainer.

MICHEL GUÉRARD
MICHEL GUÉRARD'S CUISINE MINCEUR

Stuffed Roast Chicken Toulouse-Style

Poulet à la Toulousaine

To serve 6

1.5 kg	chicken	3 lb
200 g	ham, thinly sliced and cut into 2.5 cm (1 inch) squares	7 oz
1 tbsp	chopped mixed herbs	1 tbsp
	salt and pepper	
2	garlic cloves, peeled	2
200 g	garlic sausage, left whole	7 oz
4 tbsp	brandy	4 tbsp
10 cl	oil	4 fl oz

To make the stuffing, mix the ham with the herbs, and season with salt and pepper. Stuff the chicken successively with half of the mixture, 1 garlic clove, the sausage, the other garlic clove, and finally the remainder of the stuffing. Sew up the chicken and moisten it, first with the brandy, then with the oil. Put the bird on a rack and roast it for 30 minutes at 220°C (425°F or Mark 7), then for 15 minutes at 170°C (325°F or Mark 3). Serve with puréed white haricot beans.

ODETTE KAHN
LA PETITE ET LA GRANDE CUISINE

Chicken Reshmi Kebab

Based on the recipe of the Amber restaurant, Calcutta.

To serve 2

500 g	chicken breasts, skinned, boned, and cut into 1 cm (½ inch) cubes	1 lb
	Marinade	
3 tbsp	melted butter	3 tbsp
2 tsp	ground coriander	2 tsp
1	medium-sized onion, finely chopped	1
1	garlic clove, finely chopped	1
2 tbsp	soy sauce	2 tbsp
1 tbsp	lemon juice	1 tbsp
1 tsp	brown sugar	1 tsp
	salt and black pepper	

Combine all the marinade ingredients in a bowl. Add the chicken cubes and mix thoroughly. Cover and marinate in the refrigerator for 6 to 7 hours, or overnight.

Thread the chicken cubes on skewers and place under the grill or on a charcoal fire. Grill until the chicken cubes are cooked, about 5 to 6 minutes on each side. Serve hot.

LEE FOSTER (EDITOR)
THE NEW YORK TIMES CORRESPONDENTS' CHOICE

Chicken Tandoori

This recipe is based on that of the Moti Mahal restaurant, Delhi. At the Moti Mahal, the *tandoor*—a cylindrical clay oven—in which this dish is cooked is fired with layers of wood and then with charcoal that is heated white. Western cooks may substitute an ordinary oven, an oven grill, or an outdoor grill. If using an outdoor grill, have the charcoal at white heat before the chicken is put on.

To serve 4

Two 1 kg	chickens, skinned and halved	Two 2 to 2½ lb
1 tsp	salt	1 tsp
4 to 5 tbsp	lime or lemon juice	4 to 5 tbsp
	melted butter	
2	limes or lemons cut into wedges	2
1 each	tomato and onion, sliced	1 each
	Marinade	
35 cl	natural yogurt	12 fl oz
4	garlic cloves, crushed	4
1 tsp	cayenne pepper, or to taste	1 tsp
2 tsp	ground cumin	2 tsp
1 tsp each	ground coriander and ground ginger	1 tsp each
½ to 1 tsp	red food colouring	½ to 1 tsp
	black pepper	

You can use the skinned chicken halves as they are, but it is better to cut off and discard the wings, the rib bones and the back bones.

With a sharp knife, make shallow gashes all over the skinned halves and rub the chicken with the salt and then some of the lime or lemon juice.

In a large bowl combine the yogurt, garlic, cayenne pepper, cumin, coriander, ginger, red food colouring, and black pepper. Brush the chicken thoroughly with this mixture, getting deep into the gashes. Marinate the chicken in the mixture for 4 to 5 hours, or overnight.

Preheat the oven to 230°C (450°F or Mark 8), or use a grill, or start a charcoal fire and get the coals white hot.

Thread each chicken piece along its length on a long metal skewer and cook for 5 minutes on one side, then turn and cook for 5 minutes on the other side. Brush with melted butter and cook for 10 minutes more on each side, or until the chicken is done and the surface is golden-brown.

Sprinkle with the remaining lime or lemon juice and black pepper, garnish with lime or lemon wedges, and tomato and onion slices, and serve hot.

LEE FOSTER (EDITOR)
THE NEW YORK TIMES CORRESPONDENTS' CHOICE

Grilled Chicken Breasts Sesame

To serve 3 to 6

6	chicken breasts, boned	6
	sesame seeds	
	Marinade	
60 g	butter, melted	2 oz
4 tbsp	soy sauce	4 tbsp
4 tbsp	dry white wine	4 tbsp
1 tsp	tarragon	1 tsp
1 tsp	dry mustard	1 tsp

Mix together the butter, soy sauce, white wine, tarragon, and mustard, and marinate the chicken breasts in the mixture for 2 to 3 hours.

Grill the breasts over a medium charcoal fire for 4 to 5 minutes on each side, starting with the skin side up, and basting with the marinade two or three times. Remove the chicken breasts from the fire, again brush with the marinade, then roll them in sesame seeds until they are well coated. Return the coated chicken breasts to the fire for a minute or two to brown the seeds. Serve with plain buttered rice.

JOSÉ WILSON (EDITOR)
HOUSE AND GARDEN'S PARTY MENU COOKBOOK

Grilled Skewered Chicken

Kababe Morgh

To serve 4

Two 1 kg	chickens, each cut up into 8 serving pieces	Two 2 to 2½ lb
250 g	finely grated onion	8 oz
10 cl	fresh lemon juice	4 fl oz
2 tsp	salt	2 tsp
60 g	butter, melted	2 oz
⅛ tsp	ground saffron (or saffron threads, dried in an oven, pounded with a pestle and mortar or the back of a spoon), dissolved in 1 tbsp warm water	⅛ tsp

In a stainless steel, enamelled or glass bowl combine the onion, lemon juice and salt, stirring until they are thoroughly blended. Add the chicken and turn the pieces about with a spoon to coat them well. Marinate at room temperature for at least 2 hours, or in a refrigerator for 4 hours, turning the pieces over occasionally.

Light a layer of coals in a charcoal grill and let them burn until a white ash covers the surface of all the coals, or preheat the stove grill at its highest setting.

Remove the chicken from the marinade and string the pieces tightly on 4 long skewers, pressing them together firmly. If you are using the stove grill, suspend the skewers side by side across the length of a large pan deep enough to allow about 2.5 cm (1 inch) of space under the meat.

Stir the melted butter and dissolved saffron into the marinade and brush the chicken evenly on all sides with 2 to 3 tablespoons of the mixture. Grill about 7 to 8 cm (3 inches) from the heat source for about 15 minutes, turning the skewers occasionally and basting the chicken frequently with the remaining marinade. The chicken is done if the juices that trickle out are clear rather than pink when a thigh is pierced with the point of a small, sharp knife.

THE EDITORS OF TIME-LIFE BOOKS
FOODS OF THE WORLD—MIDDLE EASTERN COOKING

Roasted Chicken

Djej Mechoui

In one of the palaces of the royal family in Marrakesh there is a huge room set aside for the spit-roasting of chickens. At least a dozen spits are slanted diagonally across piles of burning coals, each attended by two men—one to crank the spit, the other to paint the chickens with spiced butter.

To spit-roast a whole 1 kg (2 lb) chicken, count about 50 minutes cooking time. Split or quartered chickens may be grilled in the following manner.

To serve 4

Two 1 kg	chickens, split or quartered	Two 2 to 2½ lb
3	spring onions, white part only, chopped	3
1	garlic clove (optional)	1
2 tbsp	roughly chopped fresh coriander leaves and parsley, mixed	2 tbsp
1 tsp	salt	1 tsp
1½ tsp each	sweet paprika and ground cumin	1½ tsp each
¼ tsp	cayenne pepper	¼ tsp
60 g	butter, softened	2 oz

Pound the spring onions in a mortar with the garlic, herbs, salt and spices. Blend with the butter to make a paste. Rub the paste all over the prepared chicken pieces. Leave for at least 1 hour. Heat the charcoal in an outdoor grill or preheat the stove grill.

Arrange the pieces of chicken skin side up over the coals, or skin side down under the grill. After 5 minutes turn and baste with any extra paste or the juices in the grill pan. Continue turning and basting every 5 minutes for approximately 25 minutes or until the pieces are done.

PAULA WOLFERT
COUSCOUS AND OTHER GOOD FOOD FROM MOROCCO

Grilled Skewered Chicken

Yakitori

To serve 2

350 g	boned, skinned chicken meat, cut into 2.5 cm (1 inch) cubes	12 oz
250 g	mushrooms	8 oz
6 to 8	spring onions, trimmed and cut into 2.5 cm (1 inch) lengths	6 to 8
250 g	chicken livers, halved	8 oz
5 tbsp	soy sauce	5 tbsp
4 tbsp	*mirin* (sweet rice wine)	4 tbsp
2 tbsp	sugar	2 tbsp

Halve the mushrooms, if they are large. Alternate the pieces of chicken, spring onion, liver and mushroom on bamboo skewers approximately 15 to 20 cm (6 to 8 inches) long. Mix together the soy sauce, *mirin* and sugar, and baste the skewered ingredients with the mixture. Place the skewers on a *hibachi* or charcoal grill, or under a preheated stove grill and cook for 8 to 10 minutes. Baste frequently with the sauce and turn the skewers several times until the chicken and livers are cooked.

Chicken livers are often omitted from *yakitori*. Other vegetables such as pickling onions or sweet green peppers may be substituted or added.

SANDRA TAKAKO SANDLER
THE AMERICAN BOOK OF JAPANESE COOKING

Teriyaki Grilled Chicken

To serve 6

Three 1 kg	chickens, halved	Three 2 to 2½ lb
	Teriyaki marinade	
10 cl	olive, or peanut oil	4 fl oz
15 cl	Japanese soy sauce	¼ pint
2 tbsp	grated fresh ginger root	2 tbsp
2	garlic cloves, finely chopped	2
1 tbsp	grated orange rind or, preferably, tangerine rind	1 tbsp
4 tbsp	sherry	4 tbsp
	salt and pepper	

Blend all the marinade ingredients well and pour the mixture over the chicken pieces in a shallow dish or pan. Press the chicken pieces into the marinade and turn them several times while they marinate, which may be anywhere from 1 hour to 24 hours. Preheat the grill. Place the chicken pieces on the rack of a grill pan set at least 15 cm (6 inches) from the heat source, that is, a little further than normal, to prevent the soy sauce from caramelizing. Brush the pieces with a little oil and grill them for about 15 minutes on each side. Brush several times with the marinade. To serve, spoon the pan juices over the chicken.

JAMES BEARD
JAMES BEARD'S AMERICAN COOKERY

Spiced, Grilled Young Chicken

Wakadori No Nanbanyaki

To bone a chicken thigh, place it skin side down, cut along the line of the bone, cut the meat back from around the bone, and remove the bone.

To serve 4

500 g	chicken thighs, boned, with skin left on	1 lb
3 tbsp	soy sauce	3 tbsp
1 tbsp	*mirin* (sweet rice wine)	1 tbsp
1 tbsp	*sake* (strong rice wine)	1 tbsp
2	spring onions, trimmed and chopped, using white and green parts	2
2	dried, red chili peppers, seeded and chopped	2
1	egg yolk	1
12	small, fresh green chili peppers	12
	vegetable oil	
	salt	

With a fork, prick the skin of the chicken thighs all over and put them into a bowl. Add the soy sauce, *mirin* and *sake* and marinate for 10 minutes, turning 2 or 3 times. Thread the thighs on a skewer lengthwise, piercing the skin at each end. Reserve the marinade.

Pound the spring onions and dried peppers in a *suribachi* (mortar) until smooth. Add the reserved marinade and mix them together, then beat in the egg yolk. Set the mixture aside. Grill the chicken on both sides until it is about half done—allow about 4 minutes on each side. Using a pastry brush, paint the chicken with the spring onion sauce, return to the grill and cook for 1 minute on each side. Repeat the painting and grilling until the sauce is used up and the chicken is done.

Cut the stems from the fresh chili peppers. If they are very hot (check by nibbling a tiny slice), remove the seeds as well. Rinse, dry and paint with oil. Grill, turning once, for about 1 minute. Sprinkle lightly with salt.

Slice the chicken diagonally and arrange on platters; garnish with the peppers.

ELISABETH LAMBERT ORTIZ WITH MITSUKO ENDO
THE COMPLETE BOOK OF JAPANESE COOKING

Barbecued Pullets with Rice

The piquant barbecue sauce can be made in large quantities and stored for several weeks in the refrigerator.

To serve 4

Two 1.5 kg	fat pullets, split in half	Two 3 lb
250 g	rice	8 oz
	Barbecue sauce	
3 to 4 tbsp	granulated sugar	3 to 4 tbsp
3 or 4	medium-sized onions, chopped and sautéed	3 or 4
1 to 2 tbsp	salt	1 to 2 tbsp
1 tsp each	ground ginger and celery seeds	1 tsp each
½ tsp	cayenne pepper	½ tsp
2 tbsp	Worcestershire sauce	2 tbsp
6	garlic cloves, finely chopped	6
45 cl	herb vinegar	16 fl oz
1 tsp each	ground nutmeg and allspice	1 tsp each
500 g	canned tomatoes	1 lb
60 cl	flat beer	1 pint

Caramelize 1 to 2 tablespoons of the sugar by heating it in a heavy saucepan over medium heat until it is nut brown. Add the other barbecue sauce ingredients and bring to the boil. When the sauce cools, add 1 tablespoon of sugar or more, to taste. Soak the halved pullets in the barbecue sauce for 2 to 3 hours. Remove the pullets and grill them over hot embers, basting frequently with the sauce; do not be afraid to scorch the flesh a little. Use a celery stick for a barbecue brush. Serve with boiled rice to absorb the rich juices. This piquant sauce is also excellent on spare ribs or suckling pig.

PHYLLIS JERVEY
RICE & SPICE

Grilled Herbed Chicken

To serve 4

1 kg	chicken, quartered	2 to 2½ lb
90 g	butter, softened	3 oz
	several large sprigs parsley, finely chopped	
1½ tsp	thyme	1½ tsp
	salt and pepper	
1 to 2 tbsp	vegetable oil	1 to 2 tbsp

Preheat the oven to 180°C (350°F or Mark 4).

Lift the skin of each of the chicken quarters carefully with your fingers, being careful not to tear it or detach it except from the main part of the flesh. You are forming pockets in it. Blend together the butter and parsley until you have a slightly greenish paste. Add the thyme.

Smear the paste all over the flesh of the chicken under the skin until you have a good, thick coating. Fold the skin back into its normal position and press down firmly. Sprinkle the chicken with salt and pepper.

Place the chicken on a rack in the grill pan, skin side down, and cook for 20 minutes, basting the pieces once with oil. Turn them, baste and continue to cook for another 20 minutes, basting them with their juices and additional oil if necessary. The chicken will be crisp and brown when done.

JANE MOSS SNOW
A FAMILY HARVEST

Chicken à la Digoinaise

Poulet de Ferme Étuvé à la Digoinaise

This recipe is from a book dedicated to Alexandre Dumaine, chef-proprietor of the Hôtel de la Côte d'Or in Burgundy from 1931 to the mid-1960s. The eel, which your fishmonger will skin for you, has a gelatinous quality that lends body and a surprising smoothness to the sauce.

To serve 4

1 kg	chicken, cut up into serving pieces	2 to 2½ lb
90 g	butter	3 oz
1	small eel weighing about 250 g (8 oz), skinned, and cut into 2.5 cm (1 inch) slices	1
	salt and pepper	
1½ tbsp	flour	1½ tbsp
20 cl	dry white wine	7 fl oz
¼ litre	water	8 fl oz
1	bouquet garni	1
2	garlic cloves	2
	slices of coarse country bread	

Melt 60 g (2 oz) of the butter in a sauté pan. Place the chicken pieces and eel in the pan, season with salt and pepper, cover tightly and cook gently for 10 minutes. Turn the pieces, cover and cook again for another 10 minutes.

Remove the chicken and the eel, and keep them hot. Add the flour to the juice in the pan to make a *roux*, over a low heat. Stir well and do not allow to colour. Add the wine and the water, blending the sauce with a whisk. Put the pieces back in the sauté pan. Add the bouquet garni and the garlic. Cover and simmer for about 50 minutes over a low heat.

Sauté a few pieces of bread in the remaining butter in a frying pan. Place the pieces of chicken and eel on top of the bread in a hot serving dish. Pour over the sauce and serve.

ALEXANDER WATT
THE ART OF SIMPLE FRENCH COOKERY

Jambalaya of Chicken

Le Jambalaia

Chicken and rice jambalaya—a word believed to be of Arabic origin—is a traditional Provençal dish.

To serve 4 to 6

2 kg	boiling fowl	4 lb
3	medium-sized onions	3
2 or 3	carrots, whole or halved lengthwise	2 or 3
1	bouquet garni	1
1	stick celery	1
4	garlic cloves	4
½ litre each	dry white wine and water	18 fl oz each
	salt and pepper	
250 g	long-grain rice, washed and drained	8 oz
1 tbsp	olive oil	1 tbsp
¼ tsp	ground saffron	¼ tsp

Truss the chicken and place it in a pot just large enough to contain it with the vegetables placed around. Pour over the wine and water to cover. Add seasoning, bring slowly to the boil, and skim. Cook at a simmer until done (2 to 3 hours depending on the chicken). Towards the end of the cooking, fry the rice gently in the oil and add the saffron. When the rice turns opaque, moisten it with ½ litre (18 fl oz) of the degreased liquid from the pot. Cook the rice, covered, for about 18 minutes over a very low heat and leave to rest, covered, for a further 5 minutes off the heat. Carve the chicken and serve with the rice.

RENÉ JOUVEAU
LA CUISINE PROVENÇALE

Chicken Sauté with Garlic

Poulet Canaille

To serve 5

1.5 to 2 kg	chicken, cut up into serving pieces	3 to 4 lb
40 g	butter	1½ oz
4 tbsp	olive oil	4 tbsp
30	garlic cloves, unpeeled	30
10	shallots, finely chopped	10
	salt and pepper	
15 cl	dry white wine	¼ pint

Heat the butter and oil in a sauté pan or a cast-iron casserole. Place the chicken pieces in the pan and brown them lightly on one side, over a medium heat to avoid burning the fat. Turn the pieces and brown them on the other side. Add the unpeeled garlic cloves and the shallots. Sauté for 10 minutes or until the skin of the garlic is lightly coloured. Season liberally with salt and pepper. Add the wine, cover the pan, and cook gently for 30 minutes or until the meat is done. Uncover the pan and turn the heat very high until all the wine has evaporated.

Take the sauté pan to the table. Serve the chicken pieces with the garlic cloves. Eat the garlic with the chicken; bite into each clove and remove the tough skin to your plate. The taste is exquisite.

GINETTE MATHIOT
A TABLE AVEC ÉDOUARD DE POMIANE

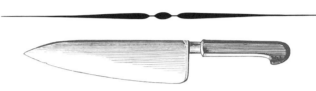

Chicken in Red Wine

Poulet en Meurette

A recipe by Austin de Croze, a distinguished gastronome of the 1920s and 1930s.

To serve 6 to 8

Two 1 kg	chickens, cut up into serving pieces	Two 2 to 2½ lb
300 g	green bacon, rind removed	10 oz
30	pickling onions	30
1	bouquet garni of parsley and thyme	1
3	garlic cloves	3
250 g	mushrooms	8 oz
	salt and pepper	
¾ litre	dry red wine (the same as will be served with the meal)	1¼ pints
100 g	butter	3½ oz
50 g	flour	2 oz
	triangles of bread, fried in butter and rubbed with garlic, for croûtons	
1 tbsp	chopped parsley	1 tbsp

Dice and blanch the bacon. Cover the bottom of a casserole with the bacon pieces, onions, bouquet garni and garlic cloves. Add the chicken pieces and mushrooms. Season with salt and pepper. Add the wine and cook for 35 to 40 minutes.

Work together the butter and flour to form a smooth paste, or *beurre manié*, and use this to thicken the braising juices slightly. Serve the dish with fried croûtons rubbed with garlic. The chicken can be prepared in the same way with white wine, in which case it is called "chicken Pauchouse".

CURNONSKY
CUISINE ET VINS DE FRANCE

Chicken in Red Wine

Coq au Vin

To serve 6 to 8

3 kg	chicken, preferably a cock, 10 to 12 months old, cut up into serving pieces	6 to 7 lb
	salt and pepper	
2	strips green streaky bacon, cut into 1.5 cm (⅔ inch) cubes	2
2 to 3 tbsp	oil or butter	2 to 3 tbsp
3	medium-sized carrots, cut into 2.5 to 5 cm (1 to 2 inch) sections	3
3	medium-sized onions, coarsely chopped	3
2 tbsp	flour	2 tbsp
4 tbsp	brandy	4 tbsp
¾ litre	good red wine	1¼ pints
1	bouquet garni, or pinch thyme, 1 bay leaf and few sprigs parsley	1
25 to 30	small white onions, peeled	25 to 30
	salt and freshly ground pepper	
175 g	butter	6 oz
250 g	mushrooms, washed rapidly and sponged dry	8 oz
6	slices firm-textured white bread, crusts removed, halved diagonally	6
1	garlic clove	1
	chopped parsley	

Parboil the pieces of bacon for 2 minutes, drain, and sponge them dry in a towel. Put them to fry, over a low heat, in a large *sauteuse* or skillet with a bit of oil (butter is nearly always called for, but it makes absolutely no difference—none of its flavour remains after cooking, and it is actually skimmed off and discarded at a later stage). When the pieces are golden-brown on all sides, remove them and put them aside.

In the same cooking fat place the carrots and the chopped onions. Keep the heat medium to low and allow them to cook, stirring regularly to avoid over-browning, for 20 to 30 minutes. Remove the vegetables, put them aside and replace them by the chicken pieces, previously salted. Cook them over a somewhat higher heat until gently browned on all sides, sprinkle with flour, and continue to cook, turning the pieces as necessary. Return the sautéed onions and carrots to the pan. When the flour has cooked for a few minutes, pour in the brandy, carefully set it alight and stir; when the flames have died, add the wine and raise the heat. Stir the chicken pieces and move them around until the liquid comes to the boil.

Transfer the chicken pieces and vegetables to an oven dish of some sort (earthenware, copper or enamelled cast-iron casserole) with a lid. Stir and scrape the first pan with a wooden spoon to loosen and dissolve the frying adherents, then pour the liquid over the chicken pieces. If they are not entirely covered, add enough wine, water or good stock (water is better than indifferent stock) to barely, but completely, cover them. Add the bouquet garni (or simply sprinkle with thyme leaves and add the bay leaf and parsley sprigs untied). Put to cook, covered, in the oven at about 170°C (325°F or Mark 3), regulating the heat so that the sauce hardly simmers. The length of cooking time depends altogether on the bird's age and "past"—from 30 to 45 minutes for a frying chicken that has never exercised to 1½ hours for a 10-month-old rooster, and an hour longer still for one that may be too old to have a fine flesh but that will produce a marvellous sauce.

Meanwhile, cook the little onions, seasoned, in butter over a very low heat, shaking the pan from time to time, for 20 to 30 minutes. Keep them covered and avoid browning them—if the saucepan is not heavy enough, you may have to use a fireproof mat over the heat source. Remove them when they are done and use the same pan to fry the mushrooms. Trim the mushroom stems and cut the caps into 2 or 4 pieces (if they are small, leave them whole). Toss them in some of the butter over a high heat, seasoned with salt and freshly ground pepper, for 2 to 3 minutes.

Transfer the chicken pieces and the carrots to a platter. Pass the cooking liquid through a very fine sieve into a saucepan, using a wooden pestle to work the residue. Discard the discernible remains of the bouquet garni. In the saucepan skim as much fat from the surface of the liquid as possible and bring it to the boil, then position the saucepan over the heat so as to permit its contents to simmer only on one side. A skin containing fat plus other impurities will begin to appear on the surface. Carefully pull it to one side with a spoon, remove it and discard it. Repeat this process regularly for approximately 30 minutes. This skimming process, in French called *dépouillement*, is too often avoided because it is time-consuming and boring. It is, however, essential to the purity and digestibility of the sauce. If, at this point, the sauce is still too thin, turn the heat up to create a fast boil and reduce it rapidly to the right consistency, stirring constantly.

Put the chicken pieces and the carrots back in the oven dish, distribute the garnish (sautéed mushrooms, glazed little onions and fried bacon sections) on top and pour the sauce over. Cover and return to the oven to simmer gently for 15 to 20 minutes.

Brown the pieces of bread in the remaining butter over low heat until golden and crisp. They will absorb an astonishing quantity of butter. They may be prepared ahead of time and rewarmed in the oven.

To serve, dispose the chicken pieces more or less symmetrically on a large, heated platter. Rub the croûton triangles with the clove of garlic, dip a corner of each in the sauce, then in the chopped parsley, and arrange them around the edge of the platter, parslied tips pointing out, pour sauce and garnish over the chicken and sprinkle with a bit of chopped parsley. Serve with steamed potatoes.

RICHARD OLNEY
THE FRENCH MENU COOKBOOK

Senator's Braised Hen

La Poule du Senateur

One of my friends, a French senator, once declared, in front of the cook of a mutual acquaintance, that an old hen was good for nothing except enriching the stock of a *pot au feu*. To show him how wrong he was, Mlle. Marthe, the cook, created the following dish and our gourmet freely admitted his error.

To serve 4

2 kg	boiling fowl	4 lb
3 or 4	thin rashers green bacon, blanched and rinsed	3 or 4
	salt and pepper	
20 cl	dry white wine	7 fl oz
1.5 kg	potatoes, peeled and diced	3 lb
100 g	butter	3½ oz
20	pickling onions	20
¼ litre	veal or chicken stock	8 fl oz
2 tsp	cornflour, mixed with a little water	2 tsp
½ tbsp	lemon juice	½ tbsp
	Marinade	
10 cl	olive oil	4 fl oz
	salt	
	peppercorns	
2 tbsp	finely chopped parsley and chives, or spring onions	2 tbsp
4	shallots, finely chopped	4
3	garlic cloves, crushed	3

Mix together all the marinade ingredients. Leave the fowl in this marinade for a day. From time to time spoon the marinade over any parts that are not immersed, and turn the bird over completely after 6 hours.

Line the bottom of a casserole with the bacon rashers; season the fowl inside, put it on top of the bacon and strain the marinade over it. Add the white wine, cover, and cook over a very low heat for about 3 hours.

Meanwhile, fry the diced potatoes in two-thirds of the butter until they are golden. In another pan, lightly colour the onions in the remaining butter. Half an hour before serving, add the potatoes to the juices in the braising vessel and add the stock. Continue cooking on a very low heat.

To serve, first put the fowl on a warm platter and surround it with the onions and potatoes arranged alternately. Then add the cornflour to the sauce in the casserole. Boil the thickened sauce for 1 minute, add the lemon juice and mix thoroughly. Carve the fowl, pour the sauce over the pieces and serve on hot plates.

RENAUDET
LES SECRETS DE LA BONNE TABLE

Chicken Vinaigrette

Pollo a la Vinagreta

To serve 4

2 kg	chicken, cut up into serving pieces	4 lb
	salt	
2 tbsp	olive oil	2 tbsp
250 g	onions, finely sliced	8 oz
1	small garlic head	1
1	bay leaf	1
1 tsp	vinegar	1 tsp

Season the chicken pieces with salt, put them in a saucepan with the olive oil, onions, garlic, bay leaf and vinegar. Cover and cook gently, over a low heat, shaking the pan from time to time, until the chicken is ready (20 to 25 minutes).

VICTORIA SERRA, TRANSLATED BY ELIZABETH GILI
TIA VICTORIA'S SPANISH KITCHEN

Chicken Sauté Suzanne

Poulet Sauté Suzanne

To serve 4

1.5 to 2 kg	chicken, cut up into serving pieces	3 to 4 lb
	salt and pepper	
4 tbsp	olive oil	4 tbsp
30 g	butter	1 oz
6 tbsp	cognac	6 tbsp
15 cl	sweet white wine, such as Grenache or Muscat	¼ pint
15 cl	double cream	¼ pint
2	egg yolks	2
	fines herbes	

Season the chicken pieces with salt and pepper. Heat a little olive oil in a sauté pan and sauté the chicken pieces rapidly on all sides. When they are golden-brown, remove and drain them. Empty any oil remaining in the pan into a bowl, and replace it with the butter. Melt the butter over a low heat, add the chicken pieces, and turn them in the butter.

Pour in the cognac and the wine, turn up the heat and reduce the liquid until it thickens. Add all but 2 tablespoons of the cream. Cover and simmer very gently for about 15 minutes. Remove the pan from the heat; stir in the egg yolks, mixed with the remaining cream, and continue stirring briskly over a very low heat until the sauce thickens, taking care not to let it boil. Sprinkle with the herbs and serve.

SUZANNE LABOURER AND X.-M. BOULESTIN
PETITS ET GRANDS PLATS

Chicken Adobo

This recipe is based on that of the Sulo restaurant, Manila.

To serve 4

1 to 1.5 kg	chicken, cut up into serving pieces	2 to 3 lb
6	garlic cloves, finely chopped	6
6	black peppercorns	6
2	bay leaves	2
10 cl	white wine vinegar	4 fl oz
2 tbsp	dark soy sauce	2 tbsp
	salt	
	oil	

In a large skillet with a cover, bring to a simmer the garlic, peppercorns, bay leaves, vinegar, soy sauce and a pinch of salt. Add the chicken pieces, stirring to coat them with the sauce. Bring again to a simmer. Cover and simmer for about 30 minutes or until the chicken is cooked, basting once or twice with the liquid in the skillet. Remove the chicken to a plate, skim the fat from the sauce in the skillet, and keep the sauce warm.

In a large frying pan, heat a thin film of oil and then brown the chicken pieces. Arrange the browned pieces on a platter and pour the sauce over them. Serve hot with plain white rice.

LEE FOSTER (EDITOR)
THE NEW YORK TIMES CORRESPONDENTS' CHOICE

Pickled Chicken

Pollo en Escabeche

To serve 6

1.5 kg	chicken, cut up into serving pieces	3 lb
	salt and freshly ground pepper	
3	medium-sized onions, thinly sliced	3
6	large garlic cloves	6
1	fresh green chili pepper, left whole	1
1	bay leaf	1
1 tsp	oregano	1 tsp
30 cl	olive oil	$\frac{1}{2}$ pint
15 cl	white wine vinegar	$\frac{1}{4}$ pint

Season the chicken pieces with salt and pepper, and place them in a heavy casserole with the onions and garlic. Tie the chili pepper, bay leaf and oregano in a small square of muslin and add to the casserole. Pour the oil and vinegar over the chicken, cover and simmer gently for 30 minutes. If the onions are very watery, continue cooking with the casserole partially covered, to reduce the sauce, for 15 minutes longer, or until the chicken is tender. Otherwise continue cooking

with the casserole covered as before. Remove and discard the muslin bag before serving. Serve with plain white rice, or any plainly cooked starchy vegetable.

This is equally good served cold. Refrigerate and serve with the jellied sauce, lettuce, sliced tomato, radishes, avocado, and olives.

ELISABETH LAMBERT ORTIZ
CARIBBEAN COOKING

Stewed Chicken from the Canary Islands

Pepitoria de Pollo a la Canaria

To serve 4 to 6

2 kg	chicken, cut up into serving pieces	4 lb
	flour	
	salt and pepper	
15 to 20 cl	olive oil	6 to 7 fl oz
2	garlic cloves, finely chopped	2
1	medium-sized onion, chopped	1
$\frac{1}{2}$ litre	dry white wine	18 fl oz
	hot chicken stock	
1	bay leaf	1
$\frac{1}{8}$ tsp	dried thyme	$\frac{1}{8}$ tsp
1 tsp	ground saffron	1 tsp
15	blanched almonds, freshly chopped	15
30 g	coarse fresh breadcrumbs	1 oz
2	hard-boiled eggs, chopped	2
	finely chopped parsley	

Coat the chicken pieces in flour that has been seasoned with salt and pepper. Shake off excess flour. Heat all but a tablespoon or two of the olive oil in a heavy skillet. Sauté the garlic and onion in it for about 5 minutes, or until soft. Add the chicken pieces and sauté over medium heat until just golden: they should not be brown. Add the white wine and enough chicken stock barely to cover the chicken. Taste for seasoning, and add salt and pepper if needed. Add the bay leaf and thyme. Cover and simmer over low heat for about 45 minutes, or until the chicken is almost tender.

Dissolve the saffron in a little hot water and add to the chicken with the almonds. Simmer about 15 minutes longer, or until the chicken is tender. If the sauce looks too thin, cook uncovered to allow evaporation.

Fry the breadcrumbs in the remaining olive oil until crisp and brown. Before serving, sprinkle the chicken pieces with chopped hard-boiled egg, breadcrumbs and parsley.

NIKA STANDEN HAZELTON
THE CONTINENTAL FLAVOUR

Chicken Célestine

Le Poulet Célestine

To serve 4

1.5 to 2 kg	chicken, cut up into serving pieces	3 to 4 lb
60 g	butter	2 oz
250 g	mushrooms, left whole	8 oz
1	medium-sized ripe tomato, skinned, seeded and diced	1
20 cl	dry white wine	7 fl oz
10 cl	veal or chicken stock	4 fl oz
1 tbsp	cognac	1 tbsp
	salt, pepper and cayenne pepper	
1 tbsp	finely chopped parsley	1 tbsp
1	garlic clove, finely chopped	1

In a casserole, heat the butter until it turns a nut-brown colour. Add the chicken pieces and sauté them over high heat to seal the juices, turning them frequently until they are golden on all sides. Add the mushrooms and tomato, and sauté for 5 minutes. Pour in the wine, the stock and the cognac. Season with salt and pepper and a pinch of cayenne pepper. Cover and simmer for 15 minutes, or until done. Remove the chicken to a hot platter, skim off any fat from the sauce, sprinkle with the parsley and garlic; if the sauce is plentiful and thin, reduce it before pouring it over the chicken.

LUCIEN TENDRET
LA TABLE AU PAYS DE BRILLAT-SAVARIN

Spiced Chicken Cooked in Milk

To serve 3 or 4

2 kg	boiling chicken	4 lb
1 tsp	coriander seeds	1 tsp
30 g	green ginger root	1 oz
1 tsp	cardamoms	1 tsp
$\frac{1}{4}$ tsp	ground cloves	$\frac{1}{4}$ tsp
	salt and ground black pepper	
2	lemons	2
2.5 litres	milk	4 pints
2	eggs, beaten	2
	pistachio nuts or roasted almonds	

Roast the coriander seeds for 2 to 3 minutes in the oven; peel the green ginger; pound both in a mortar with the cardamoms and the ground cloves; remove the husks of the cardamoms. Add salt and ground black pepper. Prick the chicken all over with a fork, rub it with lemon, then press some of the spices

into the chicken, and put some more in the inside. Leave for an hour or two.

Bring the milk to the boil with the remainder of the spices. Pour it over the chicken and cook very slowly for about $2\frac{1}{2}$ hours, for the first hour on top of the stove, with the pan covered, for the remainder of the time in the oven, without the lid. When the chicken is quite tender, take it out and leave to cool. When cold, cut all the flesh from the chicken in nice neat pieces; measure about 60 cl (1 pint) of the sauce, heat it up. Add to the beaten eggs, through a sieve, and heat it in a double boiler till thick and pour it over the chicken.

Serve cold, garnished with a few halves of pistachio nuts or roasted almonds and quarters of lemon.

ELIZABETH DAVID
SUMMER COOKING

Chicken Calypso

To serve 6

1.5 to 2 kg	chicken, cut up into serving pieces	3 to 4 lb
5 tbsp	olive oil	5 tbsp
500 g	rice	1 lb
1	medium-sized onion, finely chopped	1
1	garlic clove, chopped	1
1	sweet green pepper, seeded and chopped	1
1	small chili pepper, seeded and chopped	1
250 g	mushrooms	8 oz
$\frac{1}{2}$ tsp	ground saffron	$\frac{1}{2}$ tsp
1	5 cm (2 inch) piece lime peel	1
1 tbsp	lime juice	1 tbsp
$\frac{1}{4}$ tsp	Angostura bitters	$\frac{1}{4}$ tsp
1 litre	chicken stock	$1\frac{3}{4}$ pints
	salt and freshly ground pepper	
3 tbsp	light rum	3 tbsp

Heat 3 tablespoons of the olive oil in a frying pan and sauté the chicken pieces until brown all over. Remove them to a heavy casserole. Add the rice, onion, garlic, sweet pepper, and chili pepper to the oil remaining in the frying pan, and sauté, stirring, until the oil is absorbed, being careful not to let the rice scorch. Add to the chicken in the casserole.

Add the remaining 2 tablespoons of oil to the frying pan and sauté the mushrooms over fairly high heat for 5 minutes. Add them to the casserole with the saffron, lime peel, lime juice, bitters, chicken stock, and salt and pepper to taste. Cover and simmer gently until the rice and chicken are tender and the liquid is absorbed, about 30 minutes. Add the rum and cook, uncovered, for 5 minutes longer.

ELISABETH LAMBERT ORTIZ
CARIBBEAN COOKING

Chicken with Fresh Herbs and Cream

Jeune Poulet à l'Americaine

To serve 4

1.5 kg	chicken, cut up into serving pieces	3 lb
60 g	butter	2 oz
5	shallots, chopped	5
6 tbsp	Madeira wine	6 tbsp
10 cl	brandy	4 fl oz
2 tbsp	puréed tomato	2 tbsp
15 cl	double cream	$\frac{1}{4}$ pint
	salt and white pepper	
	ground ginger	
	fresh tarragon, basil and savory, finely chopped	

Melt the butter in a casserole, add the chicken pieces and brown them quickly on all sides. Add the shallots and make a sauce by adding the Madeira, brandy, tomato purée and double cream; season with salt, white pepper, ginger, and a large pinch of each of the fresh herbs.

Put the lid on the casserole, bring everything to the boil, and complete the cooking by placing the dish in a moderate oven, 180° C (350° F or Mark 4) for 20 minutes.

LÉON ISNARD
LA CUISINE FRANÇAISE ET AFRICAINE

Chicken with Port

Poulet au Porto

This recipe was created by Guy Nouyrigat, proprietor of the restaurant Pierre Traiteur in Paris.

To serve 4 to 6

2 kg	chicken, trussed	4 lb
2	onions, finely chopped	2
3	carrots, finely chopped	3
1	bouquet garni	1
60 g	butter	2 oz
	salt and pepper	
15 cl	port	$\frac{1}{4}$ pint
5 tbsp	double cream	5 tbsp

Cook the onions and carrots with the bouquet garni in 15 g ($\frac{1}{2}$ oz) of the butter for 10 minutes in a covered pan.

Put the rest of the butter into a casserole. Sauté the chicken until golden all over. Add the onions and carrots. Season with salt and pepper, cover and cook gently for about 1 hour. Turn the chicken from time to time so that it cooks evenly. Add the port 5 minutes before the end of the cooking time. When the chicken is cooked, lift it out and place it on a heated plate. Pour the cream into the casserole. Let it bubble for a few minutes to reduce, then pour the sauce over the chicken.

Serve with chanterelle mushrooms sautéed in butter, tomatoes and green beans.

ROBERT COURTINE
MON BOUQUET DE RECETTES

Chicken California

A remarkable old San Joaquin Valley recipe which has some authentic Mexican touches but is more interesting as an excellent example of California ranch cookery at the beginning of the century.

To serve 4 to 6

2 to 2.5 kg	chicken, cut up into serving pieces	4 to 5 lb
10 cl	olive oil	4 fl oz
100 g	cornmeal, stone-ground if possible, plus extra for thickening sauce	$3\frac{1}{2}$ oz
	salt	
1	large onion, finely chopped	1
3	garlic cloves, finely chopped	3
$\frac{1}{2}$ tsp	grated nutmeg	$\frac{1}{2}$ tsp
1 tsp each	cumin seeds and ground coriander	1 tsp each
$\frac{1}{4}$ litre	water	8 fl oz
$\frac{1}{4}$ litre	red wine	8 fl oz
4 tbsp	chili powder	4 tbsp
125 g	blanched almonds	4 oz
150 g	green olives	5 oz
	fresh, chopped coriander leaves (*cilantro*), if available	
1 tsp	sesame seeds	1 tsp

Heat the olive oil in a deep braising pan or heavy iron or cast aluminium skillet. Roll the chicken in the cornmeal and brown quickly on both sides. Salt while it is browning. When nicely coloured, add the onion, garlic, nutmeg, cumin and ground coriander. Turn the chicken so that the flavours blend. Add the water and wine and reduce the heat. Cover and simmer till the chicken is just tender—about 45 minutes to 1 hour. Do not let it overcook. Add the chili powder, turn the chicken pieces, and simmer a few minutes more.

Transfer the chicken to a hot platter. Add the almonds and olives to the sauce. Blend a little cornmeal with water and stir it into the sauce. Continue to stir until it thickens slightly. Correct the seasoning and pour over the chicken. Sprinkle with chopped coriander leaves and the sesame seeds.

Serve with rice or cornmeal and a good salad of oranges and onions flavoured with a little rosemary.

JAMES BEARD
JAMES BEARD'S AMERICAN COOKERY

Chicken with Aubergines

Braniya

To serve 4 to 6

2 to 2.5 kg	chicken, cut up into serving pieces	4 to 5 lb
4 tbsp	olive oil	4 tbsp
5	garlic cloves	5
	salt and pepper	
½ tsp	ground saffron	½ tsp
3	medium-sized aubergines, peeled and cubed	3
15 cl	water	¼ pint

Sauté the chicken in olive oil with the garlic cloves. As soon as the chicken pieces have browned, season with salt, pepper and saffron, and add the aubergines. Moisten with the water, cover the pan and cook gently over a low heat for 20 minutes.

LÉON ISNARD
LA CUISINE FRANÇAISE ET AFRICAINE

Chicken with Mutton

This dish can be reheated perfectly to serve twice, or, if this amount is not required, you can buy half a boiling fowl and then halve the quantities of all the rest. It is a very old manor-house recipe from the north of England and originally did not include tomatoes, which were not known, but is much improved by their flavour and colour. Early versions have turnips and carrots or any vegetables available.

To serve 8, or to serve twice

1.5 to 2 kg	boiling fowl	3 to 4 lb
750 g	lean shoulder of mutton, boned and cut up into 4 large pieces	1½ lb
500 g	tomatoes, skinned	1 lb
500 g	onions, sliced	1 lb
250 g	mushrooms	8 oz
125 g	vegetable marrow, peeled, seeded and cubed	4 oz
½	garlic clove, crushed	½
	salt and pepper	
40 cl	dry white wine or dry cider	13 fl oz
125 g	dried haricot beans, or dried split peas	4 oz

Put the fowl in a deep and large casserole and the mutton pieces around it. Add the tomatoes, onions, mushrooms and marrow, also the crushed garlic and plenty of salt and pepper. Pour over the white wine and leave overnight. Leave the dried peas or beans soaking separately in water. In the morning, drain the peas or beans and add them to the casserole and fill up with water to cover the whole. You will need a really large casserole or Dutch oven. Put in the oven at 95°C (200°F or Mark ¼). Leave all day in the oven.

To serve: In the evening, lift out the fowl and divide it into joints, removing the rather glutinous skin. It will almost fall apart without being carved. Arrange the pieces with the mutton carved into thick slices on a large shallow dish, with the vegetables around it in a border. Stir and season the stock and pour all over, serving the surplus in a separate jug. The stock can be thickened if preferred.

The dish should be accompanied by plain boiled potatoes.

ELISABETH AYRTON
THE COOKERY OF ENGLAND

Chicken with Tomatoes and Honey

Poulet aux Tomates et au Miel

To serve 4

1.5 kg	chicken, whole or cut up into serving pieces	3 lb
2.5 kg	tomatoes, skinned, seeded and chopped	5 lb
150 g	butter	5 oz
⅛ tsp	ground saffron	⅛ tsp
1	onion, grated	1
	salt and pepper	
3 tbsp	thick honey	3 tbsp
2 tsp	ground cinnamon, or to taste	2 tsp
75 g	blanched almonds	2½ oz
	oil	
2 tsp	sesame seeds, toasted	2 tsp

Place the chicken or chicken pieces in a casserole together with the giblets. Cover with the tomatoes, and add the butter, saffron, grated onion, salt and pepper. Cover and cook over moderate heat, stirring and shaking frequently.

After about 50 minutes (or longer for a whole chicken), when the chicken is cooked so that the flesh comes away easily from the bones, remove the chicken. Raise the heat and continue cooking the tomatoes until all their liquid has evaporated and they have the consistency of a thick stew. Stir frequently, scraping the bottom of the pot to prevent the tomato mixture from sticking, while adding the honey and cinnamon. Mix well. Return the chicken to the pot, turning it gently so that it warms through and becomes impregnated with the sauce. Remove the casserole from the stove.

A few minutes before serving, fry the almonds in a little oil. Arrange the chicken on a warm dish, pour over the tomato sauce, and decorate with the almonds and sesame seeds.

LATIFA BENNANI SMIRES
LA CUISINE MAROCAINE

Chicken Stovies

The word "stovies" comes from the French étouffer—to stew in an enclosed vessel. It is a legacy of the 17th-century "Auld Alliance" between Scotland and France, and was once a popular dish at Highland rural weddings.

To serve 4

1.5 to 2 kg	plump chicken or boiling fowl, cut up into serving pieces	3 to 4 lb
1 kg	potatoes, peeled and cut up roughly	2 lb
1	onion (or 2 shallots), sliced	1
	salt and pepper	
150 g	butter	5 oz
40 cl	water	¾ pint

In a buttered flameproof casserole, arrange alternate layers of potatoes, onion and chicken, sprinkling each layer with salt and pepper and dotting liberally with butter. Add the water and cover tightly. Simmer very gently for 2 to 3 hours, or until the chicken is tender. If necessary, add a little hot water occasionally to prevent burning.

MARIAN MCNEILL
THE SCOTS KITCHEN

Rigatoni with Chicken Gypsy-Style

Rigatoni con Pollo alla Zingara

To serve 4

1.5 kg	chicken, cut up into serving pieces	3 lb
30 g	butter	1 oz
2 tbsp	olive oil	2 tbsp
10 cl	dry white wine	4 fl oz
2	garlic cloves	2
	ground sage and dried rosemary	
1 tsp	salt	1 tsp
	freshly ground black pepper	
45 cl	chicken stock	16 fl oz
3	anchovy fillets, soaked in water and drained	3
2 tsp	wine vinegar	2 tsp
6	plum tomatoes, skinned and diced	6
250 g	*rigatoni* (grooved pasta tubes)	8 oz
	Asiago or Parmesan cheese, grated	

In a deep saucepan heat the butter and oil; sauté the chicken pieces in it, browning them evenly. Pour in the wine and continue cooking, uncovered, until the wine evaporates. Add the garlic, sage, rosemary, salt, a liberal amount of pepper and the chicken stock. Cover the pan and simmer for 1 hour, or

until the chicken is fork-tender. Transfer the chicken to a warm platter in a low oven.

Chop the anchovies, then mash them into a paste in the vinegar. Stir this into the sauce; add the tomatoes. Simmer over a low heat, uncovered, stirring often, for 20 minutes, or until the sauce is smooth and thickened. Meanwhile, cook the pasta *al dente*; drain it and place it in a large hot bowl. Pour in two-thirds of the sauce; toss well. Serve immediately in hot soup bowls. Pass the cheese, to be sprinkled on the pasta, at table. The chicken, topped with the remaining sauce, comes as the second course.

JACK DENTON SCOTT
THE COMPLETE BOOK OF PASTA

Chicken in Beer

Coq à la Bière

To serve 4

1 to 1.5 kg	chicken	2 to 3 lb
60 g	butter	2 oz
	salt and pepper	
1 tbsp	chopped shallots	1 tbsp
10 cl	gin	4 fl oz
¼ litre	double cream	8 fl oz
250 g	mushrooms, diced	8 oz
½ litre	brown ale	18 fl oz
	cayenne pepper	
2 tbsp	chopped parsley	2 tbsp

Truss the chicken. Heat 30 g (1 oz) of the butter in a casserole and turn the chicken in it until golden. Add salt and pepper, cover and cook for 30 minutes over a low heat. Remove the chicken to a heated dish and keep it, covered, in a warm place.

In the same casserole, cook the shallots. When they are golden, put back the chicken, pour on the gin and flame it. Add 15 g (½ oz) of butter, 2 tablespoons of the cream, and the mushrooms. Pour in the beer; season with salt, pepper and a little cayenne pepper, cover and simmer for 15 minutes. When the chicken is well cooked, put it on a chopping board and cut it into 4 pieces, then put it on the serving dish and keep it covered in a warm place.

Pour the rest of the cream into the casserole and boil vigorously for several minutes to thicken the liquid. Adjust the seasoning if necessary. Take the casserole off the heat and add the rest of the butter. Let it melt in the sauce, off the heat, and pour the sauce over the chicken.

Sprinkle with chopped parsley and serve hot.

RAYMOND OLIVER
LA CUISINE

Chicken with Red and Green Peppers

Le Poulet aux Poivrons de Fanny

To serve 4

2 kg	plump chicken, cut up into serving pieces	4 lb
30 g	butter	1 oz
2 tbsp	olive oil	2 tbsp
	salt and pepper	
	cayenne pepper	
1 tsp	very good paprika	1 tsp
3	onions, finely chopped	3
3	shallots, finely chopped	3
3	garlic cloves, finely chopped	3
1 kg	very ripe tomatoes, skinned, seeded and chopped	2 lb
1 kg	sweet red and green peppers, seeded and finely chopped	2 lb
1	bouquet garni of bay leaf, thyme, sage and savory	1
100 g each	black and green olives	3½ oz each

Heat the butter and olive oil in a large casserole, and sauté the chicken pieces until they are golden-brown. Season with salt, pepper, cayenne pepper to taste and paprika. Add the onions, shallots, garlic, tomatoes and sweet peppers along with the bouquet garni. Cover the pot and cook slowly for rather less than 2 hours. A few minutes before serving, add the olives and check the seasoning. Serve with boiled rice or fresh egg noodles.

MICHEL BARBEROUSSE
CUISINE PROVENÇALE

Chicken with Chicory

Poulet aux Chicons

To serve 4

1.5 kg	chicken, split down the back as for grilling	3 lb
	salt and pepper	
	flour	
30 g	butter	1 oz
1 kg	chicory, outer leaves removed, bases trimmed, sliced lengthwise into matchstick strips, washed and dried	2 lb
½ litre	double cream	18 fl oz
2 tsp	lemon juice	2 tsp

Season the chicken with salt and pepper, and coat with flour.

Heat the butter in a suitably sized casserole. Place the chicken skin downwards in the casserole and brown, then turn and brown the other side. Place the chicory around the chicken, cover and leave to sweat with the chicken for 15 minutes. Then add the cream, bring to the boil, and finish cooking on a low heat for about 30 minutes.

To be certain that the chicken is well cooked, pierce a thigh with a trussing needle: the juice released should be completely clear. If it is tinged with blood, continue for a few more minutes.

Adjust the seasoning with salt and pepper, add the lemon juice and serve in the casserole.

JEAN AND PIERRE TROISGROS
CUISINIERS À ROANNE

Sweet and Sour Chicken in Almond Sauce, Catalan-Style

Myraux ou Myrause de Catalogne

Baptiste Platine de Crémone, who published a version of this recipe in 1474, declared it to be the finest meat he had ever tasted: "very nourishing and healthy, it warms the liver and kidneys, fattens the body and relaxes the stomach".

To serve 4

1.5 kg	chicken	3 lb
	salt and pepper	
60 g	butter	2 oz
60 g	blanched almonds, roasted until lightly browned	2 oz
2	slices bread, dried out and lightly browned in a slow oven	2
10 cl	red wine vinegar	4 fl oz
1 tsp	ground cinnamon	1 tsp
1	small piece fresh ginger root (the size of a hazelnut), peeled and sliced	1
2 tbsp	sugar	2 tbsp

Season the chicken with salt and pepper, smear it with the butter, and half roast it in an oven at 190°C (375°F or Mark 5), for about 40 minutes. Remove the chicken, cut it into serving pieces and transfer them to a casserole, saving the roasting and carving juices. Pound the almonds (or grind them in a blender), first alone, then with the dried bread that has been soaked in the vinegar, and all the other ingredients—to which have been added the chicken's roasting and carving juices. If necessary, to make a smooth sauce, add a little chicken stock or water. Taste for seasoning, pour the mixture over the chicken pieces and simmer, covered, until done—about 15 minutes—over a low heat or in a moderate oven, 180°C (350°F or Mark 4). Stir occasionally to prevent sticking, and degrease, if necessary, before serving.

BAPTISTE PLATINE DE CRÉMONE
LE LIVRE DE HONNESTE VOLUPTÉ

Chicken Fricassée with Sage

Chicken Fricassée alla Salvia

To serve 4

2 kg	tender chicken, cut up into serving pieces	4 lb
15 g	butter	½ oz
1 tbsp	olive oil	1 tbsp
	salt and pepper	
30 cl	dry white wine	½ pint
60 g	*prosciutto* with fat, thinly sliced and cut into a fine *julienne*	2 oz
1 tbsp	fresh sage leaves	1 tbsp

Melt the butter in a large frying pan, and add the oil and the chicken. Sprinkle the chicken with salt and pepper, and brown it slowly and thoroughly on all sides. When it is well browned, pour the wine over the chicken and add the *prosciutto* and sage. Lower the heat, cover the pan and cook slowly until the chicken is done, about 40 minutes.

ADA BONI
THE TALISMAN ITALIAN COOK BOOK

Chicken Niçoise

Poulet Niçoise

To serve 4 or 5

1.5 kg	chicken, cut up into 10 serving pieces	3 lb
4 to 6 tbsp	olive oil	4 to 6 tbsp
2	large onions, sliced	2
300 g	sweet peppers, seeded, and cut into thin strips 6 cm (2½ inches) long	10 oz
500 g	tomatoes, skinned, seeded and chopped	1 lb
3	garlic cloves	3
	salt and pepper	
	flour	
300 g each	courgettes and aubergines, cut into cubes	10 oz each
	chopped parsley or fresh basil	

Heat 2 tablespoons of oil in a sauté pan and sauté the chicken pieces until they are golden-brown. Meanwhile, in a casserole, gently sauté the onions and peppers in 2 tablespoons of oil. When they are soft, add the tomatoes and 2 garlic cloves. Continue to cook until the vegetables are almost tender. Add them to the chicken pieces; season, and simmer, covered, for 45 minutes. Meanwhile, lightly flour the cubed courgettes and aubergines and sauté them in the oil remaining in the pan

until golden-brown; add more oil if necessary. Arrange the contents of the casserole on a serving dish, and garnish with the courgettes and aubergines. Finely chop the remaining garlic clove and sprinkle it over the dish together with the parsley or basil.

RAYMOND ARMISEN AND ANDRÉ MARTIN
LES RECETTES DE LA TABLE NIÇOISE

Chicken in Yogurt

Murghi Dehin

To serve 4

1.5 kg	roasting chicken, skinned, and cut up into serving pieces	3 lb
5 tbsp	chopped parsley or coriander leaves	5 tbsp
	Marinade	
35 cl	natural yogurt	12 fl oz
1	large sweet red pepper, grated or pounded	1
1 tsp	paprika	1 tsp
1	5 cm (2 inch) piece ginger root, grated	1
2 or 3	green chilies, crushed	2 or 3
16	large garlic cloves, crushed	16
1 tsp	salt	1 tsp

Prick the chicken pieces all over with a very sharp fork. Beat the yogurt and make a marinade with the sweet pepper, paprika, ginger root, chilies, garlic and salt. The garlic is not excessive; yogurt takes care of its pungency. Marinate the chicken for 10 to 12 hours in a cold place or in the refrigerator, turning the pieces from time to time.

Heat a heavy saucepan until the metal is very hot. Almost throw in the chicken and marinade so that it makes a light splash, producing steam. Stir in the parsley or coriander leaves, cover immediately. Cook on high heat for 5 minutes; then on medium heat until the yogurt is all dry except for a tablespoon or two at the bottom. Do not let this get brown. Stir the chicken to coat it evenly. Serve hot with all the scrapings from the pan.

DHARAMJIT SINGH
INDIAN COOKERY

Chicken Tafina

Tafina de Poule

According to religious law, Orthodox Jews are forbidden to cook on their Sabbath (Saturday). Traditionally, a hearty stew, or cholent, *was prepared on Friday evening, and was then left to cook overnight in the cooling embers of a baker's oven. The casserole was collected the following day and eaten for lunch while it was still warm. This recipe for* tafina, *a type of* cholent, *has been adapted for cooking in a normal oven.*

To serve 4

1.5 to 2 kg	chicken, cut up into serving pieces	3 to 4 lb
2 tbsp	olive oil	2 tbsp
About 10	medium-sized onions, quartered	About 10
4	large, ripe tomatoes, skinned, seeded and roughly chopped	4
1 kg	broad beans, shelled and peeled	2 lb
	salt and pepper	
½ litre	water	18 fl oz
20	small prunes, stones removed	20

In a stew pot, sauté the chicken pieces in the olive oil. When they are golden-brown add the onions and sauté them until they begin to colour. Add the tomatoes and broad beans. Season with salt and pepper, pour in the water and simmer, covered, for about 30 minutes. Add the prunes. Cook at the barest simmer over a low heat using a fireproof mat, or in a cool oven, 150°C (300°F or Mark 2), for 5 to 6 hours. Check from time to time that there is enough water and, if necessary, add some.

ÉDOUARD DE POMIANE
CUISINE JUIVE GHETTOS MODERNES

Chicken Braised with Forty Cloves of Garlic

Poulet aux Quarante Gousses d'Ail

To serve 4

1.5 to 2 kg	chicken	3 to 4 lb
	salt and pepper	
1	bouquet garni of parsley, thyme and bay leaf	1
20 cl	olive oil	7 fl oz
40	garlic cloves, unpeeled	40
	rosemary, thyme, sage, bay leaf, parsley and celery	
	flour and water paste, containing a little oil, for sealing	

Season the inside of the chicken with salt and pepper, place the bouquet garni in the cavity, and truss the bird. Put the olive oil into a casserole with the garlic cloves and the herbs. Place the chicken in the casserole and turn it several times so that it is well coated with the oil. Leave the chicken on top of the oil and all the flavourings. Seal the lid of the casserole with the flour and water paste, place the casserole in a moderate oven, 180°C (350°F or Mark 4), and cook for about 1½ hours. Transfer the casserole to the table and remove the lid

just before serving. A delicious aroma of garlic will be released. The chicken will be tender and fragrant. Serve with croûtons and let each person spread these with the garlic (let me point out that cooked garlic disagrees with no one).

JEAN-NOËL ESCUDIER
LA VÉRITABLE CUISINE PROVENÇALE ET NIÇOISE

Chicken with Cucumbers

Poularde à la Charles Monselet

To serve 6 to 8

Two 1 to 1.5 kg	chickens, cut up into serving pieces	Two 2 to 3 lb
	salt and pepper	
150 g	butter	5 oz
4 tbsp	olive oil	4 tbsp
500 g	mushrooms, quartered	1 lb
16	medium-sized young onions, finely chopped	16
6	large, ripe tomatoes, skinned, seeded and chopped	6
¼ litre	double cream	8 fl oz
2	small cucumbers, peeled, halved lengthwise, seeded, and cut into chunks the size of olives	2
	thyme flowers or dried thyme	
½ tsp	finely chopped tarragon	½ tsp

Season the chicken pieces with salt and pepper. Heat the butter and oil in a sauté pan, add the chicken pieces and cook rapidly until they are golden. Remove the pieces and keep them warm. Toss the mushrooms briefly in the butter remaining in the pan; remove them also and keep them warm.

Place the onions in the pan, put the chicken pieces on top of them, and cover with the mushrooms. Cover the pan with a piece of buttered paper beneath the lid, so that the cooking takes place in a sealed, moist atmosphere and the onions do not colour. Place over a low heat.

After 15 minutes, add the tomatoes and adjust the seasoning if necessary. After a further 10 to 12 minutes, add the cream, tilting the pan from side to side to mix it in thoroughly. Discard the buttered paper but replace the lid and leave the pan at a slow simmer.

While the dish is cooking, blanch the cucumber pieces in boiling water until they are tender, drain them, and add them to the chicken pieces in the pan.

Now comes the final delicate touch: add a pinch of thyme and the tarragon to the pan and simmer for a few minutes. To serve, arrange the chicken pieces on a platter and pour the contents of the sauté pan over them.

CURNONSKY
CUISINE ET VINS DE FRANCE

Chicken in Cream with Ham and Asparagus

Poulet à la Montagnarde

To serve 4

1.5 to 2 kg	chicken, cut up into serving pieces	3 to 4 lb
	salt and pepper	
	flour	
40 g	butter	1½ oz
30 cl	double cream	½ pint
1 tbsp	lemon juice or white wine vinegar	1 tbsp
	cooked ham, diced	
	asparagus tips, cooked but still crisp	

Season the chicken pieces with salt and pepper, and coat them with flour. Cook the pieces gently in the butter without allowing them to brown. When they have become firm, put them in an earthenware casserole or deep pan, and pour over the cream. Simmer gently, covered, for about 20 minutes. Adjust the seasoning, add the lemon juice or vinegar, and scatter diced ham and the asparagus tips over the dish.

SIMIN PALAY
LA CUISINE DU PAYS

Chicken Fricassée

La Fricassée de Poulet

To serve 8

Two 1.5 kg	chickens, cut up into serving pieces	Two 3 lb
60 g	butter	2 oz
2	medium-sized onions	2
1	sprig thyme	1
	salt	
2 tbsp	flour	2 tbsp
4 tbsp	water	4 tbsp
¾ litre	single cream	1¼ pints
4 tbsp	dry white wine	4 tbsp
	freshly ground pepper	
2	egg yolks	2

Place the chicken pieces in a sauté pan with the butter, onions and thyme. Season with salt, cover the pan and place it over a moderate heat so that the meat gives up its moisture but does not brown. When the pieces are tender and almost cooked, remove the thyme and the onions; sprinkle the chicken with flour and stir frequently. After 10 minutes, stir in the water, scraping any residues from the bottom and sides of the pan.

Pour about 6 tablespoons of the cream, and the wine, over the dish. Simmer gently and add a further 60 cl (1 pint) of cream, a little at a time. The sauce should be rich, smooth and of a consistency that will coat a spoon.

Simmer for 25 to 30 minutes and, if the sauce becomes too thick, add more cream. Taste and see if it is sufficiently salted; and season with a little pepper.

Remove the pan from the heat and let it stand for 1 minute. Beat the egg yolks into the remaining cream and stir them into the fricassée.

LUCIEN TENDRET
LA TABLE AU PAYS DE BRILLAT-SAVARIN

Chicken Fricassée

Fricassée de Poulets

This recipe has been adapted from the original version, published in 1674 and held in the Bibliothèque Nationale in Paris. The author is known only by his initials, L.S.R.

To serve 6

1.5 kg	chicken, cut up into serving pieces	3 lb
60 g	green bacon, diced	2 oz
60 g	butter	2 oz
	salt and pepper	
1	bouquet garni	1
1 or 2	cloves	1 or 2
2 tbsp	chives, finely chopped	2 tbsp
125 g	mushrooms, raw or briefly sautéed	4 oz
2 or 3	artichoke bottoms, quartered and parboiled	2 or 3
100 g	asparagus tips	3½ oz
¼ litre	veal or chicken stock	8 fl oz
2	sweetbreads, parboiled, skinned and sliced	2
2 or 3	egg yolks mixed with 1 tbsp juice of unripe grape or lemon juice	2 or 3

Fry the bacon in the butter. Add the chicken pieces, salt, pepper, bouquet garni, cloves, chives, mushrooms, artichokes and asparagus tips. Sauté, stirring and turning regularly over a moderate heat for 8 to 10 minutes. Pour in the stock, scrape the bottom of the pan, and simmer, covered, until done—another 15 minutes or so.

Skim off the fat. Stir in the sweetbreads. Mix the egg yolks and unripe grape or lemon juice with a ladleful of the cooking liquid. Away from the heat, stir the mixture back into the stew and continue stirring over a low heat until the sauce is lightly bound.

Decorate as you see fit with lemon slices, fried parsley, nasturtium flowers or pot marigold petals, pomegranate slices or *foie gras*.

L.S.R.
L'ART DE BIEN TRAITER

Sautéed Chicken with Sorrel

To serve 6

Two 1.5 kg	chickens, cut up into serving pieces	Two 3 lb
	salt and freshly ground black pepper	
30 g	butter	1 oz
1 tbsp	olive oil	1 tbsp
250 g	fresh sorrel leaves	8 oz
3 tbsp	finely chopped shallots	3 tbsp
¼ litre	dry white wine	8 fl oz
20 cl	double cream	7 fl oz
1	egg yolk	1

Sprinkle the chicken pieces with salt and pepper.

Heat the butter and oil in a heavy skillet with a lid. Add the chicken pieces, skin side down, and cook them for about 5 minutes or longer until golden-brown. Turn over the pieces, and reduce the heat. Cook for about 10 minutes, uncovered.

Meanwhile, cut the sorrel leaves into fine shreds. This is called a *chiffonade* of sorrel. Set aside.

Scatter the shallots around the chicken pieces and cook briefly. Sprinkle the chicken with the *chiffonade* and add the wine. Cover and cook for about 5 minutes. Uncover and add about half of the cream. Turn the chicken pieces in the sauce, but leave them skin side up. Cover, and remove the skillet from the heat.

When ready to serve, uncover the skillet. Cook the chicken in the sauce over high heat for about 5 minutes. Blend the remaining cream with the egg yolk and stir it into the sauce. Cook just until the sauce bubbles up: no longer or the sauce may curdle. Serve the chicken with the sauce spooned over.

CRAIG CLAIBORNE
CRAIG CLAIBORNE'S FAVORITES FROM THE NEW YORK TIMES

Creamed Chicken with Jerusalem Artichokes

Poulet aux Topinambours

To serve 4

1.5 kg	chicken, cut up into 8 serving pieces	3 lb
500 g	Jerusalem artichokes	1 lb
	salt and freshly ground pepper	
15 g	unsalted butter	½ oz
¼ tsp each	crushed thyme and oregano	¼ tsp each
20 cl	dry white wine	7 fl oz
20 cl	double cream	7 fl oz

Break the artichokes into segments so that they may be peeled more easily. Cut each segment into 2 or 3 pieces, depending on size, and trim each piece with a knife or vegetable peeler. The peeled pieces should be about the same size and shape—3 to 5 cm (1½ to 2 inches) in diameter. Put the artichoke pieces in a casserole and cover with cold water, add ½ teaspoon of salt, and bring to the boil over high heat. Simmer for 8 minutes. By this time the pieces should be half cooked and floating on the surface of the water. Drain in a colander.

Salt and pepper the pieces of chicken. Melt the butter in a large, heavy saucepan with a cover. Sauté the chicken on all sides, starting skin side down, until all the pieces are nice and brown (about 6 to 8 minutes on medium heat). Add the thyme, oregano, the wine and the artichokes. Bring to a boil and simmer for 15 minutes. Add the cream, ½ teaspoon of salt, ½ teaspoon of ground pepper, and boil on high heat for 5 to 6 minutes, uncovered, to reduce and thicken the sauce. Place the pieces of chicken on a serving platter, taste the sauce for seasoning. Pour the sauce and artichokes over the chicken and serve immediately.

JACQUES PÉPIN
A FRENCH CHEF COOKS AT HOME

Chicken with Vegetables

Poulets à la Medina-Coeli

This recipe originally appeared in L'Art de la Cuisine Française au 19ème Siècle, *by Antonin Carême, who was called "the chef of kings and the king of chefs".*

To serve 8

Two 1.5 kg	chickens, cut up into serving pieces	Two 3 lb
60 g	butter	2 oz
125 g	green bacon, rind removed, diced and blanched	4 oz
20	small onions, parboiled	20
125 g	carrots, shaped into small olives and parboiled	4 oz
1	bouquet garni	1
1	garlic head, unpeeled	1
250 g	button mushrooms	8 oz
	salt and pepper	
1 tsp	paprika	1 tsp
¼ litre	Malaga wine or sweet fortified wine	8 fl oz

Sauté the chickens in butter. Add the bacon, onions, carrots, bouquet garni, garlic, mushrooms, salt, pepper and paprika. Moisten with two-thirds of the Malaga wine and cook, covered, for approximately 40 minutes; the wine should be reduced to a light syrupy consistency. Remove the chicken, discard the bouquet garni and the garlic, and garnish the chicken pieces with the bacon, carrots and mushrooms. Add the remaining Malaga wine to the pan. Simmer for a few minutes, then pour the sauce over the chicken and serve.

BERTRAND GUÉGAN
LA FLEUR DE LA CUISINE FRANÇAISE

Chicken in Saffron and Garlic Sauce
Gallina en Pepitoria

To toast saffron, fold it in a piece of paper, and place the paper on a hotplate or other hot surface until it begins to brown. Crush the toasted saffron with a pestle in a mortar or bowl.

To serve 6

2 to 2.5 kg	boiling chicken, cut into rather small serving pieces, liver reserved	4 to 5 lb
4 to 5 tbsp	olive oil	4 to 5 tbsp
1	medium-sized onion, finely chopped	1
2	garlic cloves, finely chopped	2
2 tbsp	pine nuts	2 tbsp
1	slice white bread, crusts removed	1
2	sprigs parsley, chopped	2
2	hard-boiled egg yolks	2
¼ tsp	ground saffron, or saffron threads, toasted	¼ tsp
	salt and pepper	

Heat 2 to 3 tablespoons of the olive oil in a casserole. When the oil begins to smoke, fry the chicken, carefully dried, with the onion and garlic. In another pan, boil enough water to cover the chicken.

In a skillet, fry the pine nuts in 2 tablespoons of olive oil. Remove them to a mortar. Fry the bread and the chicken liver (cover the pan until the liquid has cooked out of the liver in order to avoid spattering grease). Remove the bread and chicken liver to the mortar with the pine nuts, and mash them to a fine paste with the parsley, egg yolks and saffron. Dilute with a little boiling water.

When the chicken is golden but not brown, sprinkle it with salt and pepper, pour the mixture from the mortar over it, and add boiling water to cover. Stir. Cook slowly, covered, until the chicken is almost tender, then remove the lid to allow the sauce to thicken. To serve, remove the chicken to a serving dish and strain the sauce over it.

Note: A boiling chicken will take 1½ to 2½ hours to cook. The recipe can be made with young chickens, which may be tender in just 30 minutes. If the sauce is too thin when the chicken is done, remove the chicken, boil the sauce, then reheat the chicken in the sauce.

BARBARA NORMAN
THE SPANISH COOKBOOK

Kubab Chicken

If any readers interested in the intricacies of spice cookery should ever come across an old book called *Indian Domestic Economy and Receipt Book*, published in Madras in 1850, and acknowledged simply to the author of *Manual of Gardening for Western India* without further clue to his identity, they should snap it up. This is the pot-roasted chicken eventually evolved from one of the recipes given in that book.

To serve 4

1 kg	chicken	2 to 2½ lb
2 tsp	coriander seeds	2 tsp
12	black peppercorns	12
	seeds from 6 cardamom pods	
½ tsp	ground cloves	½ tsp
1 tsp	salt	1 tsp
15 g	green ginger, peeled and sliced	½ oz
75 g	butter, preferably clarified	2½ oz
1 or 2	lemons	1 or 2

Pound together all the spices and seasonings until they are a paste, then work them with 15 g (½ oz) of butter.

Draw back the skin of the chicken and with a small knife make incisions in the legs and breast. Spread the spice mixture into the incisions and draw the skin back into place. Leave for a couple of hours before cooking.

Put 60 g (2 oz) of clarified butter into a deep heavy oven pot and heat it. Put in the chicken, lying on its side. Cover the pot closely. Bake in a moderate oven at 180°C (350°F or Mark 4), for 50 minutes to an hour, turning it over at half-time. Then remove the lid and turn the chicken breast upwards for 10 minutes.

Serve the chicken with the cooking liquid poured over it, and lemon quarters round the dish. Boiled rice or saffron rice makes a good accompaniment, although I prefer a salad.

On occasion I have varied the spice mixture, omitting the green ginger and cloves, using cinnamon, saffron, cardamom and a little ground ginger. The salt is important.

ELIZABETH DAVID
SPICES, SALT AND AROMATICS IN THE ENGLISH KITCHEN

Stuffed Chicken
Pullus Farsilis

The discourses of Apicius, the 1st-century Roman gourmet and writer, whose cookbook gives this recipe for boned, stuffed chicken, have come down to us through a succession of translators. The edition used here is a recent translation by Barbara Flower and Elisabeth Rosenbaum of a 4th- or 5th-century compilation of his work.

Apicius is not specific but, prepared in this way, chicken can be either pot-roasted or poached. Not all of the ingredients cited are familiar today. Spelt—"bearded wheat" or "German wheat" (French: épeautre)—is a small, hard wheat grain similar in flavour to barley, and barley or rice can be substituted for it. Liquamen is the name of the salty fermented fish sauce that the ancient Romans used as a basic seasoning.

Alternatives are pounded anchovies or one of the oriental fermented fish sauces. For boning instructions see page 20.

	To serve 4	
2 kg	chicken, boned through the neck	4 lb
	Stuffing	
3 or 4	sprigs lovage	3 or 4
	pepper	
1	small piece ginger root, peeled and chopped	1
125 g	lean veal or pork, chopped	4 oz
100 g	boiled spelt-grits	3½ oz
1	lamb's brain (or ½ calf's brain), cooked in chicken stock and roughly cut up	1
2	eggs	2
2 tsp	*liquamen*	2 tsp
2 tbsp	oil	2 tbsp
	whole peppercorns	
100 g	pine kernels	3½ oz

Using a large mortar and pestle, pound the lovage, pepper, ginger, chopped meat, boiled spelt-grits; then pound in the brain, break the eggs into the mortar and work all this into a smooth mixture. Blend it with the *liquamen* and add the oil, peppercorns and pine kernels. Stuff the chicken with this mixture, leaving a little room. Truss. Cook it.

BARBARA FLOWER AND ELISABETH ROSENBAUM
THE ROMAN COOKERY BOOK

Chicken Braised en Cocotte

Poulet en Cocotte à la Fermière

	To serve 4	
1.5 to 2 kg	chicken, seasoned inside with salt and pepper, and trussed	3 to 4 lb
90 g	butter	3 oz
1	medium-sized onion, finely sliced	1
4	young carrots, thinly sliced	4
1	small celery heart, finely sliced	1
3 or 4	thin slices raw ham	3 or 4
60 g each	fresh peas, shelled, and fresh green beans, trimmed and sliced	2 oz each
10 cl	chicken or veal stock	4 fl oz

Melt 60 g (2 oz) of the butter in a small sauté pan. Add the onion and cook gently for 4 to 5 minutes; it should be no more than straw-coloured. Add the carrots and celery. Sweat them gently over a very low heat for 15 minutes; shake the pan to toss them, rather than risk breaking them up by turning them

with a spoon. They should be nicely softened but not at all brown. The onion should be a golden colour and the butter should remain clear. Set the pan aside.

Melt the remaining butter in a casserole over a low heat. When it is hot, add the chicken and brown it lightly.

Remove the chicken from the casserole and line the casserole with the slices of ham. Replace the chicken, breast-up, and surround it with all the cooked and raw vegetables mixed together. Add the stock and cover.

Place the casserole in the oven and cook for 45 to 50 minutes. Make sure that the heat does not go above moderate, 180°C (350°F or Mark 5), since the vegetables will burn if the liquid reduces, while the cooking of the chicken will not be speeded up. Test for doneness, and serve.

MADAME SAINT-ANGE
LA CUISINE DE MADAME SAINT-ANGE

Indonesian Simmered Chicken

Ajam Smoor

	To serve 5 or 6	
1.5 kg	chicken, trussed	3 lb
¼ litre	water	8 fl oz
4 tbsp	Indonesian soy sauce (or 2 tbsp dark molasses mixed with 1 tbsp dark soy sauce)	4 tbsp
1	onion, thinly sliced	1
6	black peppercorns, crushed	6
4 tbsp	vegetable oil	4 tbsp
6	slices fresh ginger root	6
3 tbsp	chopped onion, fried in oil	3 tbsp
4	cloves	4
¼ tsp	grated nutmeg	¼ tsp
1	slice lemon	1
125 g	cellophane noodles, soaked in water	4 oz
	salt	
4 tbsp	crumbled rusk or dried breadcrumbs	4 tbsp

Place the chicken in a saucepan with the water, soy sauce, onion slices and peppercorns, and simmer for 15 to 20 minutes. Remove the chicken, and pat it dry. Either leave the chicken whole or cut it up into serving pieces before browning it rapidly in the oil in a frying pan.

Place the chicken in a heavy casserole with the ginger, fried onion, cloves, nutmeg and lemon slice. Pour in the cooking liquid from the saucepan. Cover and simmer slowly until well done. Add the noodles for the last 10 minutes of cooking. Add salt if necessary, and thicken the liquid slightly with the rusk crumbs. Serve with boiled rice.

HUGH JANS
VRIJ NEDERLAND

Chicken with Country Herbs

Poulet aux Herbes de Province

The herb butter that is the heart of this recipe must be made with fresh herbs.

To serve 4

1.5 kg	chicken, seasoned inside with salt and pepper	3 lb
40 g	parsley	1½ oz
15 g	tarragon sprigs	½ oz
10 g	chervil sprigs	⅓ oz
30 g	basil sprigs	1 oz
3 or 4	mint leaves	3 or 4
275 g	butter, softened	9 oz
	salt and pepper	
1 tbsp	lemon juice	1 tbsp
1	sprig thyme	1
1	small bay leaf	1
1	sprig rosemary	1
1	sage leaf	1
175 g	rice, washed and drained	6 oz

Wash the parsley, tarragon, chervil, basil and mint, drain and squeeze them dry in a cloth. Remove the leaves from one-third of the herbs and chop them into shreds. Mix them with two-thirds of the softened butter, then add salt, pepper and the lemon juice and mix well together.

Place the chicken on its back with the breast facing you. Detach the skin from the whole surface by sliding your fingers along the flesh, taking care not to tear the skin. Make a long slit in the flesh of each breast and stuff with half the herb butter, spreading the rest under the skin. Truss the bird and season it inside and out with salt and pepper.

Melt the remaining butter in an oval casserole. Lay the bird on its side and allow to turn golden, then turn it on to the other side. Check the progress of the browning, then turn the chicken on to its back. This operation should take about 10 minutes.

Place the rest of the herbs, together with the thyme, the bay leaf, the rosemary and the sage, around the bird. Cover the casserole and leave it to cook very slowly over a very low heat or on a fireproof mat. Since the herbs must not burn, baste frequently during cooking. The cooking time should be about 1 hour 10 minutes.

Plunge the rice into plenty of boiling, salted water and cook for 18 minutes. Cool slightly, drain it in a sieve, and put the sieve, covered, in a pot in a low oven, 150°C (300°F or Mark 2).

Remove the chicken, place it on a warm serving dish. Remove the thyme, bay leaf, rosemary and sage from the casserole. Cover the chicken with the remaining herb garnish. Leave the casserole on the heat.

Place the rice on a dish and sprinkle with 8 tablespoons of the cooking butter left floating on top of the casserole juices. Season with salt, cover with greaseproof paper, and place in the oven.

Caramelize the juices in the bottom of the casserole if necessary, taking care not to burn them. Add 10 cl (4 fl oz) of water, and reduce this liquid until about 2 good tablespoons per person are left.

Serve the chicken on a shallow dish on its back, covered with the herbs and coated with its cooking juice. Serve the rice separately.

JEAN AND PIERRE TROISGROS
CUISINIERS À ROANNE

Chicken Stuffed with Parsnips

To serve 4

1.5 kg	roasting chicken	3 lb
15 g	chicken fat or butter	½ oz
1	small parsnip, diced	1
1	small onion, chopped	1
	salt and pepper	
30 cl	stock	½ pint
1	bouquet garni	1
30 g	butter, kneaded	1 oz
1 tbsp	chopped parsley	1 tbsp
	Stuffing	
250 g	parsnips, peeled, halved lengthwise and cores removed before weighing	8 oz
15 g	chicken fat, or butter	½ oz
1	small onion, chopped	1
125 g	bacon, chopped	4 oz
2 tsp	chopped sage	2 tsp
	salt and pepper	

Preheat the oven to 180°C (350°F or Mark 4).

To make the stuffing, boil the parsnips in salted water until tender. Mash them to a purée. Melt the fat in a small frying pan and cook the onion and bacon in this until the onion is soft. Remove from the heat and mix in the mashed parsnips, sage and salt and pepper. Stuff the chicken with this mixture and truss it.

Melt the chicken fat or butter in a large flameproof casserole on a moderate heat and brown the chicken all over. Remove it and set aside. Lower the heat, stir in the diced parsnip and onion, cover and sweat them for 5 minutes. Set the chicken on top. Season, pour over the stock and tuck in the bouquet garni. Cover and cook in the oven for 1½ hours.

Remove the chicken, carve it, arrange it on a warm serving dish with the stuffing, and put it to keep warm. Strain the juices from the casserole and skim them if necessary. Return them to the casserole on a moderate heat on top of the stove. Whisk in the kneaded butter and parsley, and simmer gently for 2 minutes. Serve the sauce and the chicken separately.

GAIL DUFF
FRESH ALL THE YEAR

Chicken Casserole Grand'mère

To serve 4

1 to 1.5 kg	chicken	2 to 3 lb
1	garlic clove	1
30 g	lard or rendered bacon fat	1 oz
	salt and pepper	
4 to 6 tbsp	water	4 to 6 tbsp
125 g	fat salt pork, diced, parboiled, and drained	4 oz
125 g	mushrooms, wiped	4 oz
12	small onions	12
	sugar	
30 g	butter	1 oz
2 or 3	medium-sized potatoes, diced	2 or 3
	chopped parsley	

Put the garlic inside the chicken cavity. Truss the bird as for roasting, and place it in a casserole with the lard or bacon fat and a little salt. Put it in an oven preheated to 200 to 220°C (400 to 425°F or Mark 6 or 7) and cook, uncovered, for about 30 minutes or until it is a good brown all over, turning it occasionally and basting with the fat. Pour off the fat from the casserole and reserve. Add 2 or 3 tablespoons of water to the casserole and stir in all the brown crust from the sides of the casserole. Set the casserole aside.

In a frying pan, sauté the salt pork in the fat reserved from the casserole. When golden-brown, remove the pork and set it aside. Cook the mushrooms in the fat left in the pan and season with salt and pepper. Put the onions in another pan with 2 tablespoons of water, a sprinkling of sugar and 7 g ($\frac{1}{4}$ oz) butter, then cook slowly until the water cooks away and the onions take on a good brown colour from cooking in the butter. Add the salt pork, mushrooms and onions to the chicken and,

if the gravy has reduced too much, add a little more water. Cover the casserole, reduce the oven heat to 180 to 190°C (350 to 375°F or Mark 4 or 5) and cook 30 minutes longer or until the chicken is done, basting often.

Cook the potatoes in the remaining butter until brown and done, and put them on top of the other vegetables in the casserole. Sprinkle with chopped parsley and serve all from the casserole. Other vegetables like peas and asparagus can be added if desired.

LOUIS DIAT
FRENCH COOKING FOR AMERICANS

Braised Capon Paesana

Cappone in Casseruola alla Paesana

To skin peppers easily, follow the instructions on page 11.

To serve 6

2.5 kg	capon	5 lb
	salt and freshly ground pepper	
90 g	butter	3 oz
2	onions, sliced	2
2	garlic cloves, crushed	2
3	sweet red or yellow peppers, skinned, seeded and cut into strips	3
1	bouquet garni made up of 3 sprigs parsley, 2 sprigs thyme (or $\frac{1}{2}$ tsp dried) and a bay leaf	1
15 cl	Marsala wine	$\frac{1}{4}$ pint
6	ripe tomatoes, skinned, seeded, drained and chopped	6
60 g	*prosciutto*, chopped	2 oz
2	medium-sized courgettes, sliced	2
4 tbsp	parsley, chopped	4 tbsp

Season the cavity of the capon with salt and pepper; and truss the bird. Heat the butter in a large, heavy pot over fairly high heat until golden, and brown the capon on all sides. Adjust the heat during the browning so that the butter does not burn.

Remove the capon from the pot, add the onions and garlic, and cook until the onion begins to colour. Add the pepper strips, cook for 3 minutes longer and then add the bouquet garni, Marsala, tomatoes and *prosciutto*.

Season with salt and pepper, bring to a simmering boil and return the capon to the pot. Place it in a moderate oven, 180°C (350°C or Mark 4), for 2 hours. About 15 minutes before the capon is fully cooked, add the courgettes and the chopped parsley, and complete the cooking. Transfer the capon to a hot serving platter. If the sauce is too liquid, reduce it slightly over high heat, and spoon it round the capon.

LUIGI CARNACINA
GREAT ITALIAN COOKING

Poached Stuffed Chicken

La Véritable Poule au Pot Agenoise

This recipe, by Charles Derennes, calls for a well-fattened young adult cockerel. If you use an old boiling fowl instead, poach it for 3 hours and add the vegetables towards the end of the cooking time. The technique for stuffing a bird under the skin is demonstrated on pages 47-49.

To serve 6

2.5 to 3 kg	cockerel or capon, liver reserved	5 to 6 lb
1	slice stale bread, rubbed with garlic	1
500 g	carrots	1 lb
500 g	turnips	1 lb
2 or 3	leeks	2 or 3
1	lettuce heart	1
	salt and pepper	
	Stuffing	
100 g	stale bread, roughly crumbled	3½ oz
100 g	green streaky bacon, diced	3½ oz
2	garlic cloves, finely chopped	2
2 tbsp	finely chopped parsley	2 tbsp
4 or 5	egg yolks	4 or 5
	reserved chicken liver, pounded to a smooth paste	

Prepare the stuffing by mixing together the breadcrumbs, bacon, garlic and parsley with the egg yolks and liver. For greater elegance and flavour, instead of simply placing the stuffing in the bird's cavity, you can introduce it carefully under the skin of the breast and the inside of the thighs, and slip a slice of bread liberally rubbed with garlic into the cavity. Sew up the skin with thick thread, and allow this amiable creature to rest in a cool place overnight.

The next day, choose a suitably sized cooking pot, which should be of earthenware. Fill it with enough water to cover the bird, and add the vegetables and seasoning. Put in your bird with due delicacy. Bring to the boil over high heat, then reduce the heat to low. From this point 1½ hours of cooking at a gentle simmer will be amply sufficient.

Along with the chicken, skilfully carved, a sophisticated host may serve curried rice. It is considered bad form to eat bread with this dish: the stuffing should suffice.

In summer, the broth, skimmed of fat and chilled, constitutes one of the tastiest of cold consommés. Served hot, with croûtons fried in chicken or goose fat, it also has its partisans, and should not be underestimated.

GASTON DERYS
L'ART D'ÊTRE GOURMAND

Stuffing for Poule au Pot

This recipe is from a book published anonymously in 1922, but thought to be by the writer and gastronome Leo Larguier.

To stuff a 2.5 kg (5 lb) boiling fowl

About 50	black olives, stoned and chopped	About 50
1	garlic clove, finely chopped	1
1	small onion, chopped	1
100 g	stale bread, crusts removed, soaked in warm water, then squeezed almost dry	3½ oz
1 tbsp	chopped parsley	1 tbsp
	salt and pepper	
1	egg, lightly beaten	1
	grated nutmeg	

Mix together the olives, garlic, onion, bread, parsley and salt and pepper. Add the egg to bind the mixture, and add a suspicion of freshly grated nutmeg.

CLARISSE OU LA VIEILLE CUISINIÈRE

Poule au Pot Henri IV

One of the classic poaching recipes, this dish is named after the French King Henri IV (1589-1610).

To serve 4 to 6

2 kg	chicken, liver chopped and reserved	4 lb
2 litres	salted water	3½ pints
250 g each	carrots and turnips	8 oz each
1	small cabbage, woody stalk removed	1
	Stuffing	
3	eggs	3
125 g	breadcrumbs	4 oz
2 to 3 tbsp	chopped parsley	2 to 3 tbsp
	reserved chicken liver	
60 g each	ham and green streaky bacon, diced	2 oz each
2 or 3	shallots, chopped	2 or 3
	salt	

Prepare the stuffing as follows. Beat the eggs in a bowl, add the breadcrumbs, parsley, chicken liver, ham, bacon and shallots. Add salt to taste and stir the mixture well.

Loosely stuff the chicken and truss it. Put it in a pot with the water and bring to the boil. If you are using old carrots and turnips, cut them into pieces and add them at this stage. Cover the pot and cook over a medium heat. If the carrots and turnips are young and tender, leave them whole and add them, along with the cabbage, after 30 to 40 minutes. Continue cooking for a further 25 to 30 minutes, or until the chicken is done.

To serve the stock, strain it into a soup tureen over oven-dried bread slices. To serve the main dish, carve the chicken, arrange it on a platter surrounded by the vegetables and the sliced stuffing. Moisten with a few spoonfuls of stock.

TANTE MARGUERITE
LA CUISINE DE LA BONNE MÉNAGÈRE

Poached Stuffed Chicken, Perigord-Style

Poule Jacou-le-Croquant, Sauce de Sorges

The original recipe—by Colette Maudonnet, proprietor of the restaurant Aux Naulets d'Anjou, near Saumur in the Loire valley—calls for goose cracklings (grillons d'oie). These crunchy remains of rendered goose fat give extra flavour to the stuffing.

To serve 6 to 8

2 kg	boiling fowl	4 lb
1	head celery, halved	1
4	leeks, trimmed, slit and cleaned	4
500 g	carrots, halved lengthwise	1 lb
1	large turnip, quartered	1
2	onions, quartered	2
1	bouquet garni	1
	chopped chervil	
	Stuffing	
500 g	coarse dry bread, roughly chopped	1 lb
2	garlic cloves, crushed	2
200 g	goose cracklings (optional)	7 oz
200 g	ham fat, chopped	7 oz
2 tbsp	chopped parsley	2 tbsp
	salt, pepper and grated nutmeg	
3	eggs	3
	Sauce	
2	eggs	2
	juice and grated rind of 1 lemon	
15 cl	natural yogurt	$\frac{1}{4}$ pint
3 tbsp	oil	3 tbsp
1 tbsp	chopped chervil and chives, mixed	1 tbsp
1 tsp	chopped tarragon	1 tsp
	salt and pepper	

Make the stuffing by mixing together in a bowl the bread, garlic, goose cracklings if you are using them, ham fat and

parsley. Season with salt, pepper and nutmeg. Break the eggs into the stuffing and stir well. Fill the chicken with the mixture, taking care not to compress the stuffing lest it burst the chicken when it expands while cooking. Sew up both cavities.

Put the stuffed bird into a pot of cold water, bring it to the boil and remove the scum, then simmer it gently for 2 hours. After $1\frac{1}{2}$ hours, add the vegetables, tied up in small bundles, and the bouquet garni.

To make the sauce, boil the eggs for $3\frac{1}{2}$ to 4 minutes. Put the yolks, still warm, into a bowl with a few drops of lemon juice. Beat them, gradually adding the yogurt alternately with the oil and the remaining lemon juice until the sauce has a rich, velvety texture. Add the chopped herbs, grated lemon rind, salt, pepper and the egg whites, gently broken up with a fork. Strain and degrease the chicken's cooking liquor by passing it through a cloth that has been folded in two, moistened, and wrung out.

Serve the liquor in soup bowls, garnished with a little coarsely chopped chervil. Carve the chicken and serve it on a platter surrounded by the stuffing cut in slices, and by the vegetables from which you have removed the strings. The sauce should be served separately.

MADELEINE PETER
GRANDES DAMES DE LA CUISINE

Boiled Fowl with Oysters

Despite the name of this recipe, the fowl is poached rather than boiled. The "jar" called for is a stoneware or porcelain pot.

To serve 3 or 4

2 kg	young fowl	4 lb
36	fresh oysters	36
15 cl	cream	$\frac{1}{4}$ pint
2	egg yolks	2
$\frac{1}{2}$ tsp	ground mace (optional)	$\frac{1}{2}$ tsp

Truss a young fowl as for boiling; fill the inside with all but a few of the oysters, which have been bearded and washed in their own liquor; secure the ends of the fowl, put it into a jar, and plunge the jar into a saucepan of boiling water. Keep it boiling for $1\frac{1}{2}$ hours, or rather longer, then take the gravy that has flowed from the oysters and fowl, of which there will be a good quantity; stir in the cream and yolks of eggs, add a few oysters scalded in their liquor; let the sauce get quite *hot*, but do not allow it to *boil*; pour some of it over the fowl, and the remainder send to table in a tureen. A blade of pounded mace added to the sauce, with the cream and eggs, will be found an improvement.

MRS ISABELLA BEETON
THE BOOK OF HOUSEHOLD MANAGEMENT

Fowl with Rice

Poule au Riz

To serve 5 or 6

2 kg	fowl, cleaned and trussed	4 lb
1 or 2	carrots	1 or 2
1 or 2	onions, studded with a clove	1 or 2
1 or 2	leeks, if available, trimmed and washed well	1 or 2
1	bouquet garni	1
1 tbsp	salt	1 tbsp
	Rice	
40 g	butter	1½ oz
1	small onion, chopped	1
250 g	rice	8 oz
45 cl	chicken stock, reserved from poaching	16 fl oz
	Sauce	
30 g	butter	1 oz
1½ tbsp	flour	1½ tbsp
35 cl	chicken stock, reserved from poaching	12 fl oz
	salt and pepper	
	grated nutmeg (optional)	
1	egg yolk	1
3 to 4 tbsp	single cream, or top of the milk	3 to 4 tbsp
	lemon juice	

Put the bird together with the other ingredients in a deep pan, and add water to cover. Bring to the boil, skim, and cook slowly for about 2 hours, or until the fowl is tender.

About half an hour before the fowl is cooked, prepare the rice as follows. Melt 30 g (1 oz) of the butter in a saucepan, add the onion and cook until it is golden-brown. Add the rice and shake the pan over the heat for a minute or two until the grains are coated with butter. Add the hot chicken stock, cover the pan closely, and cook in a medium hot oven preheated to 190°C (375°F or Mark 5) or on top of the stove over low heat for 20 to 25 minutes, or until the liquid is cooked away. When done, melt the remaining butter, and add it to the rice, tossing carefully with a fork to avoid mashing the grains.

While the rice is cooking, prepare the sauce. Melt the butter, add the flour and cook until they are mixed together. Add the stock, mix all together well and cook, stirring, until the sauce is smooth and thickened. Correct the seasoning, adding a little nutmeg if desired, and continue cooking very slowly for about 10 minutes.

Mix the egg yolk with the cream (or top of the milk) and combine with the sauce by adding a little hot sauce to the egg and cream mixture and then stirring it all carefully into the sauce. Add a few drops of lemon juice and cook just long enough to combine the ingredients, but do not allow the sauce to boil.

Make a bed of the rice in a serving dish, carve the fowl and place the pieces on top of the rice. Pour over half of the sauce and serve the remaining sauce separately.

LOUIS DIAT
FRENCH COOKING FOR AMERICANS

Steamed Chicken Stuffed with Parsley

Poulet Farci au Persil et Cuit à la Vapeur

To make the preserved lemon called for in this dish, follow the directions in the recipe for chicken with eggs, lemons and olives on page 137.

To serve 6 to 8

Two 1.5 kg	chickens	Two 3 lb
1 kg	tomatoes, skinned, seeded and chopped	2 lb
150 g	parsley, finely chopped	5 oz
2	celery sticks, finely chopped	2
	peel of 1 preserved lemon, finely chopped	
	salt and pepper	
½ tsp	chili powder or cayenne pepper	½ tsp
30 g	butter	1 oz
	ground cumin	

Mix the tomatoes with the parsley, celery and lemon peel. Season with salt and pepper and the chili powder. Stuff each chicken with this mixture, along with a knob of butter.

Place the chickens in the top of a *couscousière* or other steamer containing 3 to 4 litres (5 to 7 pints) of boiling water, and seal the top and bottom sections of the vessel together by means of a strip of cloth soaked in a paste of flour and water. Cover the chickens with a damp cloth and put the lid on.

Cook over a moderate heat. Check the chickens after 1½ hours; if the flesh can be easily detached from the bones the chickens are done. Remove the vessel from the stove. Arrange the chickens on a dish and serve at once, accompanied by a mixture of salt and cumin.

LATIFA BENNANI SMIRES
LA CUISINE MAROCAINE

Lucien Tendret's Steamed Chicken

La Poularde à la Vapeur de Lucien Tendret

In the original recipe for this dish, from La Table au Pays de Brillat-Savarin *by Lucien Tendret, the chicken was stuffed with whole truffles, a luxury even in the early 1930s, when Alexandre Dumaine, considered the finest chef of his day, was owner of the Côte d'Or restaurant in Saulieu. The oxtail, which is removed from the stock after 3 hours, will itself provide the basis for a delicious supper when placed on a bed of rice and covered with tomato sauce. To seal in the steam during cooking, you may find aluminium foil a convenient alternative to the long band of cloth called for by Dumaine.*

	To serve 4	
2 kg	chicken	4 lb
1	large truffle, thinly sliced	1
	salt	
	mixed spices	
	crushed dried herbs	
3 tbsp	Marsala wine	3 tbsp
	whole truffles (optional)	
2	leeks	2
2	carrots	2
3	medium-sized tomatoes	3
1	bouquet garni	1
	Stock	
8 litres	water	14 pints
1	whole shin or shank of veal, cut into pieces	1
150 g	pork rinds, blanched	5 oz
1	oxtail, cut into pieces	1
6	chicken necks	6
2	onions, each stuck with a clove	2
2	carrots	2
2	sticks celery	2
1	turnip	1

You will need a 12 litre (2½ gallon) flameproof earthenware pot. To make the stock, place the water, veal shin or shank, pork rinds, oxtail and chicken necks in the pot. Bring slowly to the boil and skim well. Add the stock vegetables. Allow a minimum of 3 hours' cooking after bringing to the boil. Strain this gelatinous broth and return it to the pot. You should have about 4.5 litres (8 pints) of this "super-stock" left.

Place in the pot a trivet big enough to take a large dish about 5 to 8 cm (2 to 3 inches) deep that will hold the chicken. Lay slices of the truffle between the chicken's flesh and skin; season the cavity with salt, mixed spices and dried herbs, and add the Marsala with whole truffles, if you have them. Add to the stock the leeks, carrots, tomatoes and bouquet garni. Place the chicken dish on the trivet, making sure that the dish is higher than the level of the liquid, and bring the stock back to the boil. Cover the pot; then, to seal in the steam, wrap around the lid a fairly long white cloth, dampened and wrung out.

Cook at an even heat, neither too strong nor too gentle, so that the stock maintains a light boil, for about 1½ hours.

The chicken should be brought directly to the table in the pot. When the seal and lid are removed the aroma will pervade the room and stimulate the gastronome's appetite. The chicken should be carved and the pieces served at once with the juices from the dish holding the bird. Fresh morels in cream should be served separately. (The stock should be reserved for future use as a poaching liquid.)

ALEXANDRE DUMAINE
MA CUISINE

Steamed Chicken

Djej Mafooar

This dish is quite beautiful in its simplicity. The chicken is rubbed with saffron, butter and salt, then steamed above boiling water until very tender. Its skin becomes silken, and the whole chicken acquires a delicate taste.

In Tangier small white onions are placed inside the chicken along with a few sprigs of parsley. In Tetuán the chicken is stuffed with wild greens or rice, tomatoes, olives, and pickled lemons and is spiced with cayenne pepper. Some people gently brown the chicken in butter after removing it from the steamer, but I think this method interferes with the delicacy.

One thing you should know is that a steamed chicken must be served at once if you want to eat it hot. It does not reheat well, but it is excellent served cold, accompanied by sliced raw onions and chopped parsley.

	To serve 4	
1.5 kg	chicken	3 lb
¼ tsp	ground saffron	¼ tsp
1 tsp	salt	1 tsp
60 g	butter, softened	2 oz
	ground cumin	
	coarse salt	
	cayenne pepper (optional)	

Pound the saffron with the salt and blend with the softened butter. Rub into the skin of the chicken.

Fill the bottom of a *couscousière* (or steamer) with water and bring to the boil. Dampen a strip of muslin, dust it with flour, and twist it into a strip the length of the circumference of the rim of the bottom part of the *couscousière*. Use this to seal the perforated top or colander on top of the pot. Check all sides for effective sealing: the top and bottom should fit snugly, so that steam rises only through the holes. *The perforated top should not touch the liquid below.*

Place the chicken in the top container and cover with a double layer of muslin. Close the lid tightly and steam for 1 hour without lifting the cover. Serve at once, *as is*, with accompanying bowls of ground cumin and coarse salt, or mix cumin and salt with a sprinkle of cayenne pepper.

PAULA WOLFERT
COUSCOUS AND OTHER GOOD FOOD FROM MOROCCO

Boned Pullet Italiana

Pollastra Farcita Lessata all'Italiana

To bone the chicken, follow the instructions on page 20.

To serve 6

2 kg	chicken	4 lb
	salt	
3 litres	chicken stock	5 pints
2	carrots, sliced	2
2	leeks, white parts only, sliced	2
3	celery sticks, sliced	3
125 g	beetroot greens (optional)	4 oz
1	onion, stuck with a clove	1
	Stuffing	
125 g	chicken livers, chopped and sautéed in 30 g (1 oz) butter for 3 minutes	4 oz
60 g	green bacon, diced and parboiled for 10 minutes	2 oz
60 g	*prosciutto,* or smoked ham, chopped	2 oz
1 tbsp	chopped parsley	1 tbsp
1	garlic clove, crushed	1
1	onion, chopped	1
100 g	fresh bread cubes, soaked in milk and squeezed almost dry	3½ oz
	salt and pepper	
	grated nutmeg	
2	egg yolks	2
	Sauce	
2	hard-boiled eggs	2
4 tbsp	prepared mustard, preferably Dijon-type	4 tbsp
3 tbsp	wine vinegar	3 tbsp
15 to 20 cl	oil	6 fl oz
2 tbsp	finely chopped onion	2 tbsp
	salt and pepper	

Bone the chicken whole, without breaking through the skin. If desired, the drumstick and wing bones may be left intact to help give the chicken its original appearance after it is stuffed.

Mix all of the stuffing ingredients in a bowl, season the cavity of the chicken with salt and then stuff it loosely. Sew the openings with string and wrap the chicken in muslin, tying it securely, so that it will hold its shape during the cooking. Place it in a large, heavy pot with the stock and aromatic vegetables, bring to the boil, reduce the heat, and simmer for 1½ hours.

Prepare the sauce while the chicken is cooking. Mash the hard-boiled egg yolks and mix them with the mustard and vinegar in a bowl. Pour in the oil in a slow stream, beating constantly, so that the mixture develops the smoothness and consistency of mayonnaise. Chop the egg whites and add them to the sauce with the onion, salt, and pepper.

Unwrap the chicken on a hot serving platter. Carve it crosswise into slices at the table; spoon a little of the strained cooking liquid over each serving. Serve the sauce separately.

LUIGI CARNACINA
GREAT ITALIAN COOKING

Hungarian Boiled Stuffed Chicken

Fött Töltött Csirke

To serve 8 to 10

2 to 2.5 kg	roasting chicken, boned except for wing and leg bones	4 to 5 lb
2 to 3 tsp	salt	2 to 3 tsp
1	onion, finely chopped	1
15 g	butter	½ oz
500 g	minced veal	1 lb
250 g	chicken livers, trimmed and membranes removed	8 oz
1	large bread roll, soaked in milk and pressed dry	1
2	hard-boiled eggs	2
2	tomatoes, skinned and chopped	2
1 tsp	paprika	1 tsp
2	raw eggs	2
4 tbsp	soured cream	4 tbsp
2	garlic cloves	2
1	carrot, sliced	1
1 tbsp	chopped parsley	1 tbsp
6	sprigs parsley	6
	lemon slices	
	radishes	

Rub the chicken inside and out with about 2 teaspoons of salt. Wilt the onion in the butter. Add the veal and chicken livers. Put the soaked bread roll through a strainer, together with the hard-boiled eggs and tomatoes. Combine this with the meat, paprika, raw eggs, soured cream and salt. Mix well. Stuff the chicken with this mixture; sew up all openings. Tie up the bird in a buttered napkin or a double thickness of muslin, place it in a pan with water to cover. Add the garlic, carrot and chopped parsley. Cook the bird slowly for 1½ hours or until tender. Do not overcook.

Remove the chicken, carefully unwrap it, and place it on a platter. Chill it overnight, covered. Garnish it with the remaining parsley, lemon slices, and radishes. To serve, first remove the wings, then slice the chicken crosswise.

INGE KRAMARZ
THE BALKAN COOKBOOK

———————◆———————

Hindle Wakes

The name of this recipe derives from "Hen de la Wake" or "Hen of the Wake" which means the hen to be eaten during the fair. This is a late version of a very old recipe. It was collected in its present form near Wigan, about 1900. It is a feast-day dish, dating from the Middle Ages, as good to eat as it is gay to look at with its white meat, black stuffing and yellow and green trimmings. To be eaten cold.

To serve 8

2 to 2.5 kg	boiling fowl	4 to 5 lb
15 cl	wine vinegar	¼ pint
2 tbsp	brown sugar	2 tbsp
1	lemon, quartered	1
	parsley sprigs	
	Stuffing	
500 g	large prunes, stoned and soaked (but not cooked)	1 lb
250 g	fine white breadcrumbs	8 oz
60 g	blanched almonds, roughly chopped	2 oz
	salt and pepper	
1 tbsp	finely chopped mixed fresh herbs: parsley, marjoram, thyme and chives	1 tbsp
60 g	suet, shredded	2 oz
15 cl	red wine	¼ pint
	Sauce	
1 tbsp	cornflour	1 tbsp
¼ litre	chicken stock, cooled and skimmed	8 fl oz
	grated zest and juice of 2 lemons	
	salt and pepper	
2	eggs, well beaten	2

Reserve 6 prunes for decoration. Mix all the other stuffing ingredients together and stuff the fowl, both breast and inside. Sew up the breast flap and draw together the skin at

the vent. Place the fowl in a large saucepan of water to which the wine vinegar and brown sugar have been added. Simmer for 4 hours and allow the chicken to get cold in the stock.

While the chicken is cooling, make the lemon sauce. Mix the cornflour with the stock and bring to the boil, stirring in the juice of 2 lemons as you do so. Season with salt and pepper, add the grated zest of 1 lemon and boil for 2 minutes. Allow to cool slightly and stir in the well-beaten eggs, holding the pan off the heat. Beat till thick and creamy; on no account should the sauce boil again. Leave the sauce to get cold.

Pour the sauce over the cold chicken and decorate with the remaining grated lemon zest, the quarters of lemon, halves of the reserved prunes and sprigs of parsley.

Carve with a very sharp knife.

ELISABETH AYRTON
THE COOKERY OF ENGLAND

———————◆———————

Chicken with Tarragon
Poulet à l'Estragon

To serve 4

1.5 to 2 kg	chicken	3 to 4 lb
2 to 3 tbsp	lemon juice	2 to 3 tbsp
60 g	butter	2 oz
	salt and pepper	
2 tbsp	chopped tarragon, plus a few whole leaves	2 tbsp
2	egg yolks	2
15 to 20 cl	cream	6 fl oz

Rub the outside of the chicken with lemon juice. Mash the butter with salt and pepper and 1 tablespoon of chopped tarragon, and put this inside the bird.

Poach the chicken, with water barely to cover, until it is cooked. Leave it to cool in the stock. Take out the chicken and place it whole in a deepish serving dish; strain the stock. Now beat up the yolks of the eggs with the cream and the other tablespoon of chopped tarragon. Heat about 30 cl (½ pint) of the stock in a small pan, pour a spoonful or two on to the egg and cream mixture, and then pour all back into the pan, stirring continuously until the sauce thickens, but do not make it too thick, as it will solidify slightly as it cools.

Pour the sauce over the chicken in the dish, and leave to get cold. Before serving, arrange a few whole tarragon leaves along the breast of the chicken.

ELIZABETH DAVID
FRENCH COUNTRY COOKING

Circassian Chicken

Çerkez Tavuğu

This dish, popular throughout the Middle East, exemplifies a very old tradition in which nuts, ground fine, are used to thicken and enrich a sauce.

To serve 4 to 6

2 kg	roasting chicken	4 lb
2	large onions, quartered	2
2	sticks celery	2
	salt and black pepper	
	Rice	
500 g	long-grain rice	1 lb
30 g	butter	1 oz
1 litre	stock, reserved from poaching	1¾ pints
	Sauce	
125 g	shelled nuts (almonds, hazelnuts or walnuts, or a mixture)	4 oz
40 cl	stock, reserved from poaching	¾ pint
60 g	fine dry breadcrumbs (optional)	2 oz
	salt and pepper	
2 tbsp	oil	2 tbsp
1 tsp	paprika	1 tsp

Wash the chicken and put it in a large saucepan. Cover with water and add the onions, celery, salt and pepper. Bring to the boil and simmer, covered, for about 1 hour, or until the chicken is tender, skimming off scum as it comes to the surface. Drain the chicken, reserving the stock; cut the bird into serving pieces and keep it warm.

The sauce is traditionally made with walnuts only, but other nuts and breadcrumbs are often added. Pound the nuts in a mortar or grind them in an electric blender. Sieve 40 cl (¾ pint) of the reserved stock into a clean pan, and stir in the nuts and breadcrumbs. Bring to the boil and cook, stirring until the mixture has thickened. Add more stock or water if it becomes too thick, and season to taste with salt and pepper.

Mix the oil with paprika until it becomes bright red.

Cook the rice by frying it gently in the butter for a minute or so then adding about 1 litre (1¾ pints) of the reserved chicken stock. Simmer, covered, until all the liquid is absorbed.

Arrange the chicken pieces in the centre of a large serving dish. Surround them with a ring of cooked rice. Pour the nut sauce over both the chicken and rice, and decorate with a dribble of red oil. This dish is often served cold with salads.

CLAUDIA RODEN
A BOOK OF MIDDLE EASTERN FOOD

Kentucky Burgoo with Rice

To serve 12

2.5 kg	boiling fowl	5 lb
	salt and pepper	
500 g	minced beef	1 lb
6	thick bacon rashers	6
175 g	fresh butter beans, or Lima beans	6 oz
175 g	green beans, sliced	6 oz
125 g	okra	4 oz
6	tomatoes, skinned, seeded and chopped	6
250 g	onions, diced	8 oz
2	potatoes, diced	2
	Tabasco sauce	
1 tbsp	lemon juice	1 tbsp
1 tbsp	sugar	1 tbsp
175 g	corn-on-the-cob, kernels scraped off	6 oz
	grated nutmeg	
30 g	butter	1 oz

Simmer the chicken in seasoned water to cover in an iron pot or Dutch oven for an hour or until tender enough to bone. Dice the chicken, discarding the bones. Return it to the pot with the broth and add all the other ingredients except the corn, nutmeg and butter. Simmer for about 45 minutes, adding more water when necessary—there should always be enough liquid to cover the vegetables while cooking.

Stir often with a long-handled spoon. Add the corn towards the end. When the mixture begins to thicken, but is still "soupy", add the grated nutmeg and butter. Serve very hot over steaming white rice.

PHYLLIS JERVEY
RICE & SPICE

Chicken Mousseline with Sorrel in Aspic with Champagne

The poaching recipe by Richard Olney that follows incorporates many of the techniques that have been demonstrated in the front of this book. By following the meticulously described, step-by-step instructions you will create a dish that is worthy of the chef of a 3-star restaurant.

A day in advance, bone the chicken (*page 20*) and prepare the stock and basic mousseline stuffing. The chicken should be poached, chilled and covered with the aspic 6 to 8 hours before serving.

To serve 6

2 kg	plump chicken, boned, bones reserved	4 lb
2 tbsp	lemon juice	2 tbsp
10 to 12	tarragon leaves, blanched (optional)	10 to 12
6	black olives, stoned and sliced (optional)	6
2	hard-boiled egg whites, sliced (optional)	2
1	sweet red pepper, grilled, peeled, seeded and cut into thin strips (optional)	1

Stock

	reserved chicken bones	
1	veal knuckle bone	1
1 kg	meaty shin of veal	2 to 2½ lb
	chickens' necks, heads, feet and carcasses	
1	onion, stuck with 2 cloves	1
2	carrots	2
1	large bouquet garni	1
3 to 3.5 litres	water	5 to 6 pints
30 cl	Champagne	½ pint

Mousseline stuffing

300 g	chicken breast	10 oz
1	large egg, white only	1
	salt and freshly ground white pepper	
	grated nutmeg	
30 cl	double cream, chilled	½ pint

Sorrel purée

250 g	sorrel	8 oz
	salt and pepper	
30 g	butter	1 oz
1	egg yolk	1
	salt	

To prepare the stock, put all the ingredients except the Champagne together in a large pan. Bring slowly to the boil, skim and simmer for at least 6 hours. Strain through muslin.

To prepare the basic mousseline stuffing, trim the breast very carefully. Not the faintest trace of skin, fat or bone should be left. Scrape with a knife to remove any sinewy parts. Pound long and thoroughly in a mortar. Add the white of egg a little at a time and keep pounding, each time, until the egg white is completely amalgamated with the flesh. Season, and rub the raw stuffing though a fine sieve, spoonful by spoonful, with a pestle. Pack the mixture well in a bowl, cover with foil or plastic, pressed down for protection. Keep in the refrigerator.

To make the sorrel purée, wash and clean the sorrel. Blanch it for a few seconds. Allow it to drain completely, without pressing it. Season with salt and pepper, and simmer in butter very, very gently in a small, heavy pan—a tin-lined copper one preferably. Cook, stirring every 2 to 3 minutes, until the sorrel has lost all its moisture. Rub the sorrel through a fine sieve, work in the egg yolk, mixing thoroughly, spread out the sorrel on a plate, and chill in the refrigerator.

An hour before starting to mix the stuffing, put the bowl on crushed ice. Add the cream—which should be well chilled—a small quantity at a time, mixing vigorously with a wooden spoon. Put the bowl back into the refrigerator each time for 15 minutes. After about 10 tablespoons of cream have been incorporated into the mixture, it should have acquired the consistency of a paste. Work in the sorrel purée until the ingredients have amalgamated. Set aside briefly and then mix in the remaining cream, lightly whipped; it should not be stiff.

Stuff the chicken, but do not overfill (when cooking, the stuffing swells, whereas the flesh of the chicken shrinks). Truss the bird, but without drawing the string too tightly; the legs should be just pressed against the breast. Rub the whole surface lightly with lemon juice, mould the chicken with your hands so that it returns to its original shape, then wrap it in muslin.

Put the chicken in a deep, oval cooking pot, just big enough for the bird to fit comfortably. Pour over it, ladle by ladle, the stock that has been brought to the boil. Put the lid on the pot, bring to the boil, then reduce the heat and allow barely to simmer for 1½ to 2 hours. Allow the chicken to cool off in the liquor. Take it out, remove the muslin and trussing strings and leave to cool completely in the refrigerator. Strain the liquor through muslin. Let it stand and remove all the fat. There should be about 1.25 litres (2 pints) of liquid left. When completely cool, but before it starts setting, add the Champagne—which should be duly chilled.

Put the chicken in an earthenware pot just large enough to hold it comfortably and pour over the jelly—or, to make it more elegant, put the bird on a long, shallow, oval serving dish and decorate with blanched tarragon leaves or slices of stoned olives, white of egg, sweet red pepper, that have first been dipped in the jelly. Stir the aspic jelly with a spoon and, just at the moment it begins to set, pour a few teaspoons at a time, taken from a small bowl on ice, over the bird.

Put the chicken in the refrigerator to allow the aspic to set completely. Repeat this several times until the outlines of the bird are dissolved in the golden mass of aspic.

Put aside some of the aspic to set, chop it and garnish the bird with the chopped aspic.

COMITÉ INTERPROFESSIONNEL DU VIN DE CHAMPAGNE
COOKING WITH CHAMPAGNE

Chicken with Fennel Seeds

The people of Florence have always loved the slightly anise flavour of fennel seeds. Fennel seeds give distinction to the adored sausage, *finocchiona*. In the 14th century, Florentine cooks were already using fennel seeds to add excitement to the blandness of chicken.

To serve 4

1.5 kg	chicken, cut up into 8 pieces	3 lb
1 tsp	fennel seeds	1 tsp
2	medium-sized onions, finely chopped	2
125 g	green bacon, diced	4 oz
90 g	peeled almonds, finely chopped	3 oz
	salt and pepper	

Place the chicken in a deep pot and add water just to cover. Boil slowly for 20 minutes. Remove the chicken. Add the fennel seeds and onions to the liquid in the pot, and simmer until the broth has been reduced by two-thirds.

Meanwhile, in a frying pan, sauté the green bacon until slightly rendered. Add the almonds and chicken pieces and sauté until golden. Pour on the broth. Add salt and pepper to taste. Cook for 5 minutes and serve it forth.

NAOMI BARRY AND BEPPE BELLINI
FOOD ALLA FLORENTINE

Chicken Casserole

Pepitoria de Gallina

To serve 4

1 to 1.5 kg	tender chicken	2 to 3 lb
1	bunch herbs (parsley, fresh thyme and a bay leaf)	1
	salt and pepper	
1	carrot	1
1	small onion	1
30 g	lard	1 oz
100 g	ham, cut into cubes	3½ oz
2 tbsp	chopped parsley	2 tbsp
4 or 5	garlic cloves	4 or 5
10	hazelnuts, toasted	10
1	clove	1
2	hard-boiled egg yolks	2
2	raw egg yolks, lightly beaten	2

First poach the chicken in water with the bunch of herbs, salt, pepper, carrot and onion until it is almost cooked (about 50 minutes). Remove the chicken and reserve the cooking liquid.

Heat the lard in a big saucepan or casserole and fry the ham and a little of the chopped parsley, then put in the chicken and carefully brown it on all sides.

In a large mortar make a paste with the garlic and hazelnuts, the clove, hard-boiled egg yolks and the rest of the chopped parsley. Dilute the paste with 2 or more ladles of the reserved stock and pour this sauce over the chicken in the casserole. Cover and cook gently for 20 minutes. Remove from the heat and stir in the raw egg yolks. Serve straight away.

ANNA MACMIADHACHÁIN
SPANISH REGIONAL COOKERY

Chicken and Lovage

To serve 4

1.5 kg	roasting chicken	3 lb
1	onion	1
1	carrot	1
	black peppercorns	
1	bunch lovage	1
	salt	
1	bunch watercress, chopped	1
2	boxes mustard and cress	2
	Sauce	
30 g	butter	1 oz
2 tbsp	chopped lovage leaves	2 tbsp
1 tbsp	flour	1 tbsp
30 cl	stock reserved from poaching	½ pint
	grated rind and juice of 2 small oranges	
4 tbsp	double cream	4 tbsp
	salt and pepper	

Put the chicken in a large saucepan with the onion, carrot, peppercorns and the bunch of lovage. Cover it with water to the thighs, season with salt, and poach it gently for 1 hour. Remove the chicken and keep it warm.

In a small saucepan, melt the butter on a moderate heat. Add the chopped lovage and cook it until it is tender. Blend in the flour and stock and bring to the boil, stirring. Stir in the orange rind and juice and the cream. Season with salt and pepper. Keep the sauce warm but do not let it boil again.

Joint the chicken and lay the joints on a bed of chopped watercress, mixed with mustard and cress. Pour the sauce over the top and serve immediately.

GAIL DUFF
FRESH ALL THE YEAR

Chicken Bouillabaisse

Bouillabaisse de Poulet

To serve 4

1 to 1.5 kg	chicken, cut up into 10 serving pieces, liver reserved	2 to 3 lb
1 tsp	ground saffron	1 tsp
2 tbsp	*pastis* (Pernod, Ricard)	2 tbsp
20 cl	olive oil	7 fl oz
	salt and pepper	
2	onions, chopped	2
4	garlic cloves, crushed	4
6	tomatoes, skinned, seeded and chopped	6
10	small sprigs fennel	10
2 tbsp	chopped parsley	2 tbsp
4	potatoes, peeled and thickly sliced	4
4	slices dry coarse bread, moistened with a little olive oil	4

Sauce

1	garlic clove	1
4	small chili peppers	4
2 tbsp	olive oil	2 tbsp
	reserved chicken liver, sautéed	
2	slices potato cooked in the bouillabaisse	2
4 to 6 tbsp	broth from the bouillabaisse	4 to 6 tbsp

Marinate the chicken pieces for 20 minutes in an earthenware bowl with the saffron, *pastis*, 10 cl (4 fl oz) of the olive oil, salt and pepper.

Heat the rest of the olive oil in a casserole and add the onions and garlic. Cook until they begin to brown. Add the tomatoes and, when everything is well blended, add the fennel, parsley, chicken pieces and marinade. Pour on boiling water until the ingredients are well covered. Season with salt, cover the casserole and simmer for 10 minutes. Add the potatoes and simmer for about 20 minutes more, until both potatoes and chicken are well cooked. Uncover the casserole and boil fast for several minutes to thicken the broth.

Pour the broth into a soup tureen over the slices of bread. Arrange the chicken pieces, potato slices and vegetables on a platter and keep them hot until the soup course is finished.

To make the sauce, pound together in a mortar the garlic clove, peppers and olive oil. Add the sautéed chicken liver and potato slices, and continue to pound. Moisten with the broth and mix well. Serve the resulting smooth sauce in a sauceboat to accompany both courses of the bouillabaisse.

RAYMOND OLIVER
LA CUISINE

Fried and Roasted Breaded Chicken

To serve 8

Two 1 kg	chickens, each quartered	Two 2 to 2½ lb
250 g	butter	8 oz
	flour	
2	eggs	2
	fine dried breadcrumbs	
¼ litre	soured cream	8 fl oz

Put the butter in a frying pan. Flour each chicken piece thoroughly. Beat the eggs in a shallow dish, coat the floured chicken thoroughly with egg, and then cover thickly with dried breadcrumbs. It is important that the chicken is thoroughly covered with flour, then with egg, then with breadcrumbs. Place the chicken pieces in melted butter in a frying pan over medium heat and brown lightly on both sides. Remove them to a fireproof earthenware dish, wings on one side and legs on the other, backs in the centre. Put the dish in an oven preheated to 150°C (300°F or Mark 2) and roast for 2 hours, basting frequently with soured cream.

ALICE B. TOKLAS
THE ALICE B. TOKLAS COOKBOOK

Cooked Chicken Breasts in Cream Sauce

Filets de Poularde à la Béchamel

To serve 4

4	cooked chicken breasts, boned and cut up into neat pieces	4
30 g	butter	1 oz
2 tbsp	chopped parsley	2 tbsp
3 or 4	Welsh or spring onions, chopped	3 or 4
1 tbsp	chopped shallot	1 tbsp
1	garlic clove, finely chopped	1
	salt, pepper and grated nutmeg	
1 tsp	flour	1 tsp
1	egg yolk, beaten	1
10 cl	cream	4 fl oz
2 tbsp	lemon juice	2 tbsp

Melt the butter in a casserole. Add the parsley, onions, shallot, garlic, salt, pepper, a pinch of nutmeg and the flour. Cook gently for a few minutes. Mix the egg yolk with the cream and stir the mixture into the casserole over a very low heat. Continue stirring until the sauce has a consistency that will coat the spoon. Add the chicken breasts and lemon juice, stir until the breasts are heated through and serve.

BERTRAND GUÉGAN
LA FLEUR DE LA CUISINE FRANÇAISE

Chicken for Chickens
Murgi Survedar

The coconut milk called for in this recipe may be obtained from stores that specialize in Caribbean or oriental foods; or you can make it at home from the flesh of a fresh coconut: $\frac{1}{4}$ litre (8 fl oz) of grated flesh mixed with $\frac{1}{4}$ litre (8 fl oz) hot tap water will yield about $\frac{1}{4}$ litre (8 fl oz) of coconut milk. Grate the coconut flesh without removing the brown skin. Measure the volume of the grated flesh and mix it with an equal volume of hot, but not boiling, tap water. (Do not use the milk from the coconut.) Press the mixture through a fine sieve lined with a double layer of dampened muslin to produce coconut milk.

To serve 4

750 g	chicken pieces	1½ lb
2 tsp	finely chopped garlic	2 tsp
1 tbsp	chopped fresh ginger root, or ¼ tsp ground ginger	1 tbsp
1 tbsp	vegetable oil	1 tbsp
2 tsp	salt	2 tsp
½ tsp	ground turmeric	½ tsp
8	unsalted cashew nuts	8
8	unsalted almonds, blanched	8
¾ litre	water	1¼ pints
90 g	clarified butter	3 oz
5 tbsp	coarsely chopped onion	5 tbsp
4 tbsp	natural yogurt, beaten smooth with a fork	4 tbsp
¼ litre	thick coconut milk	8 fl oz
2 tbsp	chopped fresh coriander leaves (optional)	2 tbsp

Spicy paste

1 tbsp	poppy seeds	1 tbsp
4	cloves	4
1	piece cinnamon stick, 3 cm (1¼ inches) long, or ¼ tsp ground cinnamon	1
4	cardamom pods, seeds only, or ¼ tsp ground cardamom	4
½ tsp	peppercorns	½ tsp
2 tsp	chopped fresh ginger root, or ½ tsp ground ginger	2 tsp
8	garlic cloves	8
2½ tbsp	finely chopped onion	2½ tbsp
4 tbsp	water	4 tbsp

Drop the garlic, ginger, and oil into a blender and purée. Pour the purée into a heavy, medium-sized pot and sauté over medium heat for 5 minutes. Add the chicken pieces, salt, turmeric, cashews and almonds. Stir to mix well. Raise the heat and continue frying until the chicken is golden and all the natural liquid has evaporated. Add the water. Cover and simmer until just tender. Remove the chicken and nuts, drain and reserve them. Strain the broth, reduce it to ¼ litre (8 fl oz) and reserve separately.

To make the spicy paste, one by one as listed, drop the poppy seeds, cloves, cinnamon, cardamom, peppercorns, ginger, garlic and finely chopped onion into the blender. Pulverize each ingredient before adding the next. Add the water and blend to a smooth, thick paste. Set aside.

In a heavy, medium-sized saucepan, heat the butter and fry the coarsely chopped onion until it is just turning colour. Off the heat, stir in the spicy paste. Return the pan to the heat and continue frying, scraping and turning the mixture with a spatula. Add a tablespoon of water when necessary to prevent sticking. Continue thus until butter bubbles up to the top of the paste and it moves as a single mass when stirred.

Off the heat, add the drained chicken and nuts. Stir the mixture and add the yogurt. Return the pan to a medium heat. When the yogurt is absorbed, add the broth, spoon by spoon, and finally the coconut milk. Stir constantly until the chicken is tender and enveloped in a rich, golden sauce. Serve hot over rice. Garnish with the coriander leaves just before serving.

SHIVAJI RAO AND SHALINI DEVI HOLKAR
COOKING OF THE MAHARAJAS

Chicken not in a Púcara

A classic way of cooking chicken in Portugal is in a púcara—*a closed, deep earthenware pot in which the chicken and all the seasonings steam and stew together. The seasoning is potent, almost burning with mustard and brandy. This recipe for chicken baked in a shallow casserole with a seasoned sauce represents a variation on the traditional method.*

To serve 4

1 kg	chicken, cut up into serving pieces	2½ lb
3	tomatoes, skinned, seeded and chopped	3
175 g	smoked lean ham, thinly sliced and cut into 1 cm (½ inch) squares	6 oz
8	small onions	8
1 tbsp	Dijon-type mustard	1 tbsp
1	large garlic clove, finely chopped or crushed	1
6 tbsp each	dry white wine and tawny or white port	6 tbsp each
	salt and black pepper	
60 g	butter	2 oz
6 tbsp	brandy	6 tbsp

Combine the tomatoes, ham, onions, mustard, garlic, white wine and port in a shallow baking pan or casserole. Season the chicken pieces with salt and pepper and arrange them in a single layer on top of the tomato mixture. Dot with butter. Bake in a moderate oven—180°C (350°F or Mark 4) for 1 hour or until the chicken is browned and tender. Sprinkle with brandy. Serve the chicken with the sauce spooned over.

SHIRLEY SARVIS
A TASTE OF PORTUGAL

Chicken with Eggs, Lemons, and Olives

Djej Masquid Bil Beid

Preserved lemons are one of the indispensable ingredients of Moroccan cooking. Their unique pickled taste and special silken texture cannot be duplicated with fresh lemon or lime juice. They may be used as a flavouring element in stews, marinades, pilaffs and salad dressings.

The important thing in preserving lemons yourself is to be certain they are completely covered with salted lemon juice. With my recipe you can use the lemon pickling juice over and over again. (As a matter of fact, I keep a jar of juice in the kitchen and, whenever I have a half lemon left over, I toss it into the jar and let it marinate with the rest.)

Sometimes you will see a sort of lacy, white substance clinging to preserved lemons in the jar; it is perfectly harmless, but should be rinsed off for aesthetic reasons just before the lemons are used. Preserved lemons are rinsed, in any case, to rid them of their salty taste. Cook them with both pulps and rinds, if desired.

Preserved lemons

5	lemons	5
60 g	salt, more if desired	2 oz

Safi spice mixture (optional)

1	stick cinnamon	1
3	cloves	3
5 or 6	coriander seeds	5 or 6
3 or 4	black peppercorns	3 or 4
1	bay leaf	1
	lemon juice, if necessary	

If you wish to soften the peel, soak the lemons in lukewarm water for 3 days, changing the water daily.

Quarter the lemons from the top to within 1 cm ($\frac{1}{2}$ inch) of the bottom, sprinkle salt on the exposed flesh, then reshape the fruit.

Place 1 tablespoon salt on the bottom of a sterilized 1 litre (1 quart) Kilner jar. Pack in the lemons and push them down, adding more salt and the optional spices, between layers. Press the lemons down to release their juices and to make room for the remaining lemons. (If the juice released from the

squashed fruit does not cover them, add freshly squeezed lemon juice.) Leave some air space before sealing the jar.

Let the lemons ripen for 30 days in a warm place, turning the jar upside down each day to distribute the salt and juice.

To use, rinse the lemons, as needed, under running water, removing and discarding the pulp, if desired. There is no need to refrigerate after opening. Preserved lemons will keep up to a year, and the pickling juice can be used two or three times over the course of a year.

To serve 6

Two 1.5 kg	chickens, cut up into serving pieces	Two 3 lb
1	large bunch parsley, chopped	1
3	garlic cloves, chopped	3
1	Spanish onion, grated	1
	salt	
$\frac{3}{4}$ tsp	ground ginger	$\frac{3}{4}$ tsp
$\frac{3}{4}$ tsp	freshly ground black pepper	$\frac{3}{4}$ tsp
$\frac{1}{8}$ tsp	ground saffron	$\frac{1}{8}$ tsp
60 g	butter, melted	2 oz
3	large (or 6 small) sticks cinnamon	3
$\frac{1}{2}$ litre	water	18 fl oz
10	eggs	10
2	preserved lemons	2
8	red-brown olives, such as Kalamatas, stoned and chopped	8
10 cl	lemon juice	4 fl oz

Place the chicken pieces in a casserole. Add two-thirds of the parsley, and the garlic, onion, salt, spices, half the butter, and the cinnamon sticks. Add the water and bring to the boil. Simmer, covered, for about 1 hour or until the chicken pieces are very tender and the flesh is almost falling off the bones. (During the cooking you may need to add more water.)

Preheat the oven to 180°C (350°F or Mark 4).

Transfer the chicken (but not the sauce) to an ovenproof serving dish. Remove any loose bones and cinnamon sticks from the sauce in the casserole and, by boiling rapidly, uncovered, reduce to 40 cl ($\frac{3}{4}$ pint). Pour over the chicken.

Beat the eggs to a froth with the remaining parsley. Rinse and dice the preserved lemons, using the pulp if desired. Stir the lemons and chopped olives into the eggs, and pour the egg mixture over the chickens. Cover the dish with aluminium foil and bake on the middle shelf of the oven for 20 minutes.

Raise the oven heat to the highest setting, remove the aluminium cover, and dot the eggs with the remaining melted butter. Transfer the dish to the upper shelf of the oven and bake for 10 minutes more, or until the eggs are completely set and the chickens have browned slightly. Sprinkle with lemon juice and serve at once.

PAULA WOLFERT
COUSCOUS AND OTHER GOOD FOOD FROM MOROCCO

Chicken Breasts Baked with Onion

Oignonnade à la Bretonne

To serve 6

6	chicken breasts, skinned, boned and halved	6
250 g	mushrooms, finely sliced	8 oz
60 g	butter	2 oz
300 g	onions, finely sliced	10 oz
10 cl	reduced veal stock	4 fl oz
½ litre	double cream	18 fl oz
	salt and white pepper	

Sauté the mushrooms in 30 g (1 oz) of the butter. In another pan, gently cook the onions in the remaining butter until they are transparent and put half of them in a shallow casserole. Lay the chicken breasts on top, and cover with the rest of the onions and the mushrooms. Pour over the veal stock and the cream; add salt and pepper, and cook uncovered in the oven at 170°C (325°F or Mark 3). When the cream has reduced to a coating consistency, serve immediately with peas.

ÉDOUARD NIGNON
ÉLOGES DE LA CUISINE FRANÇAISE

Chicken Gratin with Cheese

Poulet au Fromage

To serve 4 to 6

Two 1.5 kg	chickens, split down the back and flattened	Two 3 lb
90 g	butter	3 oz
8 cl	white wine	3 fl oz
8 cl	veal or chicken stock	3 fl oz
1	bouquet garni	1
1	onion, chopped	1
1	small garlic clove, finely chopped	1
2	cloves	2
1	small bay leaf	1
	fresh thyme	
	fresh basil	
	salt and coarsely ground pepper	
1 tbsp	flour	1 tbsp
100 g	Gruyere cheese, grated	3 oz

Brown the chickens in a casserole in 60 g (2 oz) of the butter; moisten with the wine and stock; add the bouquet garni, onion, garlic, cloves, bay leaf, and a pinch each of thyme and basil. Season with salt and pepper. Cook for an hour in a slow oven, 150°C (300°F or Mark 2). Remove the chickens and add to the cooking liquid a *beurre manié*—the remaining butter mixed with the flour. Bring the sauce to the boil over a moderate heat. Pour some of it on the bottom of a heatproof serving dish and over it sprinkle half the cheese. Place the chickens on top, and pour over the rest of the sauce and then the remaining cheese.

Put the dish in a moderate oven, 180°C (350°F or Mark 4) to heat through, and finish under the grill until the cheese is golden-brown. Serve very hot.

OFFRAY AINÉ
LE CUISINIER MÉRIDIONAL

Chicken Loaf with Watercress Sauce

To serve 6 to 8

1 kg	chicken breasts, skinned and boned	2 lb
125 g	finely chopped onions	4 oz
2	egg yolks	2
125 g	fine, fresh breadcrumbs	4 oz
15 cl	double cream	¼ pint
1	bunch watercress, finely chopped	1
¼ tsp	grated nutmeg	¼ tsp
	salt and freshly ground pepper	
	Watercress sauce	
90 g	butter	3 oz
4 tbsp	flour	4 tbsp
¾ litre	chicken stock	1¼ pints
1	bunch watercress	1
¼ litre	double cream	8 fl oz
	salt and freshly ground pepper	
¼ tsp	grated nutmeg	¼ tsp

Preheat the oven to 200°C (400°F or Mark 6). Cut the chicken into cubes, place them in an electric blender or food processor and blend, stirring down as necessary. This may have to be done in two or more steps.

Scrape the mixture into a mixing bowl; then add the remaining ingredients and blend together well. Pour the mixture into a 22 by 12 by 8 cm (9 by 5 by 3 inch) buttered loaf tin and cover with greaseproof paper, and a close-fitting lid. Stand the mould in a roasting pan and pour boiling water around it. Bake for 1½ hours or until the loaf is set and cooked through.

To make the watercress sauce, melt 60 g (2 oz) of the butter in a saucepan and add the flour, stirring with a wire whisk. When blended, add the stock, stirring rapidly with the whisk. Cook about 20 minutes, stirring often.

Meanwhile, cut off and discard the tough bottom stems of the watercress. Drop the cress into a small saucepan of boiling water and simmer about 30 seconds. Drain, squeeze to extract most of the liquid, and chop. Set aside.

Add the cream to the sauce. Add salt and pepper to taste, and the nutmeg. Simmer about 15 minutes. Strain the sauce through a very fine sieve. Return it to a saucepan and stir in the watercress. Swirl in the remaining butter.

Serve the chicken loaf sliced and hot, with the watercress sauce.

CRAIG CLAIBORNE
CRAIG CLAIBORNE'S FAVORITES FROM THE NEW YORK TIMES

Chicken Velvet

Fu-Jung Chi-P'ien

To serve 4

2	chicken breasts, skinned	2
2 tsp	iced water	2 tsp
40 cl	cottonseed oil, or peanut or other vegetable oil	$\frac{3}{4}$ pint
10 cl	chicken stock	4 fl oz
	salt	
	sugar	
6	mange-tout	6
6	button mushrooms	6
60 g	Virginia ham, shredded (optional)	2 oz
	Marinade	
1 tbsp	cornflour, blended with enough water to make a flowing paste	1 tbsp
1	egg white	1
	salt	
2 to 4 tbsp	Chinese rice wine or dry sherry	2 to 4 tbsp

Pick out the tendon of each chicken breast with the tip of a cleaver or knife, and lay the breast on a board. Hold a cleaver almost parallel to the breast, which has been flattened out a little, and cut it in half lengthwise.

Scrape off the meat to make a paste, always along the breast in the direction of the fibres. Add the iced water to make the paste even smoother. Put the paste into a bowl with the marinade ingredients, and mix very thoroughly with your fingers to ensure a smooth texture, free from bubbles.

Heat a *wok*, put in the oil, and bring to 75°C (160° to 170°F). The oil should not be hotter than that or the chicken will brown. Mould the chicken paste into pieces about the size of a large almond. Place them in the heated oil all at the same time, and cook for 30 seconds. Scoop them all out. At this stage the pieces are cooked around the edges and already white, while the centres are still slightly underdone. Pour the oil out

of the *wok*. Put the chicken stock, the salt and the sugar into the *wok* and stir. Add the chicken pieces, mange-tout and button mushrooms and, if you like, a little Virginia ham, and stir-fry rapidly. This rapid *ch'ao*-cooking will take only another 30 seconds, when the dish should be borne to the table, admired for a few seconds, and then dispatched with celerity.

CECILIA SUN YUN CHIANG
THE MANDARIN WAY

Shaker Chicken Pudding

The Shakers—or Shaking Quakers, so-called because of their shaking movements in the course of worshipping—originally settled in America from Europe during the 18th and 19th centuries. Mainly farming people, their distinctive fare, like the functional and attractive furniture for which they are also famous, expressed their belief in the rich rewards of simple and natural living.

To serve 4 to 6

500 g	cooked chicken meat, diced	1 lb
1	apple, peeled and diced	1
1	medium-sized onion, chopped	1
1	stick celery, chopped	1
90 g	butter	3 oz
10 cl	dry cider	4 fl oz
$\frac{1}{2}$ tsp	salt	$\frac{1}{2}$ tsp
$\frac{1}{4}$ tsp	pepper	$\frac{1}{4}$ tsp
	grated nutmeg	
90 g	dry breadcrumbs	3 oz
	Sauce	
2 tbsp	flour	2 tbsp
30 g	butter	1 oz
$\frac{1}{4}$ litre	double cream	8 fl oz

Gently sauté the apple, onion and celery in 60 g (2 oz) of the butter until they are soft. Add the cider, salt and pepper, and a pinch of nutmeg. Simmer, covered, for 30 minutes, or until the vegetables are very soft. Uncover the pot and continue to cook them until the mixture thickens.

To make the sauce, cook the flour in the butter in a saucepan for a few minutes, stirring until the mixture just begins to change colour. Add the cream and cook, stirring, until the sauce thickens. Mix into this sauce the cooked vegetable hash and the chicken. Pour into a buttered baking dish, and sprinkle with breadcrumbs and the remaining butter, melted. Bake in an oven preheated to 180°C (350°F or Mark 4) for 20 minutes.

CARL LYREN
365 WAYS TO COOK CHICKEN

Williamsburg Chicken Pudding

This recipe has been adapted from the original version in Mrs. Mary Randolph's Virginia Housewife, *1831.*

To serve 4 to 6

2 to 2.5 kg	fowl, cut up into serving pieces	4 to 5 lb
1	onion	1
	celery tops	
	parsley sprigs	
1 tsp	dried thyme	1 tsp
	salt and pepper	
¼ litre	strained broth, reserved from poaching	1 pint
	Batter	
60 cl	milk	1 pint
3	eggs, well beaten	3
30 g	flour	1 oz
60 g	butter, melted	2 oz
1 tsp	salt	1 tsp

Put the chicken pieces in a pot with water to cover, along with the onion, a few celery tops, parsley, thyme, salt and pepper. Simmer gently until the meat is just tender. Take the chicken pieces from the broth, remove the skin and place the pieces in a shallow baking dish. Pour over the strained broth. Make a batter with milk, eggs, flour, melted butter and salt. Pour this over the chicken and bake in a moderate oven, 180°C (350°F or Mark 4), for about 35 minutes, or until the batter topping is set and an inserted knife comes out clean. Serve immediately with a gravy, made of broth thickened by a butter and flour *roux*, passed separately.

MRS HELEN CLAIRE BULLOCK
THE WILLIAMSBURG ART OF COOKERY

Kentish Chicken Pudding

In medieval days, farmyard fowl were kept strictly for egg-laying; not until they became old and scraggy were they killed. By then they were so tough that only by prolonged steaming, usually in a suet pastry, could they become edible. The traditional Sussex Goose or Chicken Pudding is a survival from those days, but is superseded by this recipe for young, tender chickens.

The suet pastry called for in this recipe may be made with fresh suet or the shredded commercial variety. If you use fresh suet, remove the papery skin and chop it finely, using a little flour to prevent sticking. Mix together 1 kg (2 lb) plain flour, 7 g (¼ oz) salt and 250 g (8 oz) suet. Gradually add about 30 cl (½ pint)

cold water and work the dough until it has a stiff, elastic consistency.

To serve 8

Two 1.5 kg	chickens, each quartered, giblets reserved for stock	Two 3 lb
500 g	salted belly pork, diced	1 lb
1 kg	suet pastry	2 to 2½ lb
	salt and pepper	
250 g	onions, chopped	8 oz
2 tsp	finely chopped parsley	2 tsp
30 cl	strained chicken stock	½ pint

Use the chickens' wing tips, trimmings and giblets to make stock. Blanch, refresh and drain the diced pork.

Line a 2 litre (3 to 4 pint) greased pudding basin with three-quarters of the suet pastry; put in the chicken pieces, seasoned with salt and pepper. Mix in the pork and onions and sprinkle with parsley. Pour over the strained chicken stock and cover with the remaining pastry.

Tie down with buttered greaseproof paper or foil and a pudding cloth. Steam for 2 hours, turn the pudding out on to a serving dish and serve.

LIZZIE BOYD (EDITOR)
BRITISH COOKERY

Chicken, Ham and Veal Pie

Pâté-chaud de Poulets dans un Plat

To serve 4 to 6

Two 1 kg	chickens, cut up into serving pieces	Two 2 to 2½ lb
	salt and pepper	
4	slices *prosciutto*	4
2	thin veal escalopes, finely diced	2
1	shallot, finely chopped	1
3 or 4	hard-boiled eggs, quartered	3 or 4
20 cl	cold chicken or veal stock	7 fl oz
	rough-puff, or shortcrust pastry (*page 167*)	
1	egg, mixed with a little water	1

Remove the wing tips from the chicken pieces; break the leg joints and remove the thigh bones. Season the pieces.

Line the bottom of a pie dish with the slices of *prosciutto* and cover these with veal. Sprinkle in the shallots and season with salt and pepper. Add the dark chicken flesh, then the breast pieces and wings. Tuck the eggs into the spaces around the chicken; then pour in the stock. Roll out the pastry dough. Moisten the edge of the dish with water and cover the edge with a strip of pastry. Dampen this strip and cover the dish with a lid of pastry. Seal well, trim and pinch the edges. Decorate the pie with leaves made out of the pastry and glaze the surface with the egg mixed with water.

Cook in a moderate oven, 180°C (350°F or Mark 4), for 1 hour, remembering to cover the pastry with a sheet of paper as soon as it becomes golden-brown. Place on a platter and serve.

URBAIN DUBOIS
L'ÉCOLE DES CUISINIÈRES

Charter Pie

A Cornish recipe from a Victorian recipe book, compiled by Lady Sarah Lindsay.

To serve 8 to 10

	Filling	
Two 1.5 kg	chickens, cut up into serving pieces	Two 3 lb
1	large onion, chopped	1
90 g	butter	3 oz
	flour	
	salt and pepper	
2	bunches parsley, chopped	2
15 cl	milk	$\frac{1}{4}$ pint
40 cl	double cream	$\frac{3}{4}$ pint
	Shortcrust pastry	
250 g	flour	8 oz
60 g each	butter and lard	2 oz each
2 tsp	icing sugar	2 tsp
1	egg	1
	salt	
	top of the milk, or beaten egg	

Make the pastry (*page 167*) and leave it to rest.

Sweat the onion in a frying pan in half of the butter until transparent, and put it into the pie dish (a large shallow one is best). Add the rest of the butter to the pan and fry the chicken, which should first be rolled in flour seasoned with salt and pepper. When the pieces are lightly browned, lay them on top of the onion in the dish. Simmer the parsley for 3 minutes in the milk. Pour the milk over the chicken, with half the cream. Season well.

Put a pastry rim round the pie dish, moisten it and lay on the lid (see that the chicken bones don't pierce it). Decorate

and make a central hole, which should be kept open with a small roll of white card. Brush over with top of the milk or beaten egg, and put into a hot oven, 220°C (425°F or Mark 7), for 15 minutes. Protect the top with paper or foil and lower the heat to about 180°C (350°F or Mark 4). Leave for an hour.

Just before serving, heat the rest of the cream and pour it into the pie by way of the central hole, after removing the roll of card. Charter pie is very good cold; the sauce sets to an excellent jelly.

JANE GRIGSON
GOOD THINGS

Romertopf's Beggar's Chicken

The Chinese five-spice powder called for in this recipe is a combination of star anise, Szechwan pepper, fennel seeds, cinnamon and cloves. If unavailable, use star anise or anise seed, ground to a powder with a mortar and pestle.

To serve 3 or 4

2 kg	chicken, cut up into serving pieces	4 lb
	arrowroot, mixed with a little water	
	almonds and sesame seeds (optional)	
	Marinade	
1 tsp	sesame oil	1 tsp
1 tbsp	dry sherry	1 tbsp
$\frac{1}{4}$ tsp	Chinese five-spice powder	$\frac{1}{4}$ tsp
$\frac{1}{4}$ tsp	white pepper	$\frac{1}{4}$ tsp
1	garlic clove, crushed	1
4 tbsp	soy sauce	4 tbsp
1 tsp	grated fresh ginger root	1 tsp

In a non-metal bowl, combine the ingredients for the marinade, mix well and marinate the chicken pieces for at least half a day, turning frequently. (Don't add any salt—there is enough in any good soy sauce.)

When you are ready to cook the chicken, presoak a clay pot, top and bottom, in water for 15 minutes. Add the chicken and the marinade to the pot. Place the covered pot in a cold oven. Set the oven temperature to 230°C (450°F or Mark 8). Cook for 45 minutes.

Remove the pot and pour off the liquid into a saucepan. Return the pot to the oven uncovered, for a further 10 minutes of cooking. Meanwhile, bring the liquid in the saucepan to the boil and thicken with arrowroot.

Serve with rice, liberally drenched with the sauce. For an optional Chinese touch, sprinkle the chicken with almonds and sesame seeds.

GEORGIA MACLEOD SALES AND GROVER SALES
THE CLAY-POT COOKBOOK

Baked Stuffed Poussins in Parchment

La Pochette Surprise

A recipe by Léon Abric, a member of the Académie des Gastronomes.

	To serve 2	
1	poussin, split lengthwise	1
	olive oil	
	dried fine breadcrumbs seasoned with salt and freshly ground white pepper	
	Stuffing	
3	chicken livers, chopped	3
1	chicken heart, chopped	1
7 or 8	small spring onions, finely chopped	7 or 8
2 tbsp	finely chopped fresh chives	2 tbsp
3 tbsp	finely chopped fresh chervil	3 tbsp
20	fresh tarragon leaves	20
50 g	bread, crusts removed, soaked in milk and squeezed	2 oz
15 g	butter	½ oz
1	egg	1
	salt and freshly ground white pepper	
	grated nutmeg	

To make the stuffing, mix the livers, heart, spring onions, chives, chervil and tarragon together. Put the mixture into a mortar and add the bread, butter and egg. Pound the mixture, then add the salt and pepper and a suspicion of nutmeg. Taste for seasoning.

Brush the interior of each chicken half with olive oil and fill with stuffing. Rub all surfaces generously with oil. Roll each half in the salted and peppered breadcrumbs. Then pat on the crumbs by hand to ensure a good coating. Wrap each chicken half in a large piece of well greased paper. Fold the edges of the paper securely together and tie the parcel with thread. This should be done carefully, bearing in mind that the packet, or *pochette*, will be served just as it is.

Cook the chicken in a moderate oven, 180°C (350°F or Mark 4) for 30 to 40 minutes, adjusting the heat if necessary so that the chicken is cooked through, without the packet becoming charred. This requires care but great artists often seek a challenge.

Each guest should open his or her own packet, firstly to discover what is inside, and secondly to enjoy to the full the ineffable aroma.

GASTON DERYS
L'ART D'ÊTRE GOURMAND

Turkey

Stuffed Turkey

Yemistes Yallopoules

	To serve 15	
5 to 6.5 kg	turkey, giblets reserved	11 to 14 lb
1	lemon, halved	1
	salt and pepper	
	melted butter	
	Meat stuffing	
60 to 90 g	butter	2 to 3 oz
2	onions, finely chopped	2
175 g	minced lamb	6 oz
	reserved turkey heart and liver, minced	
500 g	chestnuts, boiled, peeled and broken into small pieces	1 lb
1 tbsp	pine nuts	1 tbsp
60 cl	turkey broth, made from reserved neck and gizzard	1 pint
125 g	rice	4 oz
1	lamb's liver, minced	1
60 g	fresh breadcrumbs	2 oz
2	cooking apples, peeled, cored and chopped into small pieces	2

Wash the turkey in cold water, pat it dry inside and out, and leave it for 30 minutes while you cook your stuffing.

Heat the butter in a frying pan and fry the onions until they begin to change colour, then add the lamb and simmer gently for 15 minutes. Add the turkey heart and liver, the chestnuts and pine nuts, and simmer for another 5 minutes. Add the broth and bring this to a boil. Add the rice and cook quickly for 10 minutes, then add the lamb's liver, breadcrumbs and apples. Stir well.

To stuff the turkey, slit the skin at the back of the neck and cut off the neck down to the turkey's shoulders. Lightly fill the breast cavity, remembering that the stuffing always swells and too much swelling might cause the neck skin of the turkey to burst. Sew (or pin with a skewer) the neck flap to the back of the turkey. Just as lightly, fill the body cavity and sew or skewer this together.

Tie the legs to the tail and fix the wings snugly to the body. Do not bring the cord across the breast for it marks the skin. Rub the turkey with lemon, salt, pepper and melted butter and place it in a large, shallow pan in a moderate oven. Roast it according to its weight when stuffed, allowing 25 to 30 minutes per 500 g (1 lb).

If you have made too much stuffing for your turkey it can be roasted in the pan and served with the turkey. Or it can be made into rissoles, dipped into beaten egg and breadcrumbs and served as a garnish. Greeks prefer to have plenty of stuffing so that it can be cooked separately and served with the turkey.

ROBIN HOWE
GREEK COOKING

Brittany-Style Stuffed Turkey

Dindonneau à la Bretonne

To serve 6 to 8

4 kg	turkey	9 lb
	salt and pepper	
	thin slices pork fat	
30 g	butter, melted	1 oz
	Stuffing	
200 g	seedless raisins	7 oz
30 cl	port	½ pint
500 g	sausage meat	1 lb
30 g	butter	1 oz
24	prunes, partially cooked in tea, stones removed	24
1	turkey liver, finely chopped	1
1 tsp	dried thyme, including the flowers if possible	1 tsp
	salt and pepper	

To make the stuffing, cover the raisins in port and macerate them for 5 to 6 hours. Lightly cook the sausage meat in butter. Add the raisins, prunes, liver, thyme, salt and pepper, and mix well. Stuff the turkey with this mixture, season the bird with salt and pepper, and cover the breast with slices of pork fat. Truss the bird, pour melted butter over it, place it in a moderate oven preheated to 180°C (350°F or Mark 4) and cook for about 3 hours. Baste frequently, and from time to time moisten the bird with a spoonful of water. Serve when the turkey is done and a golden colour, steaming all over. Serve the juices separately. Above all do not add stock or any other liquid to the cooking juices.

ÉDOUARD NIGNON
ÉLOGES DE LA CUISINE FRANÇAISE

My Own Favorite Roast Turkey

Much of this fashion of roasting a turkey came from my family. I have changed and embellished it a bit, and the final recipe is the one I use for Thanksgiving or other traditional holidays.

To serve 8 to 10

8 to 9 kg	turkey, giblets reserved	18 to 20 lb
1	onion, stuck with 2 cloves	1
1	sprig parsley	1
	salt	
½ tsp	dried thyme	½ tsp
1 litre	water	1¾ pints
½	lemon	½
175 g	butter, softened	6 oz
	freshly ground pepper	
	fresh or salt pork, cut up into strips, or bacon rinds	
4 tbsp	flour	4 tbsp
4 tbsp	cognac or Madeira (optional)	4 tbsp
	Stuffing	
350 g	butter	12 oz
150 g	shallots or spring onions, finely chopped	6 oz
1½ tbsp	dried tarragon, or 3 tbsp fresh tarragon, finely chopped	1½ tbsp
	salt	
1½ tsp	freshly ground pepper	1½ tsp
75 g	pine nuts	2½ oz
500 g	fresh breadcrumbs	1 lb
1 or 2	garlic cloves, finely chopped (optional)	1 or 2

Make the stuffing first. Melt 125 g (4 oz) of the butter in a heavy skillet—a 30 cm (12 inch) one if possible. Add the shallots or spring onions and the tarragon and allow to cook until the shallots are just wilted. Add 1 tablespoon salt, or to taste, pepper, pine nuts, and then additional butter as needed—I should say another 125 to 225 g (4 to 8 oz), depending on the amount the onion has absorbed. Finally, add the crumbs and toss well. Taste the mixture and add more of any of the ingredients if required. A clove or two of garlic may also be added to the mixture.

Remove the neck from the bird if not already done, and put the neck in a 2 litre (3½ pint) saucepan with the liver, gizzard, heart, and the onion, parsley, 2 teaspoons salt, and the thyme. Add the water, bring to the boil, and boil for 5 minutes, after which reduce the heat and simmer, covered, for 1 hour. Drain and reserve the stock for the sauce. If you like, chop the gizzard, heart and liver to add to the sauce.

Rub the inside of the turkey with the lemon. Fill the body cavity and neck cavity with stuffing, but not too tightly—the crumbs should remain somewhat loose. Truss the turkey, with a trussing needle, by hand-tying the piece of neck skin to the back of the turkey, or by sewing with a needle and twine.

Close the vent of the bird, and either secure with skewers and twine or sew it up. Tie the legs together firmly, and then tie them to the tail of the bird. Massage the turkey well with about 60 g (2 oz) softened butter, and then salt and pepper it. Line a rack with strips of fresh or salt pork or with the rind of bacon, which you can sometimes buy from your butcher when he cuts down a whole slab. Set the rack in a fairly shallow roasting pan, and place the turkey breast side down on the rack. Roast for 1 hour at 180°C (350°F or Mark 4). Remove the pan from the oven, turn the turkey on one side, and rub with half of the remaining softened butter. Return the turkey to the oven and roast for another hour. Remove the pan from the oven, turn the turkey on its back, and rub the breast with the remaining butter. Return to the oven and continue roasting till the turkey is done. Remove from the oven and place on a hot platter. Allow it to rest for 15 minutes if being served hot. If being served tepid, let it cool gently at room temperature. Remove all the twine and skewers.

For the sauce, pour off all the fat, save 4 tablespoons, from the roasting pan. Discard the excess fat. Over medium heat, add the flour to the pan and blend thoroughly, scraping to loosen bits of caramelized dripping. If there are any juices on the platter beneath the turkey, add those (skimmed of fat) as well. Gradually stir in 45 cl (16 fl oz) or more of the turkey broth and cook, stirring constantly, till the mixture thickens. Correct the seasoning. Add the chopped giblets, if you like, and cognac or Madeira, and simmer about 4 to 5 minutes. Serve with the turkey and stuffing.

JAMES BEARD
JAMES BEARD'S AMERICAN COOKERY

Gratin of Vine Leaves Stuffed with Turkey

Boulettes de Dinde au Yaourt

A recipe by E. Nizan of the Comédie Française.

To serve 4

500 g	turkey breast meat, skinned and finely chopped	1 lb
12	tender young vine leaves	12
1	large onion, finely chopped	1
60 g	bread, crusts removed, soaked in milk and squeezed	2 oz
2	eggs	2
	salt and pepper	
30 g	butter	1 oz
2 tbsp	lemon juice	2 tbsp
10 cl	water	4 fl oz
	natural yogurt	

Blanch the vine leaves by immersing them in boiling water for 1 minute. Then drain them.

Prepare the stuffing by mixing together the turkey, onion, soaked bread and eggs. Season the mixture and work it together well. Place some stuffing on each vine leaf and roll it up into a parcel.

Melt the butter in a casserole, preferably earthenware, and put in the stuffed vine leaves carefully, so that they do not come apart. Add the lemon juice. Cover and cook over a very low heat, adding a little hot water from time to time. The sauce should reduce while cooking. Brown lightly under the grill for 10 minutes before serving. Serve the stuffed vine leaves very hot with yogurt.

GASTON DERYS
L'ART D'ÊTRE GOURMAND

Turkey Chili

To serve 8 to 10

2.5 to 3 kg	turkey, cut up into quarters	5 to 7 lb
1	onion, stuck with cloves	1
2	sticks celery	2
2 or 3	sprigs parsley	2 or 3
2	small dried chili peppers	2
	salt	
$\frac{1}{2}$ tsp	cayenne pepper	$\frac{1}{2}$ tsp
125 g	canned peeled green chili peppers, finely chopped	4 oz
125 g	ground almonds	4 oz
60 g	ground peanuts	2 oz
	chili powder (optional)	
1	large onion, finely chopped	1
3	garlic cloves, finely chopped	3
2	sweet green peppers, finely chopped	2
4 tbsp	olive oil	4 tbsp
150 g	small green olives, stoned	5 oz
75 g	blanched almonds	$2\frac{1}{2}$ oz

Cover the turkey pieces with water and add the onion stuck with cloves, the celery, parsley and dried peppers. Bring to the boil. Reduce the heat, skim off any scum that may rise to the top, and cover the pot. Simmer until the turkey is tender but not falling from the bones. Remove the turkey pieces and cool until they can be handled. Remove the meat from the bones in good-sized pieces.

Reduce the broth by half over a brisk heat. You should have about 90 cl ($1\frac{1}{2}$ pints) of broth. Strain and adjust the salt. Add the cayenne pepper, the green chilis, and the ground nuts. Simmer until the mixture is thickened, smooth and well blended in flavour. Taste for seasoning; you may find you wish to add a little chili powder. Sauté the onion, garlic and sweet peppers in the olive oil. Add to the sauce and cook for 5 minutes. Add the turkey meat and beat thoroughly. Add the olives and blanched almonds, and reheat for 3 minutes.

JOSE WILSON (EDITOR)
HOUSE AND GARDEN'S NEW COOK BOOK

Turkey Daube

L'Aliquid

A goose daube may be prepared in the same way, but the goose pieces should first be grilled, skin side up, for 20 minutes (see page 60), in order to draw out excess fat.

To serve 6 to 8

4 to 4.5 kg	turkey, cut up into serving pieces	9 to 10 lb
100 g	pork rinds, cut up into small pieces and blanched	3½ oz
30 g	lard	1 oz
	salt and pepper	
1	bouquet garni	1
60 g each	green bacon and ham, finely chopped	2 oz each
10 cl	brandy	4 fl oz
4 tbsp	chopped onion	4 tbsp
2	carrots, diced	2
1	garlic clove, crushed	1
1 litre	water	1¾ pints
4 tbsp	puréed tomato	4 tbsp

In a sauté pan, brown the turkey pieces and the pork rinds in the lard. Transfer the meat and rinds to a deep casserole or *daubière*, season with salt and pepper, and add the bouquet garni, bacon, ham and brandy.

In the same sauté pan lightly colour the onion and carrot, together with the garlic. Cook the vegetables for a few minutes and add the water mixed with the puréed tomato. Boil for a few minutes and add this mixture to the turkey pieces. Cover the casserole tightly, sealing the lid if necessary with a flour-and-water paste, and cook gently for 2 hours.

RENÉ JOUVEAU
LA CUISINE PROVENÇALE

Turkey Daube

Dindonneau en Daube

Goose daube can be prepared in the same way. The daube may be served cold or reheated in the oven or over a very low heat and served hot.

To serve 8 to 10

4 kg	turkey, cut up into serving pieces	9 lb
	salt, pepper and mixed spices	
100 g	piece bacon rind, blanched and cut up	3½ oz
100 g	green bacon, cut into cubes and lightly sautéed in butter	3½ oz
40 cl	veal stock	¾ pint
	Marinade	
2 to 3 tbsp	brandy	2 to 3 tbsp
2 to 3 tbsp	olive oil	2 to 3 tbsp
2 each	medium-sized onions, shallots and carrots, all chopped	2 each
60 cl	white wine	1 pint
1	bouquet garni	1
1	garlic clove, crushed	1
	orange rind	

Put the turkey pieces into a bowl with a little salt, pepper and spices. Add the marinade ingredients: the brandy, oil, chopped vegetables, wine, bouquet garni, garlic and a few strips of orange rind. Leave to marinate for 2 to 3 hours.

Put alternate layers of turkey, bacon rind and bacon into a large casserole, tucking the bouquet garni into the centre. Add the marinade and the stock. Cover very tightly and cook in a moderate oven, 180°C (325°F or Mark 4), for 2 to 2½ hours. Remove the bouquet garni and leave the turkey to get cold in the liquid.

A. ESCOFFIER
MA CUISINE

Turkey Goulash

Porkölt von Puter

This recipe, originally from Hungary, is also good for other poultry and game.

To serve 8

4 kg	turkey, cut up into serving pieces	8 lb
500 g	*paprikaspeck,* or fat bacon rubbed with paprika, cut into flat strips	1 lb
45 cl	chicken or turkey stock	16 fl oz
4 tbsp	soured cream	4 tbsp
4 tbsp	Tokay or muscat wine	4 tbsp

Lard each of the turkey pieces with the *paprikaspeck.* Brown the pieces well on all sides in a pan. Remove the pieces to a casserole. Add 40 cl (14 fl oz) of stock, cover and braise them slowly in an oven preheated to 150°C (300°F or Mark 2). Halfway through the braising, add the soured cream.

When the braising is completed, remove the turkey, add the remaining stock and the wine to dissolve the deposits in the casserole, and bring to the boil. This liquid can be served as a gravy with no further thickening.

IDA SCHULZE
DAS NEUE KOCHBUCH FÜR DIE DEUTSCHE KÜCHE

Turkey Turnovers

To serve 4

250 g	cooked turkey meat (white and/or dark), chopped	8 oz
1 tbsp	finely chopped fresh parsley	1 tbsp
1 tbsp	chopped fresh chives	1 tbsp
1 tbsp	finely chopped baby white onions	1 tbsp
1 tbsp	chopped sweet green pepper	1 tbsp
10 cl	turkey gravy	4 fl oz
2 tbsp	dry sherry	2 tbsp
	salt and pepper	
1	egg yolk	1
2 tbsp	double cream	2 tbsp
	Pastry	
125 g	plain flour	4 oz
$\frac{1}{4}$ tsp	salt	$\frac{1}{4}$ tsp
100 g	unsalted butter	$3\frac{1}{2}$ oz
5 to 10 cl	iced water	2 to 4 fl oz

Mix the turkey, parsley, chives, onion, and green pepper with the turkey gravy. Add the sherry and season well to taste.

Preheat the oven to 190°C (375°F or Mark 5). For the pastry, sift the flour and salt into a bowl. Cut the butter into the flour and rub the mixture with the fingertips until it resembles breadcrumbs. Add just enough iced water (the least possible) to work the ingredients up quickly to a firm dough.

On a lightly floured board, roll the dough out very thin, about 3 mm ($\frac{1}{8}$ inch) thick, and cut it into 10 cm (4 inch) squares. Put 1 tablespoon of the prepared turkey filling on each square. Fold the dough over the filling, into a triangle shape. Brush the edges with a little water and seal them securely. Beat the egg yolk with the cream and use it to brush the tops of the turnovers. Set them on an ungreased baking sheet and bake for about 15 minutes, or until they are golden-brown.

To serve, pile the freshly baked turnovers on a hot folded napkin on a warm serving plate and serve immediately.

DIONE LUCAS AND MARION GORMAN
THE DIONE LUCAS BOOK OF FRENCH COOKING

Turkey Tetrazzini-Style

To serve 6

250 g	cooked turkey meat, cut into thin strips	8 oz
90 g	cooked spaghetti, drained and chopped	3 oz
60 g	mushrooms, sliced and sautéed	2 oz
30 g	breadcrumbs	1 oz
	butter	
4 to 5 tbsp	grated Parmesan cheese	4 to 5 tbsp
	Cream sauce	
30 g	butter	1 oz
3 tbsp	flour	3 tbsp
$\frac{1}{4}$ litre	double cream	8 fl oz
2 or 3	thin slices onion	2 or 3
3	sprigs parsley	3
$\frac{1}{2}$	bay leaf	$\frac{1}{2}$
1	clove	1
	salt and pepper	
	grated nutmeg	

Make a cream sauce of butter, flour and cream, which has been scalded with the onion, parsley, bay leaf and clove, and then strained. Season the sauce to taste with salt, pepper and a dash of nutmeg. When the mixture is smooth and boiling, stir in the turkey, spaghetti and mushrooms. Mix well and turn the mixture into a baking dish, or 6 individual baking dishes, sprinkle with the breadcrumbs moistened with a little melted butter and mixed with the Parmesan cheese, and bake in a moderate oven preheated to 190°C (375°F or Mark 5) for

10 to 15 minutes, or until the crumbs are brown. Serve at once while still bubbling.

LOUIS P. DE GOUY
THE GOLD COOK BOOK

Pigeon squab

Braised Squabs

Pigeon Bressane

To serve 6

6	squabs, livers and hearts reserved	6
1 tsp each	salt and freshly ground white pepper	1 tsp each
15 g	butter	$\frac{1}{2}$ oz
1 each	carrot and onion, diced	1 each
10 cl each	dry white wine and water	4 fl oz each
	Stuffing	
40 g	unsalted butter	$1\frac{1}{2}$ oz
125 g	mushrooms, finely diced	4 oz
$\frac{1}{4}$ tsp	salt	$\frac{1}{4}$ tsp
$\frac{1}{8}$ tsp	ground black pepper	$\frac{1}{8}$ tsp
	reserved squab livers and hearts, roughly chopped	
100 g	onions, chopped	$3\frac{1}{2}$ oz
175 g	rice	6 oz
35 cl	chicken stock	12 fl oz

To prepare the stuffing, melt 15 g ($\frac{1}{2}$ oz) of the butter in a saucepan, add the mushrooms, and sauté for 5 to 6 minutes until all of the liquid from the mushrooms has evaporated. Add the salt and pepper and the chopped livers and hearts, and sauté for 2 minutes over a medium heat. Set aside.

Melt the remaining butter in another saucepan, add the onions and cook for 1 minute. Add the rice and mix well so that all the grains are coated with butter. Add the stock and bring to the boil. Cover and simmer slowly on top of the stove for 20 minutes. Combine with the mushroom mixture and check the seasoning. Loosely fill each squab with this stuffing, and truss in the normal way.

Season the squabs with salt and pepper. Melt the butter in a large casserole and sauté the squabs over a medium heat for about 10 minutes or until they are browned on all sides. Add the carrot and onion, reduce the heat and simmer for 15 minutes. Add the wine and water, cover and simmer for another 30 minutes. Arrange the squabs on a large serving dish, remove the trussing strings, strain the juices and pour over the squabs. Serve immediately.

JACQUES PÉPIN
A FRENCH CHEF COOKS AT HOME

Braised Stuffed Squabs Catalan-Style

Pigeonneaux à la Catalane

This dish may be served directly from the casserole. Alternatively, strain, degrease and reduce the braising liquid, pour the sauce over the squabs and garnish with the garlic cloves.

To serve 4

4	squabs, livers reserved	4
30 g	butter or rendered goose fat	1 oz
2 to 3 tbsp	raw ham, diced	2 to 3 tbsp
1 tbsp	flour	1 tbsp
8 cl	dry white wine	3 fl oz
4 tbsp	chicken or veal stock	4 tbsp
24	garlic cloves, peeled, blanched for 5 minutes in boiling salted water and drained	24
1	bouquet garni	1
	Stuffing	
	reserved squab livers, finely chopped	
1 tbsp	finely chopped cooked ham	1 tbsp
75 g	fresh breadcrumbs	$2\frac{1}{2}$ oz
1	egg	1
1 tbsp	chopped parsley	1 tbsp
$\frac{1}{2}$ tsp	finely chopped garlic	$\frac{1}{2}$ tsp
	salt and pepper	
	dried thyme and crumbled bay leaf	
1 tsp	cognac	1 tsp

Mix together all the stuffing ingredients, adding a pinch each of the thyme and bay leaf. Stuff the squabs and truss them. In an earthenware casserole, lightly fry the squabs in the butter (or goose fat, as is done in Catalan country) together with the ham. When the squabs are golden-brown on all sides, remove them to a warm platter. Add the flour to the fat in the casserole and cook, stirring, over a low heat until golden. Add the wine and stock and mix well. Return the squabs to the casserole and add the garlic cloves. Do not be afraid of using this quantity of garlic: when blanched, garlic has neither the bitterness nor the pungency that it has when fried raw. Add the bouquet garni and cook, covered, in the oven at 170°C (325°F or Mark 3) for 45 minutes.

PROSPER MONTAGNÉ
MON MENU

Sautéed Squabs Languedoc-Style

Pigeonneaux à la Languedocienne

To serve 2

2	squabs, split down the back, boned and flattened, bones and giblets reserved	2
	salt and pepper	
	paprika	
2	eggs, beaten together with 1 tbsp oil	2
	fresh breadcrumbs	
	clarified butter	

Sauce

	reserved squab bones and giblets	
30 g	butter	1 oz
1	medium-sized onion, coarsely diced	1
1	carrot, coarsely diced	1
	salt and pepper	
1 tbsp	flour	1 tbsp
10 cl	white wine	4 fl oz
20 cl	veal or chicken stock	7 fl oz
1	small garlic clove, crushed	1
1	bouquet garni	1
2 tbsp	Dijon mustard	2 tbsp
1 tbsp	lemon rind, cut into a fine *julienne*, blanched and drained	1 tbsp
1 tbsp	capers	1 tbsp
1 tbsp	lemon juice	1 tbsp

Garnishes

500 g	new potatoes, thinly sliced	1 lb
60 g	butter	2 oz
	salt and pepper	
2	aubergines, peeled and coarsely diced	2
4 tbsp	olive oil	4 tbsp
1 tbsp	onion, finely chopped	1 tbsp
4	tomatoes, skinned, seeded, and roughly chopped	4
1	garlic clove, finely chopped	1
1 tbsp	chopped parsley	1 tbsp
4	lemon slices, rind removed	4

First prepare the sauce. Gently fry the squabs' bones and giblets in 15 g ($\frac{1}{2}$ oz) of butter with the onion and carrot. Season with salt and pepper and sprinkle with the flour. When the vegetables are golden, add the wine and the stock, together with the garlic and bouquet garni, and cook for 40 minutes.

Meanwhile prepare the garnishes. Cook the potatoes in the butter, seasoning them with salt and pepper, and packing them down with the back of a fork. Fry them over a brisk heat, as you would a large pancake. In another pan sauté the aubergines in 3 tablespoons of the oil and season them with salt and pepper. In a third pan, soften the chopped onion in the remaining tablespoon of oil and add the tomatoes. Season with salt and pepper and add the garlic. Cook until the tomatoes' natural liquid has evaporated, then add the parsley. Set the garnishes aside and keep them warm.

Season the squabs with salt and paprika to taste; dip them into the beaten eggs mixed with the oil and seasoned with salt and pepper. Then coat the squabs with the breadcrumbs, pressing the crumbs on with a knife blade so that they adhere firmly. Cook the squabs in clarified butter in a sauté or frying pan for about 20 minutes, or until they are done.

Place the potatoes in a round dish and arrange the squabs on top. Alternate the aubergine and the tomato garnishes round the edge. Sprinkle the squabs with the butter in which they were cooked and arrange the lemon slices on top.

Strain the sauce, return it to the pan and bring it to the boil. Remove the pan from the heat and stir in the mustard, lemon rind, capers, the remaining butter and the lemon juice. Serve separately in a sauceboat.

PROSPER MONTAGNÉ
MON MENU

Squab Pie

Adapted from an old recipe from Lynchburg, Virginia.

To serve 4

2	squabs, trussed	2
	salt and pepper	
1	onion, studded with 2 or 3 cloves	1
2 tbsp	butter	2 tbsp
2 tbsp	chopped parsley	2 tbsp
1 tsp	chopped thyme	1 tsp
2	hard-boiled eggs	2
15 cl	milk or cream	$\frac{1}{4}$ pint
2 tbsp	cracker crumbs, or crushed water biscuits	2 tbsp
250 g	shortcrust pastry (*page 167*)	8 oz

Put the squabs in a saucepan with a tight-fitting lid. Cover with boiling water and boil slowly till tender, with a little salt and an onion and a few cloves. Then take them out, drain and dry, and put in each squab a teaspoon of butter, a little pepper, salt, chopped parsley and thyme. Then put a hard-boiled egg into the cavity of each squab. Lay the birds in a large, round earthenware baking dish, 8 to 10 cm (3 to 4 inches) deep. Strain over them the liquid in which they were simmered. Add the remaining butter and the milk or cream. Add the cracker crumbs (or crushed water biscuits), the remaining parsley and thyme, and a little salt. Put in a few pieces of pastry. Cover with shortcrust pastry and bake in an oven preheated to 180°C (350°F or Mark 4) for 30 to 40 minutes.

MRS HELEN CLAIRE BULLOCK
THE WILLIAMSBURG ART OF COOKERY

To Boil Pigeon with Rice

A dish from Shakespeare's day, from a cookery book of 1609. Unusual and good.

To serve 4

4	pigeons	4
4	bunches thyme, parsley and marjoram	4
30 g	butter	1 oz
1 tbsp	vegetable oil	1 tbsp
	Mutton stock	
	meaty mutton or lamb bones	
1.25 litres	water	2 pints
1	bouquet garni	1
1	medium-sized carrot, sliced	1
1	medium-sized onion, sliced	1
	salt and black pepper	
	Rice	
40 g	long-grain rice	1½ oz
60 cl	single cream, or cream and milk	1 pint
1	large lemon, peeled thinly	1
½ tsp	ground mace	½ tsp
	sugar	

Simmer the stock ingredients for 3 to 4 hours (this can be done in advance). Strain and reduce to ¾ litre (1¼ pints). Season with salt and black pepper.

Put the rice, cream, thinly pared lemon peel and mace into a casserole. Cook in the oven at 130° to 140°C (250° to 275°F or Mark ½ to 1). Stir in the crust occasionally and, should it become too dry, add some creamy milk. Leave for 2 to 3 hours—the slower a rice pudding is cooked, the better it tastes.

Insert the bunches of sweet herbs into the pigeons' cavities. Then brown the pigeons all over in the butter and oil. Next tuck them closely together in a casserole, breast-down, and pour on the boiling stock which should barely cover them. Simmer until cooked, either on top of the stove or in the oven

with the rice—in the latter case, it's important that the casserole should be at the boil when you put it in.

When the flesh begins to show signs of parting from the breastbone, remove the breastbones and cut each pigeon into 2 pieces. Lay them on a serving dish and keep them warm.

Reduce the stock until it has a good strong flavour. It can be thickened a little if you like, but I think that a strongly flavoured thin gravy is preferable as the rice provides the desirable thickness. Season the rice pudding with sugar, and more mace to taste. Smother the pigeons with it, and squeeze the lemon over the rice.

No green vegetables should be served with this dish. They could come before, or after, as an entirely separate course.

JANE GRIGSON
GOOD THINGS

Stuffed Squabs

Pigeons Farcis

To serve 2 to 4

2	squabs, livers reserved and chopped	2
60 g	butter	2 oz
4 to 5 tbsp	chicken or veal stock, or water	4 to 5 tbsp
	Stuffing	
15 g	butter	½ oz
1 tbsp	chopped onion	1 tbsp
3 tbsp	chopped lean bacon	3 tbsp
	reserved squab livers	
1 or 2	chicken livers, chopped (optional)	1 or 2
3 to 4 tbsp	fresh white breadcrumbs	3 to 4 tbsp
1 tsp	chopped parsley	1 tsp
	salt, pepper and mixed spices	
2	egg yolks	2

To make the stuffing, melt the butter in a casserole. Add the onion, stew gently for 6 to 8 minutes, then add the bacon, cooking it 10 minutes or until soft and translucent. Then put the onion and bacon into a bowl containing the squab livers, the chicken livers if you are using them, the breadcrumbs, parsley, salt, pepper and a pinch of mixed spices. Add the egg yolks and mix together well.

Stuff the squabs with this mixture and truss them. Place them with the butter in a heavy sauté pan just big enough to hold them and cook covered over a low heat for 30 to 35 minutes, turning them from time to time. Take the birds out of the pan and remove the trussing strings, then return the birds to the pan with the stock or hot water. Boil for a few seconds until the butter and the juices are well blended.

A. ESCOFFIER
LE CARNET D'ÉPICURE

Pigeons with Peas

Pigeons aux Pois

To serve 4

2	pigeons, halved	2
500 g	shelled young peas	1 lb
60 g	butter	2 oz
1	bouquet garni of parsley, thyme and bay leaf	1
1 tsp	flour	1 tsp
20 cl	veal or chicken stock	7 fl oz
1 tbsp	reduced veal stock (*page 167*), or 3 egg yolks blended with a little cooking liquid	1 tbsp
1 tsp	sugar	1 tsp
	salt	

Put the pigeons in a pan with the peas, butter and the bouquet garni. Place over the heat, add the flour and moisten with the stock. Cover and cook gently for about 30 to 40 minutes.

When the pigeons are cooked, add the reduced stock, the sugar and some salt. (If you have no reduced stock, add a *liaison* of 3 egg yolks blended with a little cooking liquid.)

MENON
LA CUISINIÈRE BOURGEOISE

Guinea-fowl

Roast Guinea-Fowl with Bacon

Pintade Rôtie au Lard Fumé

To serve 3 or 4

1.5 kg	large guinea-fowl, or 2 small (750 g to 1 kg or 1½ to 2 lb) guinea-fowl, wishbone removed	3 lb
	salt and freshly ground pepper	
	dried oregano	
30 g	butter	1 oz
1 tsp	oil	1 tsp
175 g	thin rashers smoked bacon	6 oz
5 tbsp	dry white wine	5 tbsp

Sprinkle salt, pepper and a pinch of oregano into the bird's cavity and add the knob of butter. Truss the bird. Rub it with a few drops of oil, sprinkle it on all sides with salt, pepper and a bit of oregano. Press bacon strips, lengthwise, over the entire breast, tying around a couple of lengths of string to hold them in place. Roast the bird (or birds) in a fairly hot oven, 190°C (375°F or Mark 5), using a heavy, shallow pan (gratin dish, small skillet, etc.) as nearly as possible just the size to contain it, counting from 45 to 50 minutes for an adult bird and 30 minutes for young ones. Remove the bacon for the last 8 to 10 minutes' cooking time to permit the breast to brown lightly.

Clip the trussing strings and pull them out. Transfer the bird to a heated platter. Skim a few tablespoons of excess fat from the roasting pan, add the white wine, and scrape and stir over a high heat until all adherent material is dissolved and the wine is reduced by about half. Send this juice to the table in a heated sauceboat and serve the guinea-fowl with a chestnut purée.

RICHARD OLNEY
THE FRENCH MENU COOKBOOK

Stuffed Guinea-Fowl with Raspberries

Poulet d'Inde à la Framboise Farci

This recipe dates from the mid-17th century, when poulet d'Inde meant either guinea-fowl or turkey. A guinea-fowl is used here. The bird is boned, using the method shown on page 20: if you spit-roast the bird, you will need a cradle spit to support it. Raspberry vinegar is made by steeping fresh raspberries in red wine vinegar for about a month at room temperature. Strain the vinegar before use.

To serve 2

1.5 kg	guinea-fowl	3 lb
100 g	pork fat, chopped	3½ oz
125 g	veal, minced	4 oz
	salt and pepper	
1 or 2	cloves, pounded	1 or 2
1 tbsp	capers	1 tbsp
3	egg yolks	3
¼ litre	veal or chicken stock	8 fl oz
125 g	mushrooms, sliced	4 oz
1	bouquet garni	1
30 g	green bacon, chopped	1 oz
1 tbsp	flour	1 tbsp
2 tbsp	red wine vinegar or, preferably, raspberry vinegar	2 tbsp
1 tbsp	lemon juice	1 tbsp
	fresh raspberries	

Remove the breast flesh from the bird without damaging the skin, then chop the flesh and mix it with the chopped pork fat and minced veal. Add salt and pepper, the cloves and capers, and mix in the egg yolks. Stuff the guinea-fowl with this mixture, truss the bird and place it on a spit—or roast it in a pan in a fairly hot oven, 200°C (400°F or Mark 6), for about 30 minutes, basting after the first 20 minutes. When the guinea-fowl is almost done, put it in a casserole. Add half the stock, the mushrooms and bouquet garni and gently braise on top of the stove, covered, basting regularly, for 15 minutes.

To make the sauce, heat the bacon in a frying pan; when the fat has melted, discard the bacon and stir the flour into the fat. As soon as this is lightly browned, dilute it with the remaining stock and the vinegar. Simmer gently, then pour it into the casserole with the lemon juice, and serve. Sprinkle a handful of fresh raspberries on top.

LA VARENNE
LE CUISINIER FRANÇOIS

Duck

Peking Duck

Peking duck is a world-famous dish which is, in fact, simple to cook. It should be noted that Peking duck has achieved its justifiable fame not only because of the way it is prepared, but also because of the way it is eaten, wrapped in a pancake. The pancakes are smaller and drier than those used in pancake rolls because no egg is used.

To serve 4

1.5 to 2 kg	duck	3 to 4 lb
1 tsp	malt sugar	1 tsp
2 tbsp	soy sauce	2 tbsp
8 tbsp	plum sauce	8 tbsp
8 tbsp	sweet bean paste jam, or *hoisin* sauce	8 tbsp
10	spring onions, trimmed and cut lengthwise into segments	10
½	cucumber, peeled and cut into thin strips each about 5 cm (2 inches) long	½
	Pancakes	
¼ litre	water	8 fl oz
250 g	flour	8 oz
	vegetable oil (or sesame oil)	

Clean the duck and place it in a basin. Boil a large kettle of water and pour it over the duck, dousing it thoroughly. Remove the bird at once and dry it inside and out with a paper towel. Hang it by the neck to dry overnight in an airy place.

Dissolve the malt sugar in the soy sauce and rub the duck with this mixture. When this coating has dried, place the duck on a wire rack in a roasting tin and put in an oven preheated to 190°C (375°F or Mark 5), to roast for 1 hour. Do not baste or open the oven door.

While the duck is roasting, make the pancakes. Boil the water and add it gradually to the flour in a basin. Mix well with a wooden spoon, but do not knead. Cover with a cloth and leave to stand for 20 minutes.

Form the dough into a long roll about 5 cm (2 inches) in diameter. Cut off 1 cm (½ inch) rounds from the roll. Roll the rounds into balls and flatten them again into round cakes 0.5 cm (¼ inch) thick. When you have used up the dough, dust each cake with flour and roll them out into paper-thin pancakes. Lightly brush a heavy frying pan with oil, and cook the pancakes over a low heat for 1¼ minutes on each side. They are ready when parts of the pancake start to curl and bubble slightly; stack the cooked pancakes and cover them with a damp cloth until required.

To serve the duck, first slice off the crisp skin in 3 to 5 cm (1 to 2 inch) squares, then slice off the meat. Place the skin and the meat on separate warmed dishes and bring to the table.

The plum sauce, the jam (or *hoisin* sauce), the spring onions and cucumber strips should all be laid out in separate small dishes. Spread a spoonful of sauce on each pancake, lay pieces of cucumber and spring onion down the centre, add duck skin and meat, and roll up the pancake.

After the duck carcass has been stripped of its meat it is normally boiled with a large amount of cabbage and is traditionally served as a soup to end the meal.

KENNETH LO
CHINESE FOOD

Cantonese Aromatic Roast Duck

To serve 6

2 kg	duck	4 lb
10 cl	soy sauce	4 fl oz
2 tbsp	dry white wine	2 tbsp
½	garlic clove	½
1½ tsp	soy bean paste	1½ tsp
1 tsp each	sugar and grated orange rind	1 tsp each
1	spring onion, trimmed	1
1	piece fresh green ginger root, peeled	1
5 tbsp	oil	5 tbsp

Place the soy sauce, wine, garlic, bean paste, sugar, orange rind, spring onion and ginger in the duck's cavity. Sew up the opening.

Brush the duck's skin with oil. Roast the bird in an oven at 190°C (375°F or Mark 5) for 1 hour, brushing the skin with oil every 10 minutes. Let the bird cool; then chill it and cut into small pieces. Serve cold.

YU WEN MEI AND CHARLOTTE ADAMS
100 MOST HONORABLE CHINESE RECIPES

Roast Honey Duck

To serve 6 to 8

2 to 2.5 kg	duck	4 to 5 lb
	salt	
2	garlic cloves, crushed	2
2 or 3	spring onions, finely chopped	2 or 3
3 tbsp	soy sauce	3 tbsp
3 tbsp	sherry	3 tbsp
2 tbsp	honey	2 tbsp
¼ litre	boiling water	8 fl oz

Wipe the duck with a damp cloth. Rub it lightly, inside and out with salt. Preheat the oven to 180°C (350°F or Mark 4).

Combine the garlic and spring onions with the soy sauce and sherry. Divide the mixture in half.

Mix the honey with one half. Rub some of the mixture into the duck skin and let it stand a few minutes until dry. Then repeat. (Reserve the remainder of the honey mixture. Combine it with the boiling water for basting.)

Pour the remaining half of the soy mixture into the duck cavity. Place the bird on a rack over a drip pan containing several centimetres (2 to 3 inches) of water.

Roast until done (about 1¾ to 2 hours), basting with the reserved honey mixture at 15-minute intervals. (Add more water to the drip pan as it evaporates.)

GLORIA BLEY MILLER
THE THOUSAND RECIPE CHINESE COOKBOOK

Roasted Stuffed Boneless Duck

The technique of boning and stuffing is the same throughout China, but the stuffings used differ from region to region. This recipe is Cantonese in origin. Instructions for boning a duck appear on page 20.

To serve 4 to 6

2.5 kg	duck	5 lb
90 g	dried mushrooms	3 oz
¼ litre	warm water	8 fl oz
400 g	glutinous rice, or Piedmont rice	14 oz
60 cl	cold water	1 pint
4	Chinese sausages, or Italian *salsiccia luganica*	4
2 tbsp	vegetable oil	2 tbsp
4 tsp	salt	4 tsp
1	slice fresh ginger root, about 1 cm (½ inch) thick	1

Soak the mushrooms in the warm water for 20 minutes. Drain them, remove the stems, and cut each mushroom into dice.

Using a 2 litre (3½ pint) saucepan, put the rice in the cold water. First bring to the boil, then cover and simmer for 10 minutes. Turn off the heat, without uncovering or otherwise disturbing the rice, and let the rice rest for 20 minutes.

Boil the Chinese sausages in ¼ litre (8 fl oz) water for 6 minutes. Discard the water. Cool the sausages and then cut them into little dice.

Stir-fry the mushrooms in oil for 1 minute. Add the sausages and mix. Then add the cooked rice and mix well. Add 2 teaspoons salt and mix again.

Remove the bones of the duck, leaving the meat and skin intact. Turn the duck inside out and rub with ginger. Then sprinkle the remaining 2 teaspoons salt all over the inside. Turn the duck skin side out. Stuff, then truss. Cover a cake rack with foil, then cut slits in the foil for air circulation.

Preheat the oven to 190°C (375°F or Mark 5). Pour cold water to a depth of 4 cm (1½ inches) in the bottom of a roasting pan. Place the duck on the rack above the water and roast for 1½ hours.

To serve, cut the stuffed duck with a knife or metal spoon into 6 even pieces.

GRACE ZIA CHU
MADAME CHU'S CHINESE COOKING SCHOOL

Holstein Duck

Ente auf Holsteiner Art

To serve 2 or 3

1.5 to 2 kg	duck, liver and gizzard reserved	3 to 4 lb
	salt and pepper	
	marjoram	
¼ litre	soured cream	8 fl oz
3 to 4 tbsp	water mixed with 2 tsp salt	3 to 4 tbsp
	Stuffing	
	reserved liver and gizzard, chopped	
1 kg	cooking apples, peeled and cut into small pieces	2 to 2½ lb
1	medium-sized onion, chopped	1
250 g	raw ham, diced	8 oz
2	eggs	2
2 tbsp	fresh breadcrumbs	2 tbsp

Season the duck inside and out with salt, pepper and marjoram. Mix together the liver and gizzard, apples, onion, diced ham, eggs and breadcrumbs. Stuff the duck with this mixture and sew it up. Place it breast-down in a roasting pan that has been rinsed with water, pour a little water over the duck, and roast in a moderate oven, 180°C (350°F or Mark 4). Turn the duck after 15 minutes. Baste frequently with the cooking juices and prick below the wings and legs. Add a little more water as soon as the cooking juices begin to brown. After roasting for 60 to 70 minutes, pour the salt water over the duck so that the skin becomes crisp. Roast for another 10 minutes, remove the duck from the oven, and carve. Degrease the pan juices, deglaze with a little water and reduce. Add the soured cream and season to taste with salt and marjoram.

Goose can also be stuffed and roasted in this way.

JUTTA KÜRTZ
DAS KOCHBUCH AUS SCHLESWIG-HOLSTEIN

Basic Roast Duckling and Sauce

To serve 4

2 to 2.5 kg	duckling, giblets reserved and chopped	4 to 5 lb
1 tsp	salt	1 tsp
$\frac{1}{4}$ tsp	pepper	$\frac{1}{4}$ tsp
$\frac{1}{2}$ tsp	dried rosemary	$\frac{1}{2}$ tsp
1	celery stick, roughly chopped	1
1 each	carrot, onion, tomato, all roughly chopped	1 each
$\frac{1}{4}$ litre	beef stock	8 fl oz
	Elderberry and ginger sauce	
	basic duck sauce	
3 tbsp	sugar	3 tbsp
15 g	butter	$\frac{1}{2}$ oz
5 tbsp	cider vinegar	5 tbsp
250 g	elderberry preserves	8 oz
3 tbsp	brandy	3 tbsp
1 tsp	fresh ginger root, finely chopped, or $\frac{1}{2}$ tsp ground ginger	1 tsp

Preheat the oven to 230°C (450°F or Mark 8).

Trim the duckling of excess fat at the base of the tail and inside. Rub it inside and out with salt, pepper and rosemary. Prick the skin on the thighs and breast to allow the fat to drain. Place the duckling and chopped giblets in a pan and roast for $1\frac{1}{2}$ hours, lowering the temperature to 180°C (350°F or Mark 4) after 30 to 40 minutes. Remove the duckling from the pan and keep it warm.

Pour off all but about 2 tablespoons of fat from the roasting pan. Add the chopped vegetables and sauté for 10 minutes, stirring constantly. Add the beef stock. Stir, scraping up the brown bits in the pan, then strain the contents into a saucepan. This basic sauce may be served as is, or turned into elderberry and ginger sauce as follows.

Melt the sugar and butter in a saucepan and cook, stirring,

until the mixture is brown. Add the vinegar and continue to cook over a high heat until the mixture is reduced by half. Stir in the elderberry preserves, the basic duck sauce, the brandy and ginger. Lower the heat and simmer for 10 minutes. Taste the sauce and add salt if necessary.

Cut the duck into quarters using poultry shears, pour the sauce over it and serve.

ALBERT STOCKLI
SPLENDID FARE, THE ALBERT STOCKLI COOKBOOK

Salt Duck

To salt a duck in brine, place 3 litres (5 pints) of water in a large pan. Add 350 g (12 oz) each of coarse sea salt and granulated sugar, and 30 g (1 oz) saltpetre. Bring to the boil and allow to cool. Pour the cold brine into a well-washed crock. Remove the giblets from the duck and soak the bird in the brine for between 36 and 48 hours.

To serve 4

2.5 kg	salted duck, giblets reserved	5 lb
60 cl	water	1 pint
60 cl	dry cider	1 pint
	Onion sauce	
500 g	onions, sliced	1 lb
60 cl	milk	1 pint
30 g	butter	1 oz
30 g	flour	1 oz
	salt and pepper	
	grated nutmeg	

Remove the duck from the brine, rinse it quickly under the cold tap and put it into a deep pan. Cover the duck with the water and dry cider, and add all the giblets except the liver (which can be used up in a pâté). Put on the lid of the pan or cover it with foil, and place in a slow oven, 170°C (325°F or Mark 3), for 2 hours or until the bird is cooked.

To serve the duck hot, prepare an onion sauce in the Welsh style: cook the onions in enough milk to cover them. When they are almost cooked, melt the butter in another pan, stir in the flour and cook for 2 minutes. Add the remaining milk, stirring, until you have a smooth white sauce. Transfer the sauce to the onion pan. Simmer the mixture of sauce and onions for 30 minutes, seasoning well with salt, pepper and nutmeg. Present the sauce separately.

If you prefer cold duck, let it cool in the water and cider. Serve it with an orange and tomato salad, seasoned with sugar, salt and pepper, and dressed with wine vinegar and olive oil.

JANE GRIGSON
GOOD THINGS

Roast Duck with Cucumbers

This is adapted from a recipe, "To dress a Duck with Cucumbers", published in 1747 by Mrs Hannah Glasse, a celebrated English cookery writer.

To serve 4 to 6

Two 3 kg	ducks	Two 6 lb
3	cucumbers, peeled, halved lengthwise, seeded, and cut into 1 cm (½ inch) cubes	3
2	large onions, sliced	2
15 cl	claret	¼ pint
	flour	
	salt and pepper	
90 g	butter	3 oz
15 g	butter into which 1 tbsp flour has been worked	½ oz
30 cl	veal stock	½ pint
250 g	Patna rice	8 oz
1 tbsp	chopped parsley	1 tbsp

Mix the cucumbers with the onions, pour the claret over and leave to marinate for 2 hours.

To roast the ducks, place them in separate roasting tins and rub over the breasts and legs with flour and salt and pepper. Press 30 g (1 oz) butter in small pieces on the breasts, legs and bodies. Put the ducks in an oven preheated to 200°C (400°F or Mark 6). After 20 minutes, remove them and prick the skin over the thighs and bodies with a sharp-pronged fork or pointed skewer; pierce only the skin, not the flesh beneath, in a dozen or so places on each duck. This lets the fat run out so that the skin is thin and crisp when done and the flesh not too greasy. Put the ducks back in the oven cooled to 170°C (325°F or Mark 3). After 20 minutes, remove them, lightly prick again and, if the breasts are getting too dark, cover them with greaseproof paper or foil. After a further 20 minutes, the birds should be cooked.

When the ducks are in the oven, put on salted water for the rice; drain the cucumbers and onions, reserving the wine, and brown them a little in 30 g (1 oz) butter. Sift a very little flour over them and stir in after 3 or 4 minutes. Season well, put in the butter worked with flour (this is a very old way of thickening a sauce), and pour on the stock and reserved red wine. Stew very gently for 15 minutes.

Put the rice into the boiling water and cook until done—approximately 20 minutes. Drain the rice and toss in the rest of the butter. Remove the ducks from the roasting tins, carve them and arrange the pieces in the centre of a flat dish with a border of rice all around. Pour the cucumbers in their sauce over the duck but not over the rice. Sprinkle the rice with chopped parsley. Serve with good crusty bread.

ELISABETH AYRTON
THE COOKERY OF ENGLAND

Four Countries Duck

Vierländer Ente

When making the sauce to accompany this duck, thoroughly degrease the roasting juices before deglazing with the stock and cream.

To serve 3 or 4

2 kg	duck	4 lb
90 g	butter	3 oz
½ litre	stock	18 fl oz
5 tbsp	soured cream	5 tbsp
	Stuffing	
200 g	ham, diced	7 oz
60 g	butter	2 oz
3	medium-sized apples, peeled, cored and cut into rings	3
4 tbsp	breadcrumbs	4 tbsp

Rub the duck all over with the butter. To make the stuffing, fry the ham in the butter, then mix it with the apples and breadcrumbs. Stuff the duck with this mixture and sew up. Roast the duck for about 1 hour at 220°C (425°F or Mark 7). Make a sauce with the roasting juices, stock and soured cream and serve this separately.

MARIA ELISABETH STRAUB
GRÖNEN AAL UND RODE GRÜTT

Grilled Duckling

To serve 4

2.5 to 3 kg	duckling, quartered, washed, dried and trimmed	5 to 6 lb
	salt, preferably coarse cooking salt	
	Marinade	
15 to 20 cl	vegetable oil	6 fl oz
10 cl	red wine vinegar	4 fl oz
1 tsp	salt	1 tsp
	freshly ground black pepper	
1	large onion, thinly sliced	1
3	large garlic cloves, thinly sliced	3
2	large bay leaves, roughly crumbled	2

In a shallow bowl, large enough to hold the duck quarters in one layer, make the marinade by mixing together the oil, vinegar, salt and a few grindings of pepper. Add the onion, garlic and bay leaves. Lay the duck pieces in this marinade, baste thoroughly and marinate at room temperature for at least 3 hours, turning the pieces every half hour. When you are ready to grill the duck, remove the pieces from the marinade. Strain the marinade through a fine sieve and discard the vegetables.

Preheat the grill at its highest setting. Arrange the duck pieces, skin side down, on the grill rack, sprinkle lightly with coarse salt and grill 10 cm (4 inches) from the heat source for about 35 minutes, regulating the heat or lowering the rack so that the duck browns slowly without burning. Baste every 10 minutes or so with the marinade. Turn the pieces over, sprinkle with salt again, and grill for a further 10 to 15 minutes, basting two or three times with the marinade. When the duck is tender and a deep golden-brown, arrange the pieces on a heated serving dish, and serve immediately.

THE EDITORS OF TIME-LIFE BOOKS
FOODS OF THE WORLD—AMERICAN COOKING

Ducks à la Mode

The following is a recipe recorded by Mrs Hannah Glasse in 1747. I give it in her own words, but add one or two more notes.

"Take two fine ducks, cut them into quarters, fry them in butter a little brown, then pour out all the fat, and throw a little flour over them; add half a pint of good gravy, a quarter of a pint of red wine, two shallots, an anchovy and a bundle of sweet herbs; cover them close and let them stew a quarter of an hour; take out the herbs, skim off the fat and let your sauce be as thick as cream. Send it to table and garnish with lemon."

To serve 6 to 8

Two 3 kg	ducks	Two 6 to 7 lb
90 g	butter	3 oz
	flour	
30 cl	veal or chicken stock	½ pint
15 cl	red wine	¼ pint
2	shallots (or 1 onion)	2
4 or 5	anchovy fillets, soaked and drained	4 or 5
1	bouquet garni of thyme, parsley, marjoram and sage	1
	salt and pepper	
1	lemon, quartered	1

Cut the ducks down the backs and then across with game scissors, or joint them in the ordinary way. They are better if lightly floured before browning and again after, as Mrs Glasse suggests. An onion may replace the shallot. For the "bundle of sweet herbs" use a prepared bouquet garni or a bundle of thyme, parsley, marjoram and sage. I don't think a quarter of an hour is long enough to stew the ducks; I stew them for 30 minutes. Many of Mrs Glasse's recipes give very

short cooking times. Thicken the sauce in the usual way to the consistency of cream, and season well. She doesn't mention pepper and salt, but assumes it. Better seasoned at the end, as the anchovies make it fairly salt. It is very good indeed.

ELISABETH AYRTON
THE COOKERY OF ENGLAND

Peppery Duck

Pepereend

This dish is greatly improved if the strained cooking liquid is degreased, skinned and reduced before adding the red pepper, green peppercorns and olives.

To serve 4

2 kg	duck, trussed	4 lb
1	onion, sliced	1
15 g	butter	½ oz
4	thin rashers green bacon	4
1	carrot, sliced	1
1	bouquet garni of parsley, thyme and bay leaf	1
	salt and pepper	
15 cl	dry white wine	¼ pint
30 cl	clear beef stock	½ pint
1	small sweet red pepper, diced	1
1 tbsp	green peppercorns	1 tbsp
12	stuffed green olives	12

Fry the onion slices in the butter until they are transparent. Line the bottom of an ovenproof casserole with the bacon. Spread the carrot and onion slices, with the butter, on top of the bacon and add the bouquet garni. Rub the duck all over with salt and pepper, and place it in the casserole. Cover and bake in an oven preheated to 220°C (425°F or Mark 7) for 15 minutes to colour the duck.

Remove the lid, add the wine to the casserole and reduce for a few minutes over a high heat. Add the stock and bring to the boil. Cover the casserole and place it in a hot oven, 190°C (375°F or Mark 5) for 45 minutes.

Remove the duck and keep it warm. Carefully strain the cooking liquid, and return it to the casserole. Mix in the diced red pepper, green peppercorns and olives. Return the duck to the casserole, cover and place it in the oven for a further 15 minutes at 180°C (350°F or Mark 4). Carve the duck, arrange the pieces in a hot oval dish, and cover them with the sauce. Serve with boiled rice and diced cucumber that has been simmered in butter with a pinch of ground fennel seeds, salt, pepper and sugar.

HUGH JANS
VRIJ NEDERLAND

Braised Duck with Orange

Canard à l'Orange ou à la Bigarade

It is customary to use Seville oranges, which are slightly bitter, for this recipe; but ordinary oranges may be substituted. Do not confuse the *zest* of the orange with the *peel*: the former is only the outer layer of the peel, and contains the essential oil or aroma of the fruit; it is, therefore, important that the zest should be as thin as possible, *without a trace of white pith.* The zest should be cut into a very fine *julienne* and blanched—placed in boiling water for 1 minute—before being added to the sauce.

Duck with orange can be served roasted, but only if the bird is young, tender and plump. If the duck does not meet these requirements, it is better to braise it as in this recipe.

An alternative method is to roast the duck long enough to draw off excess fat, and then braise it, as explained on page 62.

	To serve 4	
2.5 kg	duck, trussed	5 lb
50 g	butter or lard	2 oz
1	carrot, sliced	1
1	large onion, sliced	1
	salt and pepper	
20 cl	dry white wine	7 fl oz
30 cl	stock, preferably veal or duck	½ pint
1 tsp	cornflour mixed with a little water	1 tsp
2 tbsp	Seville orange juice	2 tbsp
1 tbsp	Seville orange zest, cut into a *julienne* and blanched	1 tbsp

Place the duck in a casserole with the butter or lard and the carrot and onion slices. Cook over a high heat, turning the bird until it is well browned all over. Season with salt and pepper. Add the white wine and let it reduce to three-quarters of its volume while continuing to turn the duck. Then add the stock, and let it cook very gently, covered.

When the duck is done—after about 1½ hours—transfer it to a hot platter and keep it warm. Add a little water to the braising liquid to increase the total volume to 30 cl (½ pint); strain the liquid into a small saucepan and degrease. Thicken the liquid with the cornflour; boil for 2 minutes; and finally add the orange juice and the zest.

Serve the duck on the platter, and the sauce separately.

J. B. REBOUL
LA CUISINIÈRE PROVENÇALE

Duck with Figs

Le Canard à la Mantouane

	To serve 4	
2.5 to 3 kg	duck	5 to 6 lb
24	dried figs	24
½ litre	good red port	18 fl oz
40 g	butter	1½ oz
½ litre	veal stock, lightly thickened with *roux*	18 fl oz

Soak the figs in the port for 36 hours in a china bowl with a tight-fitting cover.

Brown the duck in butter in a casserole. After 15 minutes, sprinkle over it some of the port from the figs. Continue adding port at frequent intervals for 20 to 30 minutes until all the wine has been used. Place the figs around the bird and add the stock. Braise in a moderate oven preheated to 180°C (350°F or Mark 4) for 45 minutes, basting frequently.

Place the duck on a warm serving platter, arrange the figs around it and pour over the rich braising liquid from which the fat has been removed.

ÉDOUARD NIGNON
L'HEPTAMÉRON DES GOURMETS

Polish Duck Braised in Red Cabbage

Kaczka Duszona z Czerwoną Kapustą

Cooking duck with cabbage is a common practice in eastern Europe and Scandinavia. Goose or any game bird can also be cooked in this manner with great success. The cooking time will vary, according to the type of bird used.

	To serve 4	
2.5 to 3 kg	duckling	5 to 6 lb
	salt and pepper	
1	medium-sized red cabbage, shredded	1
1 tbsp	lemon juice	1 tbsp
125 g	salt pork, diced	4 oz
1	medium-sized onion, chopped	1
2 tbsp	flour	2 tbsp
¼ litre	red wine	8 fl oz
1 to 2 tsp	sugar	1 to 2 tsp
1 tsp	caraway seeds	1 tsp

Rub the duckling's cavity and skin with a little salt and pepper. Truss the bird. Prick it all over with the tines of a fork.

Place it on a rack in a shallow roasting pan and roast for 10 minutes in an oven preheated to 220°C (425°F or Mark 7). Lower the oven temperature to 180°C (350°F or Mark 4) and roast for 50 minutes longer. Remove the duckling from the pan and keep it hot.

While the duckling is roasting, pour boiling water over the cabbage and drain it immediately. Sprinkle it with lemon juice to preserve its colour. Soak the salt pork in cold water for 10 minutes, changing the water twice. Drain the salt pork and dry it. In a heavy pan, cook the salt pork over medium heat until transparent. Be careful not to burn it. Add the onion and flour and cook for 5 minutes, stirring constantly. Add the cabbage, red wine, sugar, pepper to taste, and caraway seeds. Cover, and simmer over low heat for 30 minutes, or until the duckling is roasted. Stir occasionally.

Transfer the duckling into the pan with the cabbage. Cover and simmer for 45 minutes or 1 hour, or until the duckling is tender. Place it on a hot platter and serve the red cabbage in a separate dish. Plain boiled potatoes and a hearty vegetable, such as braised celery or turnips, are good accompaniments.

NIKA STANDEN HAZELTON
THE CONTINENTAL FLAVOUR

Duck in Almond Sauce

Pato en Salsa de Almendras

To serve 4

2.5 to 3 kg	duck, cut up into serving pieces, liver reserved and roughly chopped	5 to 7 lb
	flour seasoned with salt and pepper	
100 g	lard	3½ oz
1	onion, cut into rings	1
2	garlic cloves, chopped	2
4	tomatoes, skinned and chopped (or 1 small can tomatoes, drained and chopped)	4
About 15	almonds, blanched and toasted	About 15
4 tbsp	dry sherry	4 tbsp
1 tbsp	chopped parsley	1 tbsp

Remove any surplus fat from the duck pieces. Wash and dry them and dip them into well-seasoned flour. Heat the lard in a large shallow earthenware dish or, failing this, a heavy-based saucepan, and gently fry the liver. Remove it with a draining spoon and set aside.

Put the onion and garlic into the pan and fry them gently until the onion begins to soften, then remove them and put them aside with the liver, draining off as much fat as possible. Put the pieces of duck into the remaining fat in the pan, adding a little more fat if necessary, and brown them carefully on all sides. Add the tomatoes. Lower the heat and leave to cook gently with a lid on the pan.

Meanwhile, pound the liver, onion, garlic and almonds together in a large mortar (or use an electric blender) to make a smooth paste. Dilute this with the sherry and add it to the duck. Stir in the chopped parsley and adjust the seasoning. Cover the pan and simmer gently for about an hour or until the duck is tender. It may be necessary to add a little more liquid (stock or water) during the cooking. If you have used an earthenware dish it may be taken straight to the table. Otherwise transfer it to a hot serving dish. Creamed potatoes go well with this.

ANNA MACMIADHACHÁIN
SPANISH REGIONAL COOKERY

Duck in Sour-Sweet Sauce

Anitra in Agrodolce

To serve 3 or 4

2 to 2.5 kg	duck	4 to 5 lb
2	large onions, thinly sliced	2
60 g	butter	2 oz
	salt and pepper	
	flour	
	ground cloves	
40 cl	veal or chicken broth, or water	¾ pint
2 tbsp	chopped fresh mint	2 tbsp
2 tbsp	sugar	2 tbsp
2 tbsp	wine vinegar	2 tbsp

Melt the onions in the heated butter. Season the duck with salt and pepper, roll it in flour, and put it to brown with the onions. Add a pinch of ground cloves. When the duck is well browned pour over the heated broth or water, cover the pan, and cook gently for 2 to 3 hours. Turn the duck over from time to time so that it cooks evenly. When it is tender remove it from the pan and keep it warm in the oven. Pour off as much fat as possible from the sauce and stir in the chopped mint. Have the sugar ready caramelized—that is, heated in a pan with a little water until it turns toffee-coloured. Stir this into the sauce and add the vinegar. See that the seasoning is right and serve the sauce separately as soon as it has acquired a thick syrup-like consistency.

This dish is also excellent cold. Instead of pouring off the fat before adding the mint, sugar, and vinegar, make the sauce as directed and remove the fat—it makes the most delicious dripping—when the sauce is cold.

ELIZABETH DAVID
ITALIAN FOOD

Iranian Braised Duck with Walnut and Pomegranate Sauce

Fesenjan

To serve 4

2.5 kg	duck, cut into quarters and trimmed of all exposed fat	5 lb
4 tbsp	olive oil	4 tbsp
2	medium-sized onions, thickly sliced	2
½ tsp	ground turmeric	½ tsp
500 g	shelled walnuts, pulverized in a blender or with a mortar and pestle, plus 1 tbsp coarsely chopped walnuts (optional)	1 lb
1 litre	water	1¾ pints
2 tsp	salt	2 tsp
	freshly ground pepper	
4 tbsp	bottled pomegranate syrup, or juice squeezed from the fresh fruit	4 tbsp
5 tbsp	lemon juice	5 tbsp
60 g	sugar	2 oz

In a heavy, 30 to 35 cm (12 to 14 inch) skillet, heat the olive oil over a moderate heat. Add the onions and turmeric and, stirring frequently, cook for 8 to 10 minutes, or until the onions are richly browned. With a slotted spoon, transfer them to a heavy 5 to 6 litre (8 to 10 pint) casserole and set the skillet aside. Add the pulverized walnuts, water, salt and a few grindings of pepper to the onions in the casserole and stir until thoroughly blended. Bring to the boil over high heat, reduce the heat to low and simmer, partially covered, for 20 minutes.

Meanwhile, return the skillet to the stove, heat the oil remaining in the pan until a light haze forms above it, and add the duck.

Brown the duck lightly, turning it with tongs or a spoon and adding more oil if necessary. Regulate the heat so that the duck colours evenly on all sides without burning.

Transfer the duck to the simmering walnut mixture, turning the pieces about with a spoon to coat them evenly. Bring to the boil, reduce the heat to low, cover tightly and simmer for about 1½ hours or until the duck is almost tender.

With a large spoon, skim as much fat as possible from the surface of the walnut sauce. Combine the pomegranate syrup or juice, lemon juice and sugar. Add them to the sauce. Simmer for 30 minutes longer and taste for seasoning.

To serve, arrange the pieces of duck on a deep, heated platter and moisten with 30 cl (½ pint) or so of the sauce. Sprinkle it, if you like, with the coarsely chopped walnuts. Serve the rest of the sauce separately in a sauceboat.

THE EDITORS OF TIME-LIFE BOOKS
FOODS OF THE WORLD—THE COOKING OF THE MIDDLE EAST

Duckling with Green Peas

Canetons Nantais

To serve 2 or 3

3 kg	duckling	6 to 7 lb
2 kg	fresh green peas, shelled	4 lb
12	pickling onions	12
30 g	butter	1 oz
100 g	smoked streaky bacon, cut up into small pieces, blanched and drained	3½ oz
1	bouquet winter savory	1
4 tbsp	veal stock	4 tbsp

Roast the duckling at 220°C (425°F or Mark 7). When it is two-thirds cooked (after about 45 minutes), take it from the oven and degrease the pan juices. Then cook the green peas in boiling water for a few minutes and drain them. Lightly cook the onions in the butter. Mix together the bacon pieces, the onions and the peas, and put them around the duckling. Do not forget to add the bouquet of savory, which is indispensable for the green peas cooked in this way. Season the duckling and vegetables, moisten them with the veal stock, then cook them very slowly, 170°C (325°F or Mark 3), until the duckling is perfectly done—about 20 to 30 minutes.

AUSTIN DE CROZE
LES PLATS RÉGIONAUX DE FRANCE

Goose

Roast Goose with Potato Stuffing

Gänsebraten mit Kartoffelfüllung

To serve 7 or 8

4.5 kg	goose, seasoned with salt	10 lb
	Stuffing	
500 g	potatoes, diced small	1 lb
6 tbsp	chopped onion	6 tbsp
3 tbsp	chopped parsley	3 tbsp
20 g	butter	¾ oz
	salt and pepper	
	dried marjoram	

Boil the potatoes in salted water for 8 minutes and drain them. Fry the onion and parsley gently in butter, add the potatoes, shake, season and add a small pinch of marjoram. Place this stuffing in the goose and sew it up. Roast in the usual manner.

HANS KARL ADAM
DAS KOCHBUCH AUS SCHWABEN

Goose with Pears

Based on the recipe of the restaurant Tinell in Barcelona.

To serve 6

3 to 4 kg	goose	7 to 9 lb
	salt	
1	large onion	1
1	carrot	1
6	pears	6
1	lemon, halved	1
2 tbsp	cognac	2 tbsp
$\frac{1}{4}$ litre	chicken stock	8 fl oz

Preheat the oven to 180°C (350°F or Mark 4).

Wipe the goose with a damp cloth. Remove the visible fat from inside the bird and set the fat aside for rendering. Salt the cavity of the bird and place the onion and carrot inside. Puncture the skin of the goose in several places, especially below the legs and breast, to allow fat to run off during roasting.

Place the goose on a rack in a shallow roasting pan and roast it, allowing about 20 minutes to the pound. A meat thermometer inserted into the thigh, without touching the bone, should register 85°C (180°F) when the goose is done. During the cooking, fat that has dripped from the goose should be removed frequently and carefully saved. In the roasting process the goose will lose about 40 per cent of its original weight.

About 30 minutes before the goose is done, cut the pears in halves or quarters, scoop out the cores with a spoon, and rub the cut fruit with the lemon. Put a cup of the goose fat you have been taking from the roasting pan into a baking dish and add the pears, coating them with the fat. Bake them for 20 to 30 minutes, or until the pears are tender, in the same oven as the goose. In a small saucepan over medium heat, reduce the cognac to half its volume and sprinkle it over the pears when they are done.

When the goose is done, transfer it to a warm platter. Pour off and save for future use any fat still in the roasting pan. Scrape loose the goose's body juices that have solidified on the bottom of the pan and combine them over low heat with the chicken stock.

Carve the goose. Remove the baked pears from the fat. Mix the goose slices with the pears. Pour over the juices and serve.

LEE FOSTER (EDITOR)
THE NEW YORK TIMES CORRESPONDENTS' CHOICE

Roast Goose with Giblet Sauce

To serve 6 to 8

4.5 to 5 kg	goose, giblets reserved	10 to 12 lb
8	apples, peeled, cored and quartered	8
1 tbsp	salt	1 tbsp
15 g	butter	$\frac{1}{2}$ oz
$\frac{1}{4}$ litre	boiling water	8 fl oz
1	bunch watercress	1
	Giblet sauce	
	reserved goose giblets	
$\frac{1}{2}$ litre	chicken stock	18 fl oz
1	onion	1
	salt	
	dried thyme	
$\frac{1}{2}$	carrot	$\frac{1}{2}$
$\frac{1}{2}$	stick celery	$\frac{1}{2}$
30 g	butter	1 oz
4 tbsp	goose fat, reserved from roasting	4 tbsp
2 tsp	potato starch	2 tsp

Stuff the apples into the cavity of the goose and truss the legs with string. Secure the neck skin to the back with a skewer, and twist the wings behind the back. Rub the bird with salt and prick it all over with a fork. Spread the butter over the breast and place the bird on a rack in a roasting pan. Add boiling water to the pan and put the goose in an oven preheated to 190°C (375°F or Mark 5). Count 20 minutes per pound cooking time. Turn the goose so that it browns lightly on all sides, and baste frequently during roasting with the simmering giblet stock.

To make the giblet stock, simmer the neck, heart and gizzard in chicken stock to cover, adding the onion, salt to taste, a pinch of thyme, the carrot and the celery. After 2 hours, strain the stock and set it aside. Meanwhile, chop the heart and gizzard. Sauté the liver in the butter and chop it.

When the goose is done, remove the trussing strings and skewer, place the bird on a serving platter and keep it warm while you complete the giblet sauce.

Pour off all but about 4 tablespoons of fat from the roasting pan and stir into it the potato starch. Cook, stirring, over high heat for about 5 minutes. Gradually add about 35 cl (12 fl oz) of strained giblet stock to the pan and cook, stirring, for another 5 minutes. Add the chopped giblets and serve the sauce separately.

Decorate the serving platter with watercress.

JULIE DANNENBAUM
MENUS FOR ALL OCCASIONS

Michaelmas Goose

There is an old saying in Ireland that if you eat goose on Michaelmas Day (September 29) you will never want money all year round. At that time geese weigh about 4.5 kg (10 lb) and are very tender. A traditional Irish stuffing for goose is potato: this cuts the grease and absorbs the rich flavour.

To serve 6

4.5 kg	goose, liver reserved	10 lb
	the goose neck, gizzard and heart, cooked in salted water	
	Stuffing	
750 g	cooked potato	1½ lb
1	medium-sized onion, chopped	1
125 g	salt bacon, diced	4 oz
	salt and pepper	
	reserved goose liver, chopped	
1 tbsp	chopped parsley	1 tbsp
1 tsp	chopped sage	1 tsp
	Onion sauce	
500 g	onions, sliced	1 lb
10 cl each	milk and water	4 fl oz each
1	slice turnip	1
30 g	butter	1 oz
	nutmeg	
	salt and pepper	
	cream (optional)	
	Apple sauce	
250 g	peeled, cored apples	8 oz
10 cl	water	4 fl oz
30 g	butter	1 oz
2 tbsp	sugar	2 tbsp
	nutmeg	
	salt	

Mix all the stuffing ingredients together and season very highly, then put the stuffing into the body of the bird and secure the vent. Place the bird in a roasting pan with ¼ litre (8 fl oz) of the goose giblet stock. Cover the bird with foil and roast in a hot oven at 200°C (400°F or Mark 5) for the first 30 minutes, then lower the heat to 180°C (350°F or Mark 4) and cook for 20 minutes to the pound. Baste at least twice during the cooking and add another ¼ litre (8 fl oz) of stock if it is running dry. Remove the foil for the last 15 minutes to allow the skin to crisp up.

In the 18th and 19th centuries, onion sauce was always served with goose. The onions were cooked in half milk and half water with a slice of turnip. When soft they were mashed, mixed with a knob of butter, a pinch of nutmeg, pepper and salt, and beaten until smooth—sometimes finished with a little cream. Nowadays apple sauce is more usual.

Cook the apples in water until tender. Sieve or mash them and add the butter, sugar and a pinch each of nutmeg and salt. Reheat the sauce and serve hot.

THEODORA FITZGIBBON
A TASTE OF IRELAND

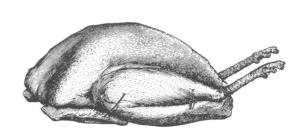

Roast Goose

Oie Rôtie

Despite its name, this Jewish recipe from Poland braises the goose for several hours: the goose pieces are roasted for only a few minutes before serving. The broth may be saved for a soup.

To serve 6 to 8

3 to 4 kg	goose, cut up into 8 pieces, giblets reserved	7 to 9 lb
250 g	pearl barley, washed and drained	8 oz
2 each	onions, carrots, and leeks, cut up into pieces	2 each
1	bouquet garni	1
4 litres	salted water	7 pints
	salt	

Put the barley, vegetables, bouquet garni and the giblets in the salted water, and simmer for at least 4 hours. In the mean time, salt the goose pieces and let them stand at room temperature for 30 minutes; then wash them in cold running water. Place the goose pieces in the barley broth and cook at a simmer until the flesh is tender. The time required will vary according to the type of goose and its age. Young geese are tender after an hour; older birds may need 2 hours or more.

When you judge that the goose is ready to eat, remove it from the pot. Drain the pieces and place them on an oven-proof dish. Baste them with goose fat skimmed from the broth and place them in a very hot oven, 230°C (450°F or Mark 8), until they become nicely browned. Serve without any garnish. The same treatment is suitable for boiling fowl, turkey or duck, and the dish is as good cold as hot.

ÉDOUARD DE POMIANE
CUISINE JUIVE GHETTOS MODERNES

Ragout of Goose with Apples

Ragoût d'Oie aux Pommes

To serve 6 to 8

4.5 to 6 kg	goose, cut up into serving pieces	10 to 13 lb
	salt	
60 g	rendered goose fat	2 oz
2	large onions, thinly sliced	2
4.5 to 6 kg	large russet or other sweet apples, peeled, cored, and cut into eighths	10 to 13 lb
2 tsp	paprika	2 tsp
10 cl	water	4 fl oz

Salt the pieces of goose, leave them for 30 minutes, then rinse them in cold water and dry. In a casserole, brown the goose pieces in the goose fat; add the onions and sauté until they are a golden colour. Salt lightly. Add the apples, sprinkle with the paprika, and pour in the water. Cover and cook slowly for at least 2 hours, or until the goose is tender. Add more salt to correct the seasoning if necessary. You may have to add a little water from time to time during the cooking, but when the goose is ready to serve there should be no water left in the casserole; the apples should be bathed only in the goose fat.

ÉDOUARD DE POMIANE
CUISINE JUIVE GHETTOS MODERNES

Old-Fashioned Braised Goose

La Compôte d'Oie Comme Autrefois

The marc *called for in the following recipe is a brandy distilled from the grape skins and pips after wine is made.*

To serve 6

3 kg	goose	6 to 7 lb
60 g	butter	2 oz
1 kg	onions, finely chopped	2 to 2½ lb
500 g	shallots, finely chopped	1 lb
10	garlic cloves, finely chopped	10
1 litre	dry white wine	1¾ pints
6	large, ripe tomatoes, skinned, seeded and chopped	6
1	bouquet garni	1
	salt and pepper	
10 cl	brandy or *marc*	4 fl oz

Brown the goose lightly in butter in a large casserole. Add the onions, shallots and garlic and fry for a few minutes more until they are soft but not browned. Pour in the wine and add the tomatoes and bouquet garni.

Salt and pepper lightly, cover the casserole, and braise in a low oven, 150°C (300°F or Mark 2), for about 5 hours, or until the goose flesh separates from the bones. Remove and bone the goose, discarding the bones. Keep the meat warm in a covered dish. Reduce the liquid in the casserole to a syrupy consistency, and add the brandy or *marc*. Remove the bouquet garni, taste the sauce and adjust the seasoning. Pour the sauce over the goose. Serve very hot.

MAURICE BÉGUIN
LA CUISINE EN POITOU

Goose or Turkey à-la-Daube

This recipe has been adapted from E. Smith's Compleat Housewife, *Williamsburg, 1742.*

To serve 6 to 8

4.5 kg	goose or turkey	10 lb
5 or 6	rashers bacon	5 or 6
1.25 litres	white wine	2 pints
2 to 3 litres	strong goose, turkey or veal broth	3½ to 5 pints
60 cl	vinegar	1 pint
¼ tsp	whole allspice	¼ tsp
2	bay leaves	2
¼ tsp each	chopped, fresh, sweet marjoram and winter savory	¼ tsp each
1	bunch spring onions, trimmed	1
250 g	mushrooms, sliced and sautéed	8 oz
1	lemon, peeled and diced	1
2 or 3	anchovies, pounded	2 or 3
30 g	butter, cooked over low heat until it browns	1 oz
1	lemon, thinly sliced	1

Lard the goose or turkey with bacon, and half roast it at 190°C (375°F or Mark 5), for about 1 hour; then take it off the spit or out of the oven, and put it in as small a pot as will hold it. Add the white wine, and enough strong broth to cover the bird. Add the vinegar, allspice, bay leaves, sweet marjoram, winter savory and spring onions. Simmer over low heat for another hour. When the bird is ready, lay it in the serving dish and make a sauce by adding to the liquor the mushrooms, diced lemon and the pounded anchovies. Thicken the sauce by swirling in the brown butter off the heat, and garnish the fowl with slices of lemon.

MRS HELEN CLAIRE BULLOCK
THE WILLIAMSBURG ART OF COOKERY

Poached Goose with Garlic Cream Sauce

L'Oie à l'Instar de Visé

Poached goose with garlic cream sauce is a traditional Belgian dish. The recipe given here is by Maurice des Ombiaux, a noted gastronome of the 1920s and 1930s. The method for binding the sauce with egg yolks and cream is described in the recipe for fowl with rice on page 128.

To serve 6 to 8

5 kg	goose	11 lb
1	bouquet garni	1
2	large onions	2
4	carrots	4
1	garlic head	1
	peppercorns	
15 g	butter	½ oz
15	garlic cloves, peeled	15
1 litre	milk	1¾ pints
5	egg yolks	5
20 cl	double cream	7 fl oz

Place the goose in a cooking pot containing salted water. Bring to the boil, skimming off any scum that rises to the surface. Add the bouquet garni, onions, carrots, the whole garlic head and a few peppercorns. Reduce the heat to low and simmer for about 2 hours or until the goose is tender. Remove the goose, cut it up into serving pieces, pat the pieces dry and brown them lightly in a frying pan with the butter.

Meanwhile, prepare the sauce by first simmering the garlic cloves in the milk for about 15 minutes. Add the egg yolks and cream to bind the sauce.

Arrange the goose pieces on a platter. Pour on the butter from the frying pan; then add the sauce, garlic and all.

GASTON DERYS
L'ART D'ÊTRE GOURMAND

Sweet and Sour Goose Legs

Goosküül Söötsuur

To serve 4

4	whole goose legs	4
60 g	butter	2 oz
1 tbsp	sugar	1 tbsp
2 tsp	cornflour, mixed with a little water	2 tsp
	Stock	
¼ litre	white vinegar	8 fl oz
4 tbsp	sugar	4 tbsp
2	large onions, peeled	2
2	bay leaves	2
1 tbsp	mustard seeds	1 tbsp
¼ tsp	ground cinnamon	¼ tsp
1 tsp	salt	1 tsp

Put all the stock ingredients into a pan. Add the goose legs to the pan, cover with water, bring to the boil, reduce the heat and simmer gently for 2 hours. Remove the goose legs, cool and cover them. Set the stock aside in a cold place for a few hours to solidify the fat. Then brown the legs in butter in a deep heavy frying pan, sprinkling them with a little of the sugar. Skim the solidified fat from the cold stock and put it in the pan with the goose legs. Add the remaining sugar, letting it caramelize over moderate heat. Remove the pieces of goose to a hot platter, pour in 35 cl (12 fl oz) of the vinegary stock, and add the cornflour mixture to thicken the sauce. Simmer a few minutes and pour the sauce over the goose pieces.

JUTTA KÜRTZ
DAS KOCHBUCH AUS SCHLESWIG-HOLSTEIN

Preserved Goose

Confit d'Oie

To serve 8 to 10

6 to 8 kg	goose	13 to 17 lb
10 cl	water	4 fl oz
	lard (if required)	
	coarse salt	
3	garlic cloves	3
12	peppercorns	12
2	cloves	2
1	bay leaf	1
	thyme	

Clean the goose. Remove the fat from inside and from around the gizzard and melt it. There should be at least 1 litre (1¾ pints); if not, add melted lard. Add the water and place the pan over a gentle heat to render the fat. In the mean time, cut the goose into 4 pieces, making 2 breast pieces and 2 whole leg pieces. Rub the pieces generously with coarse salt. Leave them in a bowl with the garlic, peppercorns, cloves, bay leaf and a little thyme for 24 hours, moving the pieces occasionally so that each is covered with salt.

After 24 hours wipe off the salt and dry the pieces with a towel; cook them in the fat for 1 hour or until done, simmering slowly and never allowing the fat to get hot enough to fry the meat. To test when done, pierce with a metal skewer. If the juice which flows out when the skewer is withdrawn is clear and shows no pink colour, the goose is cooked enough. Remove the goose pieces from the fat, drain them, and separate the meat from the bones.

Strain the fat and separate it from the gravy. Pour about 2.5 cm (1 inch) of the clear melted fat into a large jar and let it harden. Place the pieces of meat on this, then pour in the remaining fat, making sure that it covers every part of the meat, that none of the meat is uncovered and that none touches the sides of the jar. It is very important that no gravy at all be left in the fat. Let the jar stand about 2 days then pour in more fat to fill any interstices that were formed by the cooling fat. Cover closely with waxed paper and keep in the refrigerator or other cold place until ready to use.

LOUIS DIAT
FRENCH COOKING FOR AMERICANS

<hr>

Stuffed Goose Neck

You may not often eat goose; but when you do, make sure you are given the whole of the neck with the bird. The skin of the neck can make a wonderful meal. Stuff it with chopped goose liver, minced pork or veal, onion and herbs and serve it hot with red cabbage or cold with salad. Thin slices of stuffed goose neck are delicious as part of an hors d'oeuvre.

To serve 4

1	goose neck	1
1	goose liver, finely chopped	1
1	medium-sized onion, finely chopped	1
1 tbsp	chopped parsley	1 tbsp
	dried sage	
	salt and pepper	
3 tbsp	fresh white breadcrumbs	3 tbsp
2	eggs, beaten	2
125 g	rendered goose fat	4 oz

Peel off the skin from the goose neck (use the bones for stock). Combine the liver, onion, parsley, sage, seasoning and bread-

crumbs. Bind with the beaten eggs and pack the stuffing in the neck skin.

Sew up each end of the neck and roast it in the goose fat, basting frequently, for 40 minutes in a medium oven preheated to 190°C (375°F or Mark 5).

Remove the stitches and cut the neck into slices before serving.

MARIKA HANBURY TENISON
LEFT OVER FOR TOMORROW

<hr>

Sauces and Stuffings

<hr>

Bread Sauce

This sauce, a traditional accompaniment for roast chicken and turkey, may also be served with other birds. It should have the consistency of a medium-thick oatmeal porridge, creamy, and utterly free of lumps. It should also be well flavoured with onion and seasonings.

To serve 4

1	medium-sized onion, stuck with 3 cloves	1
1	bay leaf	1
40 cl	milk	$\frac{3}{4}$ pint
3 to 4 tbsp	fresh white breadcrumbs	3 to 4 tbsp
	salt and pepper	
	ground nutmeg or cayenne pepper (optional)	
15 g	butter	$\frac{1}{2}$ oz
1 tbsp	cream	1 tbsp

Put the onion stuck with cloves, the bay leaf and milk into a saucepan. Cover, and barely simmer over very low heat for 15 to 20 minutes, or until the milk is well flavoured.

Remove the onion and bay leaf, and stir the crumbs into the milk. Simmer over low heat for about 5 minutes, or until the sauce is thickened and creamy, stirring constantly.

Remove the pan from the heat and season the sauce with salt and pepper and nutmeg or cayenne pepper. Blend in the butter and cream. Reheat the sauce gently and serve at once.

Note: Depending on individual tastes, this sauce can be made thicker or thinner. If a thicker sauce is wanted, add 1 or 2 more tablespoons of breadcrumbs. If a thinner sauce is called for, decrease the breadcrumbs accordingly.

NIKA STANDEN HAZELTON
THE CONTINENTAL FLAVOUR

Cranberry Sauce

To make about 35 cl (12 fl oz)

250 g	firm, unblemished, fresh cranberries	8 oz
200 g	sugar	7 oz
10 cl	water	4 fl oz
1 tsp	finely grated orange rind	1 tsp

Wash the cranberries in a colander under cold running water. Combine the berries with the sugar and water in a small, heavy enamelled or stainless-steel saucepan and, stirring frequently, bring them to the boil over high heat. Then reduce the heat to low and, still stirring from time to time, simmer uncovered for 4 to 5 minutes, or until the skins of the cranberries begin to pop and the berries are tender. Do not overcook them to the point where they become mushy.

Remove the pan from the heat and stir in the orange rind. With a rubber spatula, scrape the entire contents of the pan into a small bowl. Refrigerate for 2 to 3 hours or until the sauce is thoroughly chilled.

THE EDITORS OF TIME-LIFE BOOKS
FOODS OF THE WORLD—AMERICAN COOKING: NEW ENGLAND

Sage and Onion Stuffing

To stuff a 6 kg (13 lb) goose, or 2 ducks

4	large onions	4
10	fresh sage leaves	10
125 g	fresh breadcrumbs	4 oz
	salt and pepper	
40 g	butter	1½ oz
1	egg yolk	1

Peel the onions and put them into boiling water. Let them simmer for 5 minutes or rather longer, and, just before they are taken out, put in the sage leaves for a minute or two to take off their rawness. Chop the onions and sage very fine, add the bread, seasoning and butter, and work the whole together with the yolk of an egg. The stuffing will now be ready for use. It should be rather highly seasoned, and the sage leaves should be very finely chopped. Many cooks do not parboil the onions in the manner just stated, but merely use them raw. The stuffing then, however, is not nearly so mild and, to many tastes, its strong flavour would be very objectionable. When made for goose, a portion of the liver of the bird, simmered for a few minutes and very finely minced, is frequently added to this stuffing; and where economy is studied, the egg may be dispensed with.

MRS ISABELLA BEETON
THE BOOK OF HOUSEHOLD MANAGEMENT

Potato Filling

The Pennsylvania Dutch are very fond of what they call potato filling for turkeys and other birds. It is not as delicate as some stuffings, but it is unusual and delicious.

To stuff a 5.5 kg (12 lb) turkey

1	large onion, finely chopped	1
1	small garlic clove, finely chopped	1
90 g	bacon or chicken fat	3 oz
250 g	turkey, pig's or chicken livers, chopped	8 oz
1	stick celery, chopped	1
400 g	mashed potato, blended with ½ tsp baking powder	14 oz
4 tbsp	sherry or white wine (optional)	4 tbsp
250 g	1 cm (½ inch) croûtons, dried in the oven	8 oz
4 tbsp	chopped parsley	4 tbsp
1 tbsp	salt	1 tbsp
1 tsp	dried thyme	1 tsp
½ tsp	freshly ground pepper	½ tsp
½ tsp	Tabasco sauce	½ tsp

In a large skillet, sauté the onion and garlic in the fat, and when they are nicely browned, add the liver. Cook, shaking the pan well, until the liver just changes colour. Add the celery and cook about 3 minutes more. Blend this mixture in with the mashed potato. Scrape the pan well, or rinse it with the sherry or white wine; add the scrapings to the stuffing along with the croûtons and the herbs and seasonings, blending thoroughly.

JAMES BEARD
JAMES BEARD'S AMERICAN COOKERY

Oyster Stuffing for Turkey

Adapted from an old Williamsburg recipe, circa 1837.

To stuff a 5 kg (11 lb) turkey

60 cl	shelled oysters	1 pint
200 g	cracker crumbs, or crumbled water biscuits	7 oz
20 cl	single cream	7 fl oz
60 g	butter, melted	2 oz
	salt and pepper	

Place the oysters and the cracker crumbs in a large bowl. Add the cream and butter. Season to taste with salt and pepper. Mix gently together. Set the mixture aside for about 1 hour before use to allow the flavours to mingle.

MRS HELEN CLAIRE BULLOCK
THE WILLIAMSBURG ART OF COOKERY

Soyer's Recipe for Goose Stuffing

To stuff a 5 kg (11 lb) goose

4	apples, peeled and cored	4
4	onions	4
4	fresh sage leaves	4
4	fresh lemon thyme leaves	4
4 or 5	boiled potatoes, mashed	4 or 5
	pepper and salt	

Boil the apples, onions, sage and thyme in a stewpan with sufficient water to cover them. When done, pulp them through a sieve, after first removing the sage and thyme. Then add sufficient pulp of potatoes to cause the stuffing to be sufficiently dry without sticking to the hand. Add pepper and salt, and stuff the bird.

MRS ISABELLA BEETON
THE BOOK OF HOUSEHOLD MANAGEMENT

Cornbread Stuffing

To stuff a 6 kg (13 lb) turkey

1 each	turkey neck, gizzard and liver	1 each
150 g	spring onions, finely chopped	5 oz
2	sticks celery, finely chopped	2
½	sweet green pepper, finely chopped	½
60 g	butter	2 oz
24	oysters, cleaned, drained (liquor reserved) and chopped	24
	salt and pepper	
	oyster liquor, stock or milk	
	Cornbread	
125 g	flour	4 oz
150 g	white cornmeal	5 oz
1 tsp	baking powder	1 tsp
½ tsp	baking soda	½ tsp
1 tsp	salt	1 tsp
2 tbsp	sugar (optional)	2 tbsp
¼ litre	buttermilk	8 fl oz
1	egg	1
2 tbsp	melted shortening	2 tbsp

The cornbread batter can be prepared several hours ahead. Put the flour, cornmeal, baking powder, soda, salt and sugar into a sifter; sift together into a bowl. Add the buttermilk and stir well. Add the egg and shortening and beat well. When ready to bake, stir the mixture, pour it into a hot, greased 22 cm (9 inch) iron skillet. Place in an oven preheated to 200°C (400°F or Mark 6) for approximately 20 minutes or until brown.

Boil the turkey neck and gizzard in enough water to obtain about 15 cl (¼ pint) stock. Chop the liver and the gizzard when cool. In a large skillet, sauté the spring onions, celery and green pepper in the butter until they are soft and transparent. Add the liver, gizzard and oysters, stirring lightly for 1 to 2 minutes. Remove from the heat and mix in crumbled cornbread. Add salt and pepper to taste. Moisten to desired consistency with oyster liquor, stock or milk.

THE JUNIOR LEAGUE OF NEW ORLEANS INC.
THE PLANTATION COOKBOOK

Louisiana Yam and Apple Stuffing

To stuff 2 ducklings, 2 capons, or a 5.5 kg (12 lb) turkey

500 g	apples, diced	1 lb
2	sticks celery, chopped	2
¼ litre	water	8 fl oz
1.5 kg	yams	3 lb
2 tbsp	lemon juice	2 tbsp
1 tsp	ground cinnamon	1 tsp
125 g	butter	4 oz
150 g	brown sugar	5 oz
	salt	
125 g	pecans, chopped	4 oz
	grated rind of 1 lemon	

Simmer the apples and celery in the water until just tender. Drain, reserving the liquid. Meanwhile boil the yams in water to cover for approximately 25 minutes. Peel the yams and mash with lemon juice, cinnamon, butter, brown sugar, and salt. Moisten with the apple and celery liquid. Add the apple, celery, pecans and lemon rind. Toss. Correct seasoning.

THE JUNIOR LEAGUE OF NEW ORLEANS INC.
THE PLANTATION COOKBOOK

Standard Preparations

A Basic White Sauce

To make about 45 cl ($\frac{3}{4}$ pint)

30 g	butter	1 oz
2 tbsp	flour	2 tbsp
60 cl	milk	1 pint
	salt	
	white pepper	
	freshly grated nutmeg (optional)	
	double cream (optional)	

Melt the butter in a heavy saucepan. Stir in the flour and cook, stirring, over a low heat for 2 to 5 minutes. Pour in all of the milk, whisking constantly to blend the mixture smoothly. Raise the heat and continue whisking while the sauce comes to the boil. Season with a very little salt. Reduce the heat to very low, and simmer for about 40 minutes, stirring every so often to prevent the sauce from sticking to the bottom of the pan. Add white pepper and a pinch of nutmeg if desired; taste for seasoning. Whisk again until the sauce is perfectly smooth, and add cream if you prefer a richer and whiter sauce.

Batter for Deep Frying

The consistency of this batter may be varied by increasing or decreasing the proportion of liquid to flour. A thin batter will cook crisper and lighter, but some of it will be lost in the oil during frying; a thicker batter clings better, but tends to be more stodgy.

To coat about 10 chicken pieces

125 g	flour	4 oz
$\frac{1}{4}$ tsp	salt	$\frac{1}{4}$ tsp
2	eggs, yolks separated from whites	2
3 tbsp	olive oil or melted butter	3 tbsp
20 cl	beer or water	7 fl oz

Mix together the flour, salt, egg yolks and oil or butter in a bowl. Gradually add the beer or water, and whisk for only as long as it takes to produce a smooth batter. Do not overwork the mixture. Leave the batter to rest for at least 1 hour at room temperature, otherwise it will shrink away from the poultry pieces and provide an uneven coating.

Beat the egg whites until they form soft peaks and fold them into the batter just before using.

Chicken Stock

Chicken stock is prepared in the same way as veal stock (see below), but it is cooked for a shorter time. All the scum and dissolved fats must be completely removed to produce a clear and digestible liquid. Old hens and roosters will produce the richest, most flavourful version. Duck, turkey or other poultry stocks are prepared in the same way as chicken stock.

To make about 2 litres ($3\frac{1}{2}$ pints)

2 kg	chicken carcasses, trimmings, necks, gizzards and hearts	4 lb
3 to 4 litres	water	5 to 7 pints
	salt	
200 g	carrots, scraped and topped	7 oz
2	large onions, 1 stuck with 2 cloves	2
1	large leek, split and washed	1
1	stick celery	1
1	large bouquet garni	1

Put all the chicken pieces in a stock-pot and cover by 5 cm (2 inches) with water. Bring to the boil over a low heat, skimming to remove the scum as it rises to the surface. Occasionally, add a little cold water to help precipitate the scum. Add the salt, vegetables and bouquet garni, pushing them down into the liquid to make sure that they are all submerged. Return the liquid to the boil, and simmer gently for 2 hours, skimming and degreasing at intervals. Strain the stock through a colander into a bowl. Discard the chicken pieces, vegetables and bouquet. Cool the stock and remove every trace of fat.

Veal Stock

To make 2 to 3 litres ($3\frac{1}{2}$ to 5 pints)

1	veal knuckle bone, sawn into 5 cm (2 inch) pieces	1
2 kg	meaty veal trimmings (neck, shank or rib tips)	4 lb
3 to 5 litres	water	5 to 8 pints
4	carrots, scraped and topped	4
2	large onions, 1 stuck with cloves	2
1	whole garlic head, unpeeled	1
1	stick celery	1
1	leek, split and washed	1
1	large bouquet garni	1
	salt	

Put the bones into a heavy stock-pot and place the meat on top of them. Add cold water to cover by 5 cm (2 inches). Bring to the boil over a low heat, starting to skim before the liquid reaches the boil. Keep skimming, occasionally adding a glass of cold water, until no more scum rises. Do not stir up the bones and meat, lest you cloud the stock.

Add the vegetables, bouquet garni and a dash of salt to the pot, pushing them down into the liquid so that everything is submerged. Continue skimming until the boil is reached. Reduce the heat to very low, and cook at a bare simmer for 4 hours, skimming off the surface fat 3 or 4 times.

Strain the stock by pouring the contents of the pot through a colander into a large bowl or clean pot. Discard the bones, veal pieces, vegetables and bouquet. Cool the strained stock and skim the last traces of fat from the surface. If there is any residue at the bottom of the container after the stock cools, decant the clear liquid carefully and discard the sediment.

To reduce veal stock. Pour the stock into a wide saucepan and bring it to the boil, removing any scum or skin that forms on the surface. Continue boiling until the liquid reaches the desired consistency or quantity.

To prepare veal stock for use as an aspic glaze. Reduce the stock further until it reaches a syrupy consistency. Test the consistency by placing a spoonful on a plate and refrigerating it for 10 minutes. If the stock sets to a trembling jelly it is ready.

To make a velouté. Thicken veal or chicken stock with a *roux*.

To make 1.5 litres (2½ pints)

60 g	butter	2 oz
4 tbsp	flour	4 tbsp
2 litres	veal or chicken stock	3½ pints

Melt the butter in a heavy saucepan over a low heat and stir in the flour until this *roux* mixture is smooth. Cook, stirring constantly, for 2 to 3 minutes. When the *roux* stops foaming and is a light golden colour, pour in the stock and whisk continuously until it reaches the boil. Move the saucepan half off the heat, so that the liquid on one side of the pan maintains a steady, but very light boil and a skin of fat and impurities forms on the surface of the other, calm side. Remove the skin with a spoon from time to time. Cook for 30 minutes or more.

Pancake Batter

To make about 20 small pancakes

45 g	flour	1½ oz
	salt	
3	eggs	3
30 cl	milk or water	½ pint
1 tbsp	brandy	1 tbsp
3 tbsp	melted butter	3 tbsp

Place the flour in a mixing bowl and make a well in the centre. Add a pinch of salt, then add the eggs, and whisk from the centre gradually outwards until the mixture is fairly smooth. Whisk in the liquids, adding the butter last. The batter should have the consistency of single cream. Add more or less of the milk or water to achieve the correct consistency. The batter can be used immediately.

Shortcrust and Rough-Puff Pastry

One simple formula produces dough for both plain shortcrust pastry and for rough-puff pastry. The difference is in how you roll it out.

To cover a 20 cm (7 to 8 inch) pie dish

125 g	flour	4 oz
¼ tsp	salt	¼ tsp
125 g	cold unsalted butter, cut into small pieces	4 oz
3 to 4 tbsp	cold water	3 to 4 tbsp

Mix the flour and salt in a mixing bowl. Add the butter and cut it into the flour rapidly, using 2 table knives, until the butter is in tiny pieces. Do not work for more than a few minutes. Add half the water and, with a fork, quickly blend it into the flour and butter mixture. Add just enough of the rest of the water to allow you to gather the dough together with your hands into a firm ball. Wrap the dough in plastic film or waxed paper and refrigerate it for 2 to 3 hours, or put it in the freezer for 20 minutes until the outside surface is slightly frozen.

To roll out shortcrust pastry. Remove the ball of pastry dough from the refrigerator or freezer and put it on a cool floured surface (a marble slab is ideal). Press the dough out partially with your hand, then give it a few gentle smacks with the rolling pin to flatten it and render it more supple. Roll out the dough from the centre, until the pastry forms a circle about 1 cm (½ inch) thick. Turn the pastry over so that both sides are floured and continue rolling until the circle is about 3 mm (⅛ inch) thick. Roll the pastry on to the rolling pin, lift it up and unroll it over the pie dish. Trim the pastry to within 1 cm (½ inch) of the edge of the dish, roll the edges under, press firmly with thumb and forefingers and crimp the edges.

To roll out rough-puff pastry. Place the dough on a cool floured surface and smack it flat with the rolling pin. Turn the dough over to make sure that both sides are well floured, and roll out the pastry rapidly into a rectangle about 30 cm (1 foot) long and 12 to 15 cm (5 to 6 inches) wide. Fold the two short ends to meet each other in the centre, then fold again to align the folded edges with each other. Following the direction of the fold lines, roll the pastry into a rectangle again, fold again in the same way and refrigerate for at least 30 minutes. Repeat this process two or three more times before using the pastry to cover a pie. Always let the pastry dough rest in the refrigerator in between rollings out.

Recipe Index

English recipe titles are listed under the name of each bird. Foreign titles are listed alphabetically.

General Index/Glossary

Included in this index are definitions of many of the culinary terms used in this book; definitions are in italics. The recipes in the Anthology are listed in the Recipe Index on page 168.

Al dente: *an Italian expression. Literally translated as "to the tooth", it is used to describe the correct texture of cooked pasta—firm to the bite, not too soft on the outside, and barely cooked through to the centre.*

Allspice: *the dried berry—used whole or ground—of a member of the myrtle family. It is called allspice because it has something of the aroma of clove, cinnamon, and nutmeg combined.*

Aluminium, 43; baking, in 74-75

Aromatics: *the term for all substances that give out their aroma and flavour when used in cooking. Herbs and spices are aromatics, but there are also many aromatic vegetables, including the onion family and most root vegetables;* 10, 53, 54-55

Artichoke heart: *the tender, edible portion of a young artichoke that remains when the inedible parts of the leaves have been removed;* 77

Artichokes, preparing as garnish, 11

Aspic: *a clear jelly made by concentrating, and then cooling, gelatinous stock. It is used as a glaze to cover cold savoury dishes;* preparation, 86

Aubergines, as garnish, 11

Bacon, in a pot-roast, 72; preparing as a garnish, 54

Bain-marie: *a large pot or vessel in which water is heated. A small pot is placed inside and the contents of the smaller pot are cooked or reheated. Used for sauces and other preparations that cannot take direct heat or boiling.*

Baking, in aluminium, 74-75; in clay pot, 74-75

Bard: *to cover meat, game or poultry with thin slices of pork fat or bacon. The fat melts during cooking, thus basting (q.v.) the meat and keeping it moist;* 40

Basil, 15

Baste: *to pour or spoon fat or liquid over food—particularly roast meats—to prevent it from drying up during cooking;* 43, 62; fatty birds, 46, 62; during grilling, 50-51

Baster, 62

Batter: *a mixture of flour, beaten egg and a liquid, such as milk, that is used to make pancakes and to coat food for deep frying;* for deep frying 31, 32; for pancakes, 80-81

Bay, 14

Beans, Broad, as garnish, 10, 11

Béchamel sauce: *a "white" or "cream" sauce made from milk thickened with a roux (q.v.). In the context of this book, it is synonymous with white sauce; but it has many variants, ranging from a simple reduction of pure cream to a roux-thickened mixture of stock and milk, to milk cooked with aromatics (onion, carrot, herbs and seasoning) before being added to a roux.*

Beer, in batter, 32, 80; as a cooking liquid, 59

Beurre manié: *a paste made by mixing flour and butter. Used to bind and thicken sauces, it is added raw to the sauce, whereas a roux (q.v.) is cooked.*

Blanch: *to plunge food into boiling water and simmer (q.v.) it for a few minutes. This is done for a number of reasons: to remove excess flavour, such as the excess saltiness of bacon; to soften or wilt (q.v.) vegetables; to facilitate the removal of skins or shells. Another meaning is "to whiten".*

Boiling fowl, 6; braising, 60-61; poaching, 66

Boning whole poultry, 20-21; chicken breasts, 28-29

Bouillon: *the French name for stock or broth.*

Bouquet garni: *a bunch of mixed herbs— the classic three being parsley, thyme, and bay leaf—used for flavouring and perfuming sauces and stews;* 14-15

Braise: *to cook meat, vegetables or both at a low heat in a covered pot with a little liquid;* 53; cleansing sauce, 57; comparison with poaching, 65; herbs for, 14; method, 53; vegetable garnishes for, 10

Brandy, in batter, 80; cooking with, 59; flaming with, 55, 59

Bread, cases, 80-81; croûtons, 57; in stuffings, 38; as test of oil temperature, 31

Brillat-Savarin, Jean Anthelme, 5, 8, 31

Brochette: *a French word for a skewer; also a dish made by threading meat or other ingredients on a skewer, and grilling them;* chicken, 50, 51

Broth, from poaching liquid, 65, 66, 67

Butter, in pastry-making, 76; in pilaff, 83; in a sauce, 29; for sautéing, 24; smearing poultry with, 38; in stuffings, 34, 35, 38, 39

Cabbage, in poached dishes, 66

Calf's feet, 60

Calvados: *an apple brandy named after a town in Normandy;* 59

Capon, history and characteristics, 6-8; roasting times and temperatures, 43

Caramelize: *to heat sugar until it turns brown and syrupy. Also used to describe the evaporation of meat juices to leave a residue on the bottom of the pan. These deposits are deglazed (q.v.) with a liquid to form the basis of a sauce.*

Carrots, coring, 11; as garnish, 10, 53, 54, 55, 56, 57, 73

Carving, 44-45; method for goose and duck, 46; method for poultry stuffed under the skin, 49

Casserole (noun): *a metal, enamelled or earthenware cooking vessel with a lid. It is also the term for a dish prepared in such a vessel;* chicken casserole, 72-73

Casserole (verb): *to cook a combination of foods slowly in a covered pot with a minimum of liquid.*

Cassoulet: *a dish from south-western France made by slowly baking haricot beans and various meats for several hours in a slow oven. Traditionally, a cassoulet includes preserved goose, but there are many versions of the dish;* 84

Celery, in a bouquet garni, 14-15; as a garnish, 11

Cep: *an edible wild mushroom that is sometimes sold in shops, fresh or dried. Found in woods in late autumn, it has a light-brown cap, shaped like a bun, a whitish stem and a spongy texture.*

Chanterelle: *an edible mushroom, yellow in colour, with a serrated, funnel-shaped cap.*

Chard, 62

Chervil, 14, 81

Chicken, ancestry, 5; in aspic, 86; baking, 74-75; boning breasts, 28, 34, 35; braising, 54-57; carving, 44-45; in casserole, 72-73; classification according to age, 5-6; coating, 26, 31, 32-33, 34-35; en cocotte, 72-73; cutting backbone, 47; deep frying, 31-35; fat, rendering, 84; as filling for pancakes and bread cases, 80-81; flattening, 47; in a gratin, 79; grilling, 6, 50-51; jointing, 16-19; leftovers, 76-82; marinating, 12, 32; pancakes, 80-81; pan frying, 23-28; pie, 77; pilaff, 82-83; poaching, 65, 66-69; pot-roasting, 72-73; roasting, 6; roasting times and temperatures, 43; sautéing, 23-28; spit-roasting, 6; stuffing cutlets, 34-35; stuffing for poaching, 66; stuffing for roasting, 6, 38-39, 47-49; testing for doneness, 24, 50, 66; with wine, 23, 24-25, 53, 54-57, 72, 77; wine to serve with, 9, 59; wrapping for poaching, 68

Chiffonade: *any green leafy herb or vegetable that has been cut into fine ribbons; the term especially applies to sorrel, lettuce, spinach and chard treated in this way.*

Chili pepper: *small, finger-shaped hot pepper native to tropical America and the West Indies. There are numerous varieties, and both red and green chilies are used in cooking, either fresh or dried. The seeds and fruit of two species are ground to make cayenne pepper. Other varieties are ground and blended in chili powder (q.v.).*

Chili powder: *a hot, pungent spice made from several varieties of chili pepper (q.v.) that are dried and ground.*

Chives, 14, 81

Choke: *the inedible fibrous part of the artichoke. It nestles immediately above the edible artichoke bottom;* removing, 11

Cider, 59

Clarified butter: *butter from which the water, milk solids and salt have been removed. The butter is gently heated until it melts and a foam appears. This foam is skimmed (q.v.) off, and the clear, golden liquid carefully decanted, leaving behind a milky sediment that is discarded. Butter treated in this way retains its freshness longer, and can be heated to higher temperatures than ordinary butter without smoking.*

Clay vessel, baking in, 74-75

Coating, with batter, 31, 32-33; with breadcrumbs, 34-35; with flour, 26

Cocotte: *a round or oval cooking vessel made of earthenware, porcelain or metal and used for braising.*

Coq au vin, 54-57

Courgettes, as garnish, 11; in stuffing, 39, 47

Couscousière: *a north African cooking vessel that works on the same principle as the double boiler (q.v.). The upper pan has perforations through which the steam rises.*

Cradle spit: *a spit in the form of a cage that holds meat in a compact shape while it is being turned.*

Cream, in sauce, 25, 26, 27, 58, 68-69

Crêpe: *the French term for a pancake;* method, 80-81

Crêpe pan: *a heavy metal pan with shallow sloping sides used for cooking pancakes;* 80

Crock: *an old-fashioned storage vessel.*

Croûtons, see Bread

Cucumber, as garnish, 11, 24, 25; removing seeds, 11

Daube: *a dish of meat, poultry and vegetables braised for several hours in a little liquid;* 8, 60-61

Daubière: *a vessel traditionally used for cooking daubes (q.v.). It is normally of earthenware, with a bulbous lower part and a narrow neck that reduces evaporation, and facilitates the removal of fat;* 60

David, Elizabeth, 8

Deep frying, 31; method, 32-33; safety measures, 32; temperatures, 31

Deglaze: *to pour a liquid—such as wine, stock, water or cream—into a pan in which meat has been sautéed or roasted, in order to incorporate the particles remaining on the bottom of the pan in a sauce;* 24, 25, 56

Degrease: *to remove fat from cooking juices and broths.*

Diat, Louis, 9

Doneness, testing for, 24, 42, 50, 66

Double boiler: *a cooking vessel consisting of two saucepans, one of which is designed to rest snugly inside the other, so that the food in it can be cooked by the heat of the steam from a small amount of water simmering in the lower pan.*

Dough, 76, 77

Dress: *to pluck, draw, singe, trim and truss (q.v.) a bird in preparation for cooking it.*

Dripping: *in general, the fat that melts out of meat as it roasts. Dripping bought from a butcher is beef fat that has been rendered (q.v.). Pork dripping is known as lard (q.v.).*

Drumstick: *the lower part of a bird's leg.*

Duck, age, 8; in aspic, 86; boned, stuffed, braised, 62-63; boning, 20-21; breeds, 8; carving, 46; Chinese treatment, 8; in a daube, 60; fat, drawing out excess, 60; fat, rendering, 84; oil glands, 9; roasting, 46; roasting times and temperatures, 43; wine to serve with, 9

Duckling, 8

Dutch oven: *a deep, heavy, metal cooking pot with a lid. It is used for slow-cooking braises or pot-roasts.*

Entrée: *originally a first course, an entrée is now usually taken to mean any main dish of meat, poultry, game or fish.*

Escoffier, Auguste, 8, 65

Fennel, as a herb, 15; as vegetable garnish, 10

Fines herbes: *a mixture of finely chopped fresh herbs that always incorporates*

parsley, and then one or more of a selection that includes chives, tarragon and chervil; 14

Flour, in braising, 55; as a coating, 26; in gravy, 26, 27; in pastry, 76; in white sauce, 78

Flouring, see Coating

Foie gras: *the liver of a specially fattened goose or duck;* 8, 84

Fowl, Boiling, 6; braising, 60-61; poaching, 66

Fricassée: *a braised dish in which the cooking liquid is thickened with a mixture of egg and cream;* 58

Frozen poultry, 9; thawing, 9

Frying, see Deep frying, Pan frying, Sauté

Garlic, for flavouring bread cases, 8; in a persillade, 57; seasoning unglazed clay vessels, 74; in stock, 55

Garnishes, vegetables for, 10-11, 24-25

Giblets: *the liver, heart, gizzard, neck, feet, and wing tips of birds. They can be cooked to make stock or the edible parts may be cut up and used in stuffings, terrines or other dishes;* 9; storing, 9; in stuffing, 38, 39

Gizzard: *the part of a bird's alimentary canal where the food is ground up. After being rinsed clean, the gizzard can be used to make stock and in stuffing;* preparation of, 39

Glaze: *in meat cookery, to baste meat with its cooking juices in the last stages of cooking. The juices evaporate, forming an attractive glaze; see also* Aspic

Goose, braising, 60-61; carving, 46; fat, 8; fat, rendering, 84; history and domestication, 8; oil glands, 9; preserving, 84-85; roasting times and temperatures, 43; stuffing, 8, 46; wine to serve with, 9; goose fat, 8; rendering, 84

Gratin: *the French term for a crust. Usually made of cheese or breadcrumbs (though some gratins contain neither), it is formed by strewing the gratin ingredients over the food and placing the dish in a hot oven or under a grill so that the top crisps. The word is also used for a dish—a "gratin"—that has such a finish;* 71; sauce, 78-79

Gravy, 26, 27

Green bacon: *unsmoked bacon.*

Grilling, 37; cooking times, 51; method, 50-51; testing for doneness, 50; using charcoal or wood, 6, 37, 50, 51

Guinea-fowl, carving, 44-45; grilling, 50; hanging, 8; roasting, 8; roasting times and temperatures, 43; stuffing, 8; wine to serve with, 9

Hen, Stewing, 6

soups and stews. Saffron is sold in threads or in powdered form. The threads are the dried orange stamens of the lilac-coloured autumn crocus (*Crocus sativus*). The dried stamens are ground to make powdered saffron; in batter, 80; in pilaff, 82

Sage, 15; and onion stuffing, 38

Salsiccia luganica: *a long, thin, fatty sausage obtainable from Italian delicatessens.*

Saltpetre: *potassium nitrate, a mineral salt used in the curing of meat for the red colour it imparts.*

Salt pork: *pork that has been treated with salt to preserve it.*

Sauce aurore: *the French term for a velouté sauce that has a "glow of dawn", or pinkish tinge, created by the addition of tomato or paprika;* 69

Sauces, cleansing, 57; eliminating taste of flour, 27, 69, 78; from pan juices, 25, 26, 27; gratin sauce, 78-79; keeping warm, 78; preventing skin forming, 78; sauce aurore, 69; sauce suprême, 68; sorrel sauce, 69, 80; velouté sauce, 68, 69; vinegar-and-butter sauce, 29; white sauce, 78; white sauce variations, 80

Sauce suprême: *a velouté sauce with cream;* 68

Sauté: *to fry food in just enough oil or fat to prevent it from sticking;* 23; Chinese method, 23; garnishes, 10-11, 24; method, 24-25, 28-29; testing for doneness, 24

Sauté pan: *a pan with straight sides and a long handle for easy manipulation over the heat source.*

Sauteuse: *a type of sauté pan.*

Savory, 14

Shallot: *(Allium ascaloricum) a member of the onion family that grows as a cluster. It has a milder, less sweet flavour than onion, and is an important ingredient in many French dishes;* 29, 60

Sherry, 59, 86

Simmer: *to cook in a liquid at just below the boiling point, so that the surface of the liquid trembles but bubbles do not burst violently;* controlling, 65

Skim or scum: *to remove from the surface of a cooking liquid the frothy, grey-white substance that is exuded by meats when they are heated;* 55, 56, 66

Skin: *the surface layer of impurities that forms on a sauce, especially a flour-thickened sauce;* 57, 69

Sorrel, 15; sauce, 69, 80

Spices, for marinades, 12-13

Spider: *a wire scoop used for turning pieces of food in deep fat without damaging the*

batter coating, and for draining food as it is lifted out; 30

Spinach, in stuffing, 39, 62

Spit-roast: *to roast a joint or fowl on a spit that is turned so the meat cooks evenly;* 6, 37

Spring chicken, 6

Spring onion, as garnish, 11

Squab, 9

Stewing hen, 6

Stir-fry: *to move small pieces of food around constantly in a frying pan or wok (q.v.) so that they cook rapidly on all sides and do not stick.*

Stock: *a base for sauces and stews that is made by simmering the giblets and carcass of poultry, or meat bones and other trimmings, in water, often with vegetables, herbs, and seasoning;* braising in, 62-63; poaching in, 68-69; veal, 54-55

Stuffing, bread, dry, 38; bread, moist, 38; buttering under skin, 8, 38, 39; for chicken, 6; for duck, 62; giblets, 38, 39; for goose, 8; for guinea-fowl, 8; method, 41; under skin, 47-49; vegetable and cheese, 8, 38, 39, 47, 62

Suet: *beef fat that is sold in its natural state or shredded and packaged. Suet comes from around the animal's kidneys;* refining, 84

Suprême: *the term for a skinned, boned and halved chicken breast;* 28-29

Sweat: *to cook vegetables in a little fat over a gentle heat in a closed vessel until they exude their juices. The process is often a preliminary of braising.*

Swede, in stuffing, 39

Sweet pepper: *used here to distinguish red or green bell peppers from the hotter chili varieties of the pepper family (the genus Capsicum);* as garnish, 11, 24; peeling, 11; in pilaff, 82; in sauce, 80

Tarragon, 14, 81, 86

Tempura pan: *a wide Japanese pan for deep frying.*

Thyme, 15

Tokay: *a sweet, white, dessert wine made near Tokaj in Hungary.*

Tomatoes, as garnish, 10, 24; in sauce, 69; seeding, 10

Tomatoes, Puréed: *the tomatoes are skinned and seeded and then passed through a sieve, or puréed in a blender;* in velouté sauce, 69

Trencher, 6

Trivet: *a metal stand or rack that is placed inside a cooking vessel.*

Truffle: *an edible fungus that grows underground. Truffles are used in stuffings, sauces, pâtés or as a garnish. They impart a heady fragrance and a unique flavour.*

Truss: *to tie a bird or joint of meat with string so that it is compactly arranged for cooking. The string may be tied round by hand or, in the case of poultry, threaded through parts of the bird, by means of a trussing needle (q.v.), then knotted by hand;* 40-41; removing strings, 42

Trussing needle: *a large needle with a big eye that is threaded with kitchen string and used to truss (q.v.) fowl.*

Turkey, braising, 60-61; carving, 44-45; deep frying, 32; history, 8; leftovers, 80, 82; roasting, 40-42; roasting times and temperatures, 43; stuffing, 8, 40, 41; trussing, 40-41; wine to serve with, 9

Turnips, as garnish, 10; in stuffing, 39

Veal stock, 54-55; 86

Vegetables, as garnishes, 10-11, 24, 54-55; in poaching, 66; in stuffings, 8, 38, 39, 47, 62

Velouté: *a sauce consisting of a roux (q.v.) to which stock has been added;* 68-69

Vinegar, in marinades, 12-13; in sauce, 29; from wine, 59

Welsh onion: *(Allium fistulosum) a small green onion. All of it can be eaten except for the brown husk on the bulb. Spring onions, although milder in taste, can be substituted.*

White sauce: *a roux-thickened sauce made with milk or cream. In the context of this book, white sauce is synonymous with béchamel sauce (q.v.);* 78, 80

Wilt: *to cook vegetables, such as onion or lettuce, briefly until they soften.*

Wine, types to serve, 9; as a cooking liquid, 53, 54-57, 59, 61, 72; deglazing with, 24, 25, 56; in a marinade, 12-13, 59; in a sauce, 24, 58; as vinegar, 59

Wishbone: *the V-shaped bone in chicken (horseshoe-shaped in duck) that links the tip of the breastbone with the shoulder joints;* removing, 20, 40

Wok: *a large round-bottomed pan used in Chinese cookery;* 23

Yam: *the starchy tuber of a tropical plant, also known as sweet potato.*

Zest: *the coloured outer rind of oranges and lemons (and other citrus fruits) when scraped or grated off for use in cooking.*

Recipe Credits

The sources for the recipes in this volume are shown below. Page references in brackets indicate where the recipes appear in the Anthology.

Adam, Hans Karl, *Das Kochbuch aus Schwaben.* © 1976 by Verlagsteam Wolfgang Hölker. Published by Verlag Wolfgang Hölker, Münster. Translated by permission of Verlag Wolfgang Hölker (*page 158*).

Ainé, Offray, *Le Cuisinier Méridional.* Imprimeur-Libraire, 1855 (*pages 101, 138*).

Ali-Bab, *Encyclopedia of Practical Gastronomy* (English Translation). Translated by Elizabeth Benson. Copyright © 1974 by McGraw-Hill, Inc. Published by McGraw-Hill Book Company, New York. With permission of McGraw-Hill Book Co. (*page 90*).

Aresty, Esther B., *The Delectable Past.* Copyright © 1964 by Esther B. Aresty. First published in Great Britain 1965 by George Allen & Unwin (Publishers) Ltd., Hemel Hempstead. By permission of George Allen & Unwin (Publishers) Ltd. (*page 104*).

Armisen, Raymond & Martin, André, *Les Recettes de la Table Niçoise.* © Librairie Istra 1972. Published by Librairie Istra, 15 rue des Juifs, Strasbourg. Translated by permission of Librairie Istra (*page 118*).

Ayrton, Elisabeth, *The Cookery of England.* Copyright © Elisabeth Ayrton, 1974. Published by Penguin Books Ltd., London. By permission of Penguin Books Ltd. (*pages 115, 131, 154 and 155*).

Barberousse, Michel, *Cuisine Normande.* Published by Éditions Barberousse, Paris. Translated by permission of Michel Barberousse (*page 89*).

Barberousse, Michel, *Cuisine Provençale.* Privately published by Michel Barberousse, Seguret. Translated by permission of Michel Barberousse (*page 117*).

Barr, Beryl & Turner Sachs, Barbara (Editors), *The Artists' & Writers' Cookbook.* Copyright © 1961 by William H. Ryan. Published by Angel Island Publications, Inc. (*pages 98, 104*).

Barry, Naomi & Bellini, Beppe, *Food alla Florentine.* Copyright © 1972 by Doubleday & Company, Inc. Published by Doubleday & Company, Inc., New York. Reprinted by permission of Brandt & Brandt and Doubleday & Company, Inc. (*page 134*).

Beard, James, *James Beard's American Cookery.* Copyright © 1972 by James A. Beard. Published by Hart-Davis, MacGibbon Ltd./Granada Publishing Ltd., Hertfordshire and Little, Brown and Company, Boston. Reproduced with the permission of Granada Publishing Limited and Little, Brown and Co. (*pages 107, 114, 143 and 164*).

Beeton, Mrs. Isabella, *The Book of Household Management.* (1861). Reproduced in facsimile by Jonathan Cape Ltd., London (*pages 127, 164 and 165*).

Béguin, Maurice, *La Cuisine en Poitou.* Published by La Librarie Saint-Denis, c. 1933 (*page 161*).

Bocuse, Paul, *La Cuisine du Marché.* © 1976, Flammarion. Published by Éditions Flammarion, Paris. Translated by permission of Éditions Flammarion and Paul Bocuse (*page 93*).

Boni, Ada, *The Talisman Italian Cook Book.* Copyright, 1950, 1978 by Crown Publishers, Inc. Published by Crown Publishers, Inc., New York. Used by permission of Crown Publishers, Inc. (*pages 99, 118*).

Bonnefons, Nicolas de, *Les Délices de la Campagne* (1654) (*page 99*).

Boyd, Lizzie (Editor), *British Cookery.* Copyright © British Farm Produce Council and British Tourist Authority. Published by Croom Helm (London). By permission of British Farm Produce Council and British Tourist Authority (*page 140*).

Bullock, Mrs. Helen Claire, *The Williamsburg Art of Cookery.* © 1938, © 1966 by the Colonial Williamsburg Foundation. Published by Colonial Williamsburg. Reprinted by permission of Holt, Rinehart and Winston, Publishers (*pages 140, 148, 161 and 164*).

Carnacina, Luigi, *Great Italian Cooking,* edited by Michael Sonino. Published in English by Abradale Press Inc., New York and The Hamlyn Publishing Group Limited, London. By permission of Aldo Garzanti Editore and Abradale Press (*pages 88, 94, 125 and 130*).

Carrier, Robert, *The Robert Carrier Cookery Course.* © Robert Carrier, 1974. Published by W. H. Allen & Co. Ltd., London. By permission of W. H. Allen & Co. Ltd. (*pages 94, 100*).

Chantiles, Vilma Liacouras, *The Food of Greece.* Copyright © 1975 by Vilma Liacouras Chantiles. Published by Atheneum, New York. By permission of Vilma Liacouras Chantiles (*pages 95, 103*).

Chiang, Cecilia Sun Yun, as told to Allan Carr, *The Mandarin Way.* Copyright © 1974 by Cecilia Chiang and Allan Carr. Published by Little, Brown and Co., Boston, in association with The Atlantic Monthly Press. By permission of Cecilia Sun Yun Chiang (*page 139*).

Chu, Grace Zia, *Madam Chu's Chinese Cooking School.* Copyright © 1975 by Grace Zia Chu. Published by Simon & Schuster, New York. Reprinted by permission of Simon & Schuster, a Division of Gulf & Western Corporation (*page 152*).

Claiborne, Craig, *Craig Claiborne's Favorites from The New York Times, Volume 1, 1975.* Copyright © 1975 by The New York Times Company. Published by The New York Times Book Company, New York. Reprinted by permission of Times Books (*page 138*).

Claiborne, Craig, *Craig Claiborne's Favorites from The New York Times, Volume 2, 1976.* Copyright © 1976 by The New York Times Company. Published by The New York Times Book Company, New York. Reprinted by permission of Times Books (*page 121*).

Clarisse ou la Vieille Cuisinière. © 1922 by Éditions de l'Abeille d'Or. Published by Éditions de l'Abeille d'Or, Paris. Translated by permission of Éditions Rombaldi, Paris (*page 126*).

Comité Interprofessionnel du Vin de Champagne, *Cooking with Champagne.* © 1970 by Comité Interprofessionnel du Vin de Champagne, Lallemand Éditeur. Published by Lallemand Éditeur, Paris. By permission of Comité Interprofessionnel du Vin de Champagne, Épernay (*page 132*).

Courtine, Robert, *Mon Bouquet de Recettes.* © Les Nouvelles Éditions Marabout, Verviers 1977. Published by Les Nouvelles Éditions Marabout, Verviers. Translated by permission of Les Nouvelles Éditions Marabout (*pages 91, 114*).

Crémone, Baptiste Platine de, *Le Livre de Honneste Volupté,* 1474 (*page 117*).

Croze, Austin de, *Les Plats Régionaux de France.* Published by Éditions Daniel Morcrette, B.P. 26,95270-Luzarches, France. Translated by permission of Éditions Daniel Morcrette (*page 158*).

La Cuisine Lyonnaise. Published by Éditions Gutenberg, 1947 (*page 103*).

Curnonsky, *A L'Infortune du Pot.* © Éditions de la Couronne, 1946. Published by Éditions de la Couronne, Paris (*page 89*).

Curnonsky, *Cuisine et Vins de France.* Copyright © 1953 by Augé, Gillon, Hollier-Larousse, Moreau et Cie. (Librairie Larousse), Paris. Published by Librairie Larousse, Paris. Translated by permission of Société Encyclopédique Universelle (*pages 88, 109, 119*).

Dannenbaum, Julie, *Menus for All Occasions.* Copyright © 1974 by Julie Dannenbaum. Published by E. P. Dutton & Co. Inc., New York. Reprinted by permission of E. P. Dutton and John Schaffner, Agency (*page 159*).

David, Elizabeth, *French Country Cooking.* Copyright © Elizabeth David, 1951. Published by Penguin Books Ltd., London. By permission of Penguin Books Ltd. (*page 131*).

David, Elizabeth, *Italian Food.* Copyright © Elizabeth David, 1954, 1963, 1969. Published by Penguin Books Ltd., London. By permission of Penguin Books Ltd. (*page 157*).

David, Elizabeth, *Spices, Salt and Aromatics in the English Kitchen.* Copyright © Elizabeth David, 1970. Published by Penguin Books Ltd., London. By permission of Penguin Books Ltd. (*page 122*).

David, Elizabeth, *Summer Cooking.* Copyright © Elizabeth David, 1955. Published by Penguin Books Ltd., London. By permission of Penguin Books Ltd. (*page 113*).

Derys, Gaston, *L'Art d'Être Gourmand.* Copyright © by Albin Michel 1929. Published by Éditions Albin Michel, Paris. Translated by permission of Éditions Albin Michel (*pages 126, 142, 144 and 162*).

Diat, Louis, *French Cooking for Americans.* Copyright 1941 by Louis Diat. Copyright © renewed 1969 by Mrs. Louis Diat. Published by J. B. Lippincott Company, New York. Reprinted by permission of J. B. Lippincott Company (*pages 125, 128 and 162*).

Dubois, Urbain, *L'École des Cuisinières.* Published by Dentu, Paris, 1876 (*pages 98, 140*).

Dubois, Urbain & Bernard, Émile, *La Cuisine Classique.* (1881) (*page 90*).

Duff, Gail, *Fresh All The Year.* © Gail Duff 1976. First published by Macmillan London Ltd., 1976. Also published by Pan Books Ltd., 1977. By permission of Macmillan London Ltd. (*pages 124, 134*).

Dumaine, Alexandre, *Ma Cuisine.* © 1972 Pensée Moderne. Published by Éditions de la Pensée Moderne, Paris. Translated by permission of Éditions de la Pensée Moderne (*page 128*).

Escoffier, Auguste, *A Guide to Modern Cookery.* Published by William Heinemann Ltd., London. By permission of William Heinemann Ltd. (*page 92*).

Escoffier, Auguste, *Ma Cuisine.* © English text 1965 by The Hamlyn Publishing Group Limited. Published by The Hamlyn Publishing Group Limited, London. By permission of The Hamlyn Publishing Group Limited (*page 145*).

Escoffier, Auguste, *Le Carnet d'Épicure.* (Magazine). 1912, no. 10 and 1914, no. 9, (*pages 90, 149*).

Escudier, Jean-Noël, *La Véritable Cuisine Provençale et Niçoise.* Published by U.N.I.D.E., Paris. Translated by permission of U.N.I.D.E. (*pages 88, 119*).

FitzGibbon, Theodora, *A Taste of Ireland.* Copyright © 1968 by Theodora FitzGibbon. First published by J. M. Dent & Sons Ltd., 1968. Also published by Pan Books Ltd., 1970. By permission of Theodora FitzGibbon and J. M. Dent & Sons Ltd. (*page 160*).

Flower, Barbara and Rosenbaum, Elisabeth, *The Roman Cookery Book, a critical translation of* The Art of Cooking *by Apicius.* © E. Rosenbaum 1958. Published by George G. Harrap & Co. Ltd., London. By permission of George G. Harrap & Co. Ltd. (*page 122*).

Foster, Lee (Editor), *The New York Times Correspondents' Choice.* Copyright © 1974 by Quadrangle/The New York Times Book Company. Published by Quadrangle/The New York Times Book Co. Reprinted by permission of Quadrangle/The New York Times Book Co. (*pages 105, 112 and 159*).

Gouy, Louis P. De, *The Gold Cook Book* (revised edition). Copyright 1948, 1969 by the author (Louis P. De Gouy). Published by Chilton Book Company. Reprinted with the permission of the publisher, Chilton Book Company, Radnor, Pennsylvania (*page 146*).

Grigson, Jane, *Good Things.* Copyright © Jane Grigson, 1971. First published by Michael Joseph 1971. Published by Penguin Books Ltd., 1973. By permission of David Higham Associates Limited for Jane Grigson (*pages 141, 149 and 153*).

Guégan, Bertrand, *La Fleur de la Cuisine Française, Vols. 1 & 2.* Published by Éditions de la Sirène, 1920. Translated by permission of Éditions Henri Lefebvre (*pages 121, 135*).

Guérard, Michel, *Michel Guérard's Cuisine Minceur.* © Macmillan London Ltd 1977. Published by Macmillan London Ltd. Originally published in French as *La Grande Cuisine Minceur.* © Éditions Robert Laffont S.A., Paris, 1976. By permission of Macmillan London Ltd. (*page 104*).

Hazelton, Nika Standen, *The Continental Flavour.* Copyright © 1961 by Nika Standen Hazelton. Published by Penguin Books, Ltd., London. Reprinted by permission of Penguin Books Ltd. and Curtis Brown Ltd. (*pages 112, 156 and 163*).

Hazelton, Nika Standen, *The Swiss Cookbook.* Copyright © 1967 by Nika Standen Hazelton. Published by Atheneum, New York. By permission of Atheneum (*page 93*).

Hibben, Sheila, *American Regional Cookery.* Copyright © 1932, 1946, by Sheila Hibben. Published by Little, Brown and Company, Boston. Reprinted by permission of McIntosh and Otis (*page 96*).

Holkar, Shivaji Rao and Shalini Devi, *Cooking of the Maharajas.* Copyright © 1975 by Shivaji Rao Holkar and Shalini Devi Holkar. Published by The Viking Press, New York. Reprinted by permission of The Viking Press (*pages 92, 136*).

Howe, Robin, *Greek Cooking.* © Robin Howe 1960. Published by André Deutsch Limited, London. By permission of André Deutsch Limited (*page 142*).

Isnard, Léon, *La Cuisine Française et Africaine.* © 1949 by Éditions Albin Michel. Published by Éditions Albin Michel, Paris. Translated by permission of Éditions Albin Michel (*pages 90, 97, 114 and 115*).

Jans, Hugh, *Vrij Nederland.* (Dutch Magazine). Published by Vrij Nederland, Amsterdam. Translated by permission of Vrij Nederland and Hugh Jans (*pages 123, 155*).

Jervey, Phyllis, *Rice & Spice.* © 1957 by Charles E. Tuttle Co., Inc. Published by Charles E. Tuttle Company Inc., Tokyo. By permission of Charles E. Tuttle Company Inc. (*pages 108, 132*).

Jouveau, René, *La Cuisine Provençale.* Copyright © Bouquet & Baumgartner, Flamatt, Switzerland. Published by Éditions du Message, 1962, Berne. Translated by permission of Bouquet & Baumgartner (*pages 109, 145*).

Junior League of New Orleans, Inc., The, *The Plantation Cookbook.* Copyright © 1972 by The Junior League of New Orleans, Inc. Published by Doubleday & Company, Inc., New York. Reprinted by permission of Doubleday & Company, Inc. (*page 165*).

Kahn, Odette, *La Petite et la Grand Cuisine.* © Calmann-Lévy 1977. Published by Éditions Calmann-Lévy, Paris. Translated by permission of Éditions Calmann-Lévy (*pages 89, 105*).

Kramarz, Inge, *The Balkan Cookbook.* © 1972 by Crown Publishers, Inc. Published by Crown Publishers, Inc., New York. Used by permission of Crown Publishers, Inc. (*page 130*).

Kürtz, Jutta, *Das Kochbuch aus Schleswig-Holstein.* © 1976 by Verlagsteam Wolfgang Hölker. Published by Verlag Wolfgang Hölker, Münster. Translated by permission of Wolfgang Hölker (*pages 152, 162*).

Labourer, Suzanne & Boulestin, X-M, *Petits et Grands Plats.* Published by Au Sans Pareil, 1928 (*page 111*).

Lo, Kenneth, *Chinese Food.* Copyright © Kenneth Lo, 1972. Published by Penguin Books Ltd., London. By permission of Penguin Books Ltd. (*pages 95, 100 and 151*).

L.S.R., *L'Art de Bien Traiter* (1674). (*page 120*).

Lucas, Dione & Gorman, Marion, *The Dione Lucas Book of French Cooking.* Copyright 1947 by Dione Lucas. Copyright © 1973 by Mark Lucas and Marion F. Gorman. Published by Little, Brown and Company, Boston. By permission of Little, Brown and Company, (*pages 93, 146*).

Lyren, Carl, *365 Ways to Cook Chicken.* Copyright © 1974 by Carl Lyren. Published by Doubleday & Company, Inc., New York. Reprinted by permission of Robert Hale & Co. and Doubleday & Company, Inc. (*pages 100, 139*).

MacMiadhacháin, Anna, *Spanish Regional Cookery.* Copyright © Anna MacMiadhacháin, 1976. Published by Penguin Books Ltd., London. By permission of Penguin Books Ltd. (*pages 134, 157*).

Massiolot, *Le Cuisinier Roial et Bourgeois* (1691). (*page 101*).

Mathiot, Ginette, *A Table avec Édouard de Pomiane.* © Éditions Albin Michel, 1975. Published by Éditions Albin Michel, Paris. Translated by permission of Éditions Albin Michel (*page 109*).

McNeill, F. Marian, *The Scots Kitchen.* Published by Blackie & Son Limited, London. Reproduced by permission of Blackie & Son Limited (*page 116*).

Médecin, Jacques, *La Cuisine du Comté de Nice.* © Julliard, 1972. Published by Penguin Books Ltd., London. Translated by permission of Penguin Books Ltd (*pages 92, 102*).

Menon, *La Cuisinière Bourgeoise* (1746) (*page 150*).

Miller, Gloria Bley, *The Thousand Recipe Chinese Cookbook.* Copyright © 1966 by Gloria Bley Miller. Published by Grosset & Dunlap, New York. By permission of Gloria Bley Miller (*pages 98, 152*).

Montagné, Prosper, *Larousse Gastronomique.* © Copyright The Hamlyn Publishing Group Limited 1961. Published by The Hamlyn Publishing Group Limited, London. Reproduced by permission of The Hamlyn Publishing Group Limited (*page 91*).

Montagné, Prosper and Gottschalk, A., *Mon Menu—Guide d'Hygiène Alimentaire.* Published by Société d'Applications Scientifiques, Paris (*pages 147, 148*).

Nignon, Édouard, *Éloges de la Cuisine Française.* Published by Éditions d'Art, Paris, 1933. Translated by permission of Éditions Daniel Morcrette, B.P. 26, 95270-Luzarches, France (*pages 138, 143*).

Nignon, Édouard, *L'Heptameron des Gourmets ou les Délices de la Cuisine Française.* Privately printed in Paris by Impr. G. de Malherbes, 1919. Translated by permission of Éditions Daniel Morcrette, B.P. 26, 95270-Luzarches, France (*page 156*).

Norman, Barbara, *The Spanish Cookbook.* Copyright © 1969 by Barbara Norman. Published by Bantam Books, Inc., New York. By permission of Bantam Books, Inc. (*page 122*).

Oliver, Raymond, *La Cuisine—sa technique, ses secrets.* Published by Éditions Bordas, Paris. Translated by permission of Leon Amiel Publishers, New York. (*pages 116, 135*).

Olney, Richard, *The French Menu Cookbook.* Copyright © 1970 by Richard Olney. Published by Simon and Schuster, New York. By permission of John Schaffner, Literary Agent (*pages 110, 150*).

Olney, Richard, *Simple French Food.* Copyright © 1974 by Richard Olney. Published by Atheneum, New York. Reprinted by permission of Atheneum and A. M. Heath & Company Ltd., Authors' Agents (*page 102*).

Ortiz, Elisabeth Lambert, *Caribbean Cooking.* Copyright © Elisabeth Lambert Ortiz, 1973, 1975. Published by Penguin Books Ltd., London. By permission of Penguin Books Ltd. and John Farquharson Ltd., Literary Agents (*pages 112, 113*).

Ortiz, Elisabeth Lambert with Endo, Mitsuko, *The Complete Book of Japanese Cooking.* Copyright © 1976 by Elisabeth Lambert Ortiz. Published by M. Evans and Company, Inc., New York. By permission of John Farquharson Ltd., Literary Agents (*pages 96, 107*).

Palay, Simin, *La Cuisine du Pays.* © 1970 Marrimpouey Jeune—Pau. Published by Éditions Marrimpouey Jeune et Cie., Pau. Translated by permission of Éditions Marrimpouey Jeune et Cie. (*page 120*).

Pépin, Jacques, *A French Chef Cooks at Home.* Copyright © 1975 by Jacques Pépin. Published by Simon and Schuster, New York. Reprinted by permission of Simon & Schuster, a Division of Gulf & Western Corporation (*pages 121, 147*).

Peter, Madeleine, *Grandes Dames de la Cuisine.* © 1977 by Éditions Robert Laffont S.A. Published by Éditions Robert Laffont S.A. Translated by permission of Holt, Rinehart & Winston, Inc. (*page 127*).

Pomiane, Édouard de, *Cuisine Juive Ghettos Modernes.* Copyright © 1929 by Albin Michel. Published by Éditions Albin Michel, Paris. Translated by permission of Éditions Albin Michel (*pages 118, 160 and 161*).

Reboul, J. B., (Editor: Librairie Tacussel), *La Cuisinière*

Provençale. Published by Tacussel, Marseille. Translated by permission of Tacussel, Éditeur (*page 156*).

Renaudet, *Les Secrets de la Bonne Table*. Published by Éditions Albin Michel, Paris. Translated by permission of Éditions Albin Michel (*page 111*).

Roden, Claudia, *A Book of Middle Eastern Food*. Copyright © Claudia Roden, 1968. Published by Penguin Books Ltd., London and Alfred A. Knopf, New York. By permission of Claudia Roden (*page 132*).

Saint-Ange, Madame, *La Cuisine de Madame Saint-Ange*. © Éditions Chaix. Published by Éditions Chaix, Grenoble. Translated by permission of Éditions Chaix (*page 123*).

Sales, Georgia MacLeod and Grover, *The Clay-Pot Cookbook*. Copyright © 1974 by Georgia MacLeod Sales and Grover Sales. Published by Atheneum, New York. By permission of Atheneum (*page 141*).

Salta, Romeo, *The Pleasures of Italian Cooking*. © Romeo Salta, 1962. Published by Macmillan Publishing Co., New York. By permission of Macmillan Publishing Co., Inc (*page 98*).

Sandler, Sandra Takako, *The American Book of Japanese Cooking*. Copyright © 1974 by Sandra Sandler. Published by Stackpole Books, Harrisburg. By permission of Stackpole Books (*page 107*).

Sarvis, Shirley, *A Taste of Portugal*. Copyright © 1967 Shirley Sarvis. Published by Charles Scribner's Sons, New York. By permission of Shirley Sarvis (*page 136*).

Schulze, Ida, *Das neue Kochbuch für die deutsche Küche*. Published by Verlag von Velhagen & Klasing, West Berlin. Translated by permission of Verlag von Velhagen & Klasing (*page 146*).

Scott, Jack Denton, *The Complete Book of Pasta*. Copyright © 1968 by Jack Denton Scott. Published by William Morrow & Company, Inc., New York. Reprinted by permission of Jack Denton Scott and William Morrow & Company, Inc. (*page 116*).

Serra, Victoria, translated by **Gili, Elizabeth,** *Tia Victoria's Spanish Kitchen*. Copyright © Elizabeth Gili 1963. Published by Kaye & Ward Ltd., London. By permission of Kaye & Ward Ltd. and Elizabeth Gili (*page 111*).

Singh, Dharamjit, *Indian Cookery*. Copyright © Dharamjit Singh, 1970. Published by Penguin Books Ltd., London. By permission of Penguin Books Ltd. (*page 118*).

Smires, Latifa Bennani, *La Cuisine Marocaine*. Published by Éditions Alpha, Casablanca (*pages 115, 128*).

Snow, Jane Moss, *A Family Harvest*. Copyright © 1976 by Jane Moss Snow. Published by The Bobbs-Merrill Company, Inc., Indiana. Reprinted by permission of The Bobbs-Merrill Company, Inc., Jane Moss Snow and Julian Bach Literary Agency, Inc. (*pages 96, 108*).

Stockli, Albert, *Splendid Fare, The Albert Stockli Cookbook*. Copyright © 1970 by Albert Stockli, Inc. Published by Alfred A. Knopf, Inc., New York. By permission of Alfred A. Knopf, Inc. (*page 153*).

Straub, Maria Elisabeth, *Grönen Aal und Rode Grütt*. © LN-Verlag Lübecker Nachrichten GmbH, Lübeck, 1971. Published by LN-Verlag Lübeck. Translated by permission of LN-Verlag Lübeck (*page 154*).

Tante Marguerite, *La Cuisine de la Bonne Ménagère*. Published by Éditions de L'Épi, Paris (1929) (*page 126*).

Tendret, Lucien, *La Table au Pays de Brillat-Savarin*. Published by Librairie Dardel, Chambery, 1934. Translated by permission of Éditions Rabelais Grancher. (*pages 113, 120*).

Tenison, Marika Hanbury, *Left Over for Tomorrow*. Copyright © Marika Hanbury Tenison, 1971. Published by Penguin Books Ltd., London. By permission of Penguin Books Ltd. (*page 163*).

Time-Life Books, Dale Brown and the Editors of, *Foods of the World—American Cooking*. © 1968 Time Inc. Published by Time-Life Books, Alexandria (*pages 97, 154 and 164*).

Time-Life Books, Jonathan Norton Leonard and the Editors of, *Foods of the World—American Cooking: New England*. © 1970 Time Inc. Published by Time-Life Books, Alexandria (*page 164*).

Time-Life Books, Linda Wolfe and the Editors of, *Foods of the World—The Cooking of the Caribbean Islands*. © 1970 Time Inc. Published by Time-Life Books, Alexandria (*page 94*).

Time-Life Books, Harry G. Nickles and the Editors of, *Foods of the World—Middle Eastern Cooking*. © 1969 Time Inc. Published by Time-Life Books, Alexandria (*page 106, 158*).

Toklas, Alice B., *The Alice B. Toklas Cook Book*. Copyright © 1954 by Alice B. Toklas. Published by Harper & Row, Publishers, Inc. By permission of Harper & Row, Publishers, Inc. (*page 135*).

Troisgros, Jean and Pierre, *Cuisiniers à Roanne*. Éditions Robert Laffont, S.A., 1977. Published by Éditions Robert Laffont, Paris. Translated by permission of Éditions Robert Laffont (*pages 117, 124*).

Varenne, La, *Le Cuisinier François*. (1651). (*page 150*).

Watt, Alexander, *The Art of Simple French Cookery*. © 1960 by Alexander Watt. Published by MacGibbon & Kee, 1960 and Doubleday & Company, Inc., New York. By permission of Curtis Brown Ltd., London, on behalf of the Estate of Alexander Watt (*page 108*).

Wilson, José (Editor), *House and Garden's New Cook Book*. Copyright © 1967 by The Condé Nast Publications Inc. Published by The Condé Nast Publications Inc., New York. By permission of The Condé Nast Publications Inc. (*page 144*).

Wilson, José (Editor), *House and Garden's Party Menu Cookbook*. Copyright © 1973 by The Condé Nast Publications Inc. Published by The Condé Nast Publications Inc., New York. By permission of The Condé Nast Publications Inc. (*page 106*).

Wolfert, Paula, *Couscous and Other Good Food from Morocco*. Copyright © 1973 by Paula Wolfert. Published by Harper & Row, Publishers, Inc., New York. Reprinted by permission of Harper & Row, Publishers, Inc. and Paula Wolfert (*pages 106, 129 and 137*).

Yu Wen Mei and Adams, Charlotte, *100 Most Honorable Chinese Recipes*. Copyright © 1963 by Charlotte Adams. Published by Thomas Y. Crowell Company, Inc., New York. Reprinted by permission of Curtis Brown, Ltd. (*pages 99, 151*).

Acknowledgements and Picture Credits

The editors of this book are particularly indebted to Elizabeth David, Jeremiah Tower and Elisabeth Lambert Ortiz.

They also wish to thank the following: Pat Alburey; R. Allen & Co. (Butchers) Ltd.; John Baily & Son (Poulterers) Ltd.; Naomi Barry; British Poultry Meat Association; Ginny Buckley; Michael Carter; The Copper Shop; Sue Crowther; Richard Dare; Elizabeth David, Ltd.; Dickins and Jones Ltd.; Divertimenti; Electricity Council; Irene Ertugrul; S. Ferrari and Sons (Soho) Ltd.; Habitat Designs Ltd.; Heal's; Maggi Heinz; Marion Hunter; Leon Jaeggi and Sons; John Lewis; Ruth Lynam; David Lynch; David Mellor; The National Book League; Jo Northey; William Page & Co. Ltd.; Helena Radecka; Glenn Recchia; Selfridges Ltd.; Ursula Whyte.

All photographs are by Alan Duns except: page 2-Louis Klein. 6, 7-Illustration by Charles Pickard. 10, 11-Stak. 12, 13-Bob Cramp. 14, 15-Illustration by Leonora Box. 16, 17-far right, Paul Kemp. 18, 19-Bob Cramp. 30 to 33-Roger Phillips. 34-Bob Cramp. 35-Roger Phillips, except bottom, Alan Duns. 39-top and bottom left, Paul Kemp. 43-Illustration by Richard Bonson. 44-bottom left, Bob Cramp. 47-Paul Kemp. 48, 49-Paul Kemp. 50, 51-Stak. 55-top right, Roger Phillips. 57-top left, Roger Phillips. 58-Roger Phillips. 60, 61-Bob Cramp. 64-Bob Cramp. 72, 73-Roger Phillips. 74-top, Bob Cramp. 75-top, Bob Cramp. 82, 83-Roger Phillips. 84, 85-Bob Cramp. 86-Roger Phillips.

Colour separations by Gilchrist Ltd—Leeds, England
Typesetting by Camden Typesetters—London, England
Printed and bound by Brepols SA—Turnhout, Belgium

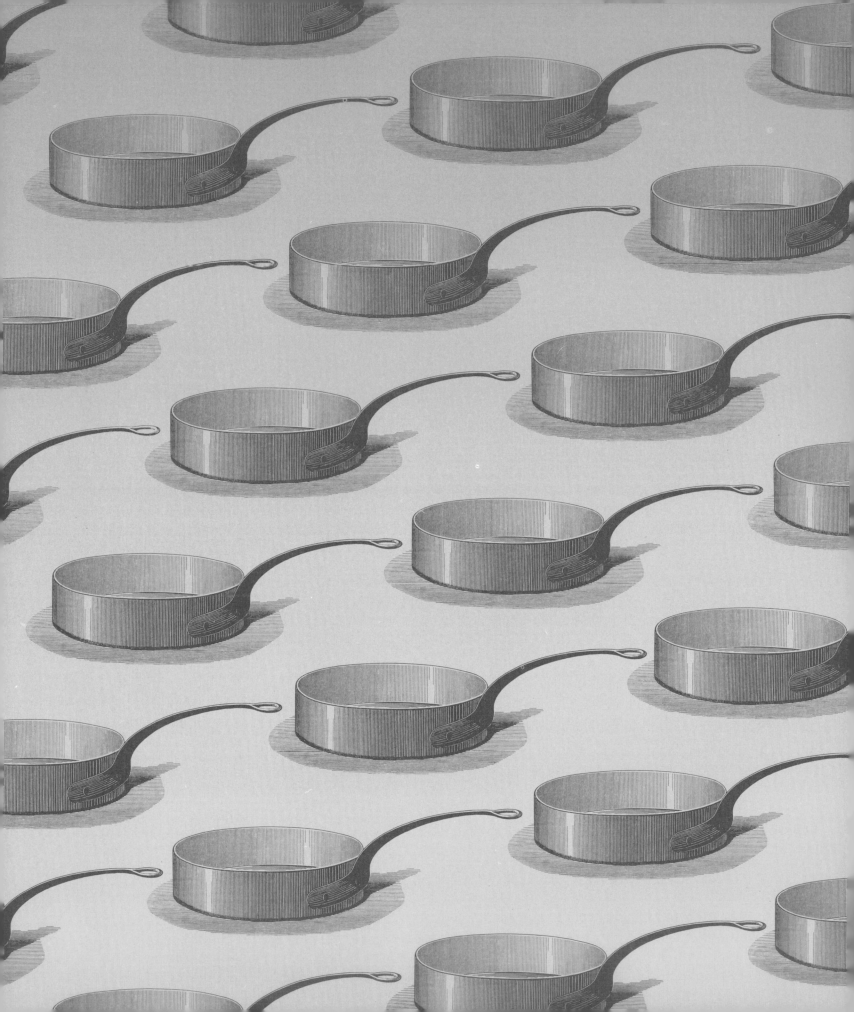